OCTOBER
SURPRISE

OCTOBER SURPRISE

How the FBI Tried to Save Itself
and Crashed an Election

Devlin Barrett

PublicAffairs
New York

PublicAffairs
Hachette Book Group
1290 Avenue of the Americas, New York, NY 10104
www.publicaffairsbooks.com
@Public_Affairs

Printed in the United States of America
First Edition: September 2020

Published by PublicAffairs, an imprint of Perseus Books, LLC, a subsidiary of Hachette Book Group, Inc. The PublicAffairs name and logo is a trademark of the Hachette Book Group.

The Hachette Speakers Bureau provides a wide range of authors for speaking events. To find out more, go to www.hachettespeakersbureau.com or call (866) 376-6591.

The publisher is not responsible for websites (or their content) that are not owned by the publisher.

Editorial production by Christine Marra, *Marra*thon Production Services. www.marrathoneditorial.org

Book design by Jane Raese
Set in 11-point Minion

Library of Congress Cataloging-in-Publication Data has been applied for.

ISBN 978-1-5417-6197-1 (hardcover); ISBN 978-1-5417-5868-1 (ebook)

LSC-C

10 9 8 7 6 5 4 3 2 1

TO MY WIFE, MIRANDA,

AND TO MY LATE MOTHER, BLAIR GIBB,
co-author of *When Good Companies Do Bad Things*

*Never let your sense of morals
get in the way of doing what's right.*
—ISAAC ASIMOV

Can't fix stupid.
–SHOE

Contents

PART ONE. FIDELITY

PART TWO. BRAVERY

PART THREE. INTEGRITY

PART 1
FIDELITY

Missile Fire

FRIDAY, JULY 6, 2012

Of all the elements of the 2016 election that made Donald Trump president, the most surprising and hotly debated—to this day—was the role of the FBI. The combination of presidential politics, classified intelligence, and bureaucratic backbiting combined to inject a toxic level of anger and distrust into the body politic and the highest levels of the world's premier law enforcement agency.

The debate over why Trump won, why Hillary Clinton lost, and how much of that result was due to the FBI has never really ended. Even in 2020, the political schism of those questions often seems as fresh as it was on Election Day, with us all trapped in a kind of feedback loop of recriminations over Clinton's emails, Russia, and Trump.

As part of that feedback loop, I found myself in the extremely odd and uncomfortable situation of becoming a player in some of the key events in October 2016, which led to one of the FBI's top officials nearly being indicted over my reporting. But as Republicans and Democrats fought over the FBI in the following years, it seemed the true lessons of that tumultuous election year grew further away rather than closer. In

2016, the FBI, an agency whose motto is "Fidelity, Bravery, Integrity," and which has long held itself out to the public as above reproach and above politics, proved just how susceptible it was to the same anger, mistrust, and misunderstanding that plagued the political process.

There were many ingredients that combined to make 2016 an election like no other. But to understand just how decisive a role the FBI played in American politics, one has to look back further in time to see the forces that were building not just inside the FBI and the Justice Department—two organizations whose inner workings are closely guarded secrets shrouded from public view—but also inside Congress and the American electorate. Many of the events of 2016 were difficult if not impossible to predict. This book is an attempt, after years of partisan spin and bureaucratic bluster, to help people at least understand what did and didn't happen in 2016 inside the FBI and, most importantly, why things turned out the way they did.

Strange as it may seem, that story begins years ago on the other side of the world, in a remote town in northern Pakistan called Zowi Sidgi. As the sun began to set on July 6, 2012, a number of men in the village gathered to eat dinner under a tent. Some residents noticed drones circling above them in the sky. Suddenly, they heard the sound of missiles rushing toward them. The missiles struck the tent, creating an explosion of gases moving at thousands of feet per second. The force of the blast killed at least eight people, witnesses said. Neighbors rushed to help and found a blast site littered with severed body parts.

"The people tried to collect their bodies, some were carrying stretchers, blankets and water," a witness, Junaid, would later tell an investigator with the human rights group Amnesty International. Witnesses said minutes after the first attack, while people scrambled to help the injured and the dead, the drones fired a second volley at the site, killing some of those responding to help. At least six people died in the second strike. The final death toll would rise to eighteen, including, according to witnesses, a fourteen-year-old boy named Saleh Khan who sold wood in the town. More than twenty others were wounded. "The bodies were burnt and it was not possible to recognize them," said Nabeel, another villager.

In the big picture of the Obama administration's war on terror, the missile strike was fairly routine. Zowi Sidgi was in the Waziristan region bordering Afghanistan. To terror networks like the Taliban, crossing the Afghanistan-Pakistan border was an essential part of their strategy to strike in Afghanistan, then slip back over the border to safety in Pakistan. To counter that tactic, the Obama administration had adopted and expanded a program known as "signature strikes": missiles were fired from CIA drones even when US counterterrorism officials did not know the identities of the people they were killing. Instead, analysts working with classified information gathered evidence about the types of activity they observed—their signatures—to be confident the target was a terrorist hot spot.

US intelligence had concluded the tent at Zowi Sidgi was a meeting point for militants. In the moral calculus of the US drone program, that made it an acceptable target. Due to the inaccessibility and danger for Westerners to travel to such areas, it was often hard for the rest of the world to learn the details about drone strikes, which is why most of the available information about what happened that day comes from Amnesty International. Villagers told the human rights group that those killed were not Taliban fighters, but farmers and miners.

Counterterrorism officials were confident in the accuracy of their intelligence. Within hours news agencies issued the first public reports about the drone strike. "U.S. Drone Strike Kills 4 Militants in Pakistan," the first Associated Press headline read. Datelined from Pakistan's capital, Islamabad, the story began: "Pakistani intelligence officials say missiles fired by a U.S. drone have killed at least four suspected militants near the Afghan border." The US government kept the drone strike program highly classified—even using the word "drone" was considered a serious violation of the classification rules.

Senior staff of the US embassy in Islamabad were closely involved in the CIA's drone strikes. Such remote-controlled missile strikes were deeply unpopular in Pakistan, and in order to try to manage the diplomatic and political aftershocks of such strikes, the senior State Department official in the country, either the ambassador or whoever was acting in his or her stead when they were away, had to give the okay. The US embassy also was under strict orders to keep their superiors at the State Department in Washington, DC, up to date at all times on developments that could affect their relationships with the governments of Pakistan and Afghanistan.

The July 6 strike was particularly important to the State Department because just three days earlier, Secretary of State Hillary Clinton had issued an apology, while carefully avoiding using what her advisers referred to as the "A-word," to the government of Pakistan for a 2011 airstrike that killed twenty-four Pakistani soldiers. The Pakistan government was so angry about the attack that they cut off critical supply lines used by the US and its allies to supply soldiers in Afghanistan; this created a logistical nightmare for NATO forces that added more than $1 billion to the shipping and transportation costs of the decade-long military conflict.

The bombing of the Pakistan military site put the relationship into a deep freeze that lasted six months, until a delicate conversation between Clinton and Pakistan's foreign minister, Hina Rabbani Khar, finally got the supply line reopened. "We are sorry for the losses suffered by the Pakistani military," Clinton said after her call with Khar. "We are committed to working closely with Pakistan and Afghanistan to prevent this from ever happening again."

Even after the impasse was over, the State Department was still highly sensitive to other drone strikes or developments that might derail the delicate alliance. Further complicating matters, in a matter of days Clinton was due to meet Khar again at a global summit on Afghanistan's future. If a new assault just over the border was going to affect the meeting, Clinton's people wanted to know about it as soon as possible. So a flurry of communications ensued, mostly by email.

At the time of that particular strike, the US ambassador to Pakistan, Cameron Munter, was in the United States for a NATO meeting. Munter's wife forwarded him the news email alert about the strike. Munter, in turn, forwarded it to his deputy, Richard Hoagland, who was acting as chief of mission in Munter's absence. Hoagland replied with what he knew about the situation, adding, "If I get more, I'll let you know immediately."

Munter forwarded Hoagland's response to three of his superiors in Washington with a note, mentioning the Pakistan foreign minister only by her initials. "Heads up for HRK meetings with Secretary," he wrote. Jake Sullivan, a senior aide to Hillary Clinton, forwarded the email chain to the secretary of state, adding only "fyi."

When, the next day, Clinton met with Afghanistan president Hamid Karzai, the two talked about US efforts to stabilize the country, reduce corruption, and fight the Taliban. Clinton and Karzai then flew to Japan for a seventy-nation summit on Afghanistan. In Tokyo, Clinton met with Khar, and the two were photographed shaking hands and smiling.

In the United States, neither the drone strike nor the Clinton meeting would garner much attention, particularly since most of the country was still enjoying the July 4 holiday weekend. By 2012, the war in Afghanistan, and the poorly kept secret of lethal strikes in Pakistan, were mostly old news. There was nothing about the drone strike that would suggest it was exceptional, or momentous.

Speaking to reporters in Tokyo, Clinton said she and Khar had "put the recent difficulties behind us," but said the two countries have "a challenging but essential relationship . . . I have no reason to believe it will not continue to raise hard questions for us both."

She was talking about the US-Pakistan relationship, but the hard questions she would face would not be issues of diplomacy or statecraft. The internal State Department discussions of the missile strike would sit on an email server in the basement of her Chappaqua, New York, home, like unexploded political ordinance that would, when detonated, cause a chain reaction that would destroy her chances of becoming president, open the door to her unorthodox rival, and alter the trajectory of US history.

MONDAY, JULY 6, 2015

The three-year anniversary of the drone strike in Zowi Sidgi went unnoticed inside the US government and media. But it was observed nevertheless, albeit in a backhanded, bureaucratic way. That day, the inspector general of the Intelligence Community (IGIC) sent a letter to the FBI. The letter was what intelligence officials called an "811," a formal referral for investigation of a possible crime. The letter was about Hillary Clinton's use of a private email server during the time she was secretary of state.

The inspector general of the Intelligence Community—a mouthful of a title hinting at the sprawl of spy agencies the office was meant to police—had been wrestling for months with batches of Clinton's emails the State Department was preparing to release in response to lawsuits.

Inside the FBI, the 811 referral was not particularly surprising. The FBI receives hundreds of 811s every year, whenever another federal agency like the CIA or NSA thinks it has found possible evidence someone may have shared classified information without authorization.

The Bureau, or as many agents refer to it, the "Bu" (rhymes with "few"), only opens criminal investigations on a small percentage of them, about one in five. But when the Clinton email referral arrived, senior FBI leaders were certain they would investigate. By that point, the gears of government had been rolling in that direction for months. The House Select Committee on Benghazi created by Republicans had been at work for more than a year, investigating the attack on the US consulate that killed US ambassador Christopher Stevens and three other Americans. Republicans had accused the Obama administration generally, and Clinton in particular, of covering up the facts of the attack and the response.

As the State Department dealt with congressional requests for documents related to the investigation, officials at the agency contacted Cheryl Mills, a lawyer for Clinton, trying to locate the former secretary's emails. The State Department asked Mills to produce Clinton's emails from her time as a cabinet official, and reminded her of government policy that it was Clinton's responsibility to filter out any personal messages.

Clinton had her lawyers do the sorting of the sixty-thousand-plus emails in her private, nongovernment clintonemail.com account. Rather than go through the time-consuming process of reading each one individually, the lawyers used keyword searches to identify messages related to her work as secretary of state. The keywords included the names of State Department officials, lawmakers, foreign leaders, or words like "Afghanistan" and "Benghazi." Her lawyers also read the subject lines for all of the emails, but did not open the emails to examine their contents. When the lawyers finished their sorting, Hillary Clinton handed over roughly 30,490 work-related emails to the State Department, in a stack of some fifty-five thousand printed pages.

Clinton's lawyers also asked an IT contractor, Paul Combetta, to remove any of the Clinton emails that had been copied to their laptops, which he did using widely available software called BleachBit that writes over the file space to ensure deleted files can't be recovered. Approximately 31,830 emails were wiped clean from the lawyers' computers with this method. The lawyers also instructed the IT contractor to modify Clinton's email policy for the clintonemail.com account so it didn't retain any emails more than sixty days old. That change was not made until later, after her emails had become a political football.

Clinton's use of the clintonemail.com account became public knowledge on March 2, 2015, when the *New York Times* reported Clinton had exclusively used a personal email account to conduct government business, in possible violation of federal records laws. The following day, the Benghazi committee sent legal notice to Clinton requiring her to preserve any emails on her servers. It was only then that the IT contractor Paul Combetta deleted emails that were still lingering on a server at his company, after what he called an "oh shit" moment when he realized they were there, and that he had never carried out the Clinton lawyers' instruction to shorten the retention time on Clinton emails. Combetta was eventually granted immunity in exchange for his cooperation with investigators, and a lawyer for the IT company has insisted the FBI found no wrongdoing.

The emails that had previously been sorted by Clinton's legal team and sent to the State Department, meanwhile, were being processed by Freedom of Information Act (FOIA) officials, leading to their release in batches. But as the first three hundred or so messages were posted online, officials at other government agencies saw a problem. There appeared to be discussions of sensitive, possibly classified topics in the emails.

One in particular was flagged to the FBI, because it concerned their investigation into the Benghazi attack. The November 12, 2012, email relayed news reports that "Libyans [sic] police have arrested several people today who may/may have some connection to the Benghazi attack." A senior State Department official forwarded the message to others, noting: "FBI in Tripoli is fully involved."

To the consternation of the FBI's counterterrorism division, the email referred to a local official who had been helping the FBI in their investigation, potentially endangering a source. Even though the email did not name the local official, they worried someone might be able to figure out who it was, which "could be fatal for whoever cooperated with us."

By May 21, the back-and-forth between the Bureau and the State Department had come to a head. Mike Steinbach, then the assistant director for the Counterterrorism Division, talked to Pat Kennedy, the senior State Department official who had been trying to convince the Bureau not to decide that the email contained classified material. Steinbach told Kennedy it was settled: the email was classified and the Bureau wasn't going to budge. In a note to colleagues memorializing the conversation, Steinbach wrote: "I would not change the original determination made by the FBI."

The implications of Steinbach's move were clear to many inside the FBI. What may have seemed, on the surface, a bureaucratic debate about the redactions of a single, years-old government email meant far more. Federal workers who handle classified information often refer to their two worlds of communications as the "high side," where classified material is shared, and the "low side," where unclassified discussions take place. Clinton's private server threw a monkey wrench into that binary world, by putting emails she considered "low side" outside the government on a private server. It was against the law to put classified information in a low-side government email, so in criminal law terms it didn't matter very much whether such classified information was in an unclassified government email or a personal email. But within the bureaucracy of secrecy, it mattered a great deal. To people who lived and worked in the classified world on a daily basis, Clinton's decision to use a private server had taken a fairly frequent and commonplace problem—government secrets sometimes spilling into the unclassified government space—and put them somewhere outside the government entirely.

When the FBI first got wind of the Clinton email server, some senior officials felt they should try to avoid launching a criminal investigation. Better, they argued, to conduct a "spillage" review—the term used when classified information escapes into the wild. A spillage review is different from a criminal investigation, in that the main effort is to see where the sensitive information traveled and retrieve it or delete it in order to keep it from spreading any further. It's primarily a cleanup job, not a hunt for a suspect.

But the Clinton investigation would not be a spillage case. The IGIC made its referral on July 6, 2015. Three years to the day after the drone attack on Zowi Sigdi, a legal and political missile was primed inside the FBI. On July 10, the FBI formally opened a full investigation of Clinton's use of a private email account "to detect, obtain information about, and protect against federal crimes or threats to national security," according to an internal FBI document. More than any other person, the trajectory and timing of that missile would be decided by the seventh director of the FBI, James B. Comey.

The Comey Effect

JAMES COMEY'S STAR inside the Justice Department shone brightly, beginning with a stint as an assistant US attorney in Manhattan in the late 1980s and early 1990s. After a brief period in private practice, he went back to the Justice Department, running the federal prosecutor's office in Virginia's capital, Richmond. After 9/11, Comey was tapped for one of the biggest jobs in the Justice Department, running the US attorney's office in lower Manhattan where he'd worked years earlier as an assistant. At the time of his confirmation to the job, he still had many friends in the prosecutor's office, but was less known in the broader New York legal community.

Comey decided that one way to fix that was to meet directly with a large group of defense lawyers on neutral ground: the ceremonial courtroom of the federal courthouse in lower Manhattan, a cavernous room of wooden benches. In some ways, courtrooms are like churches. A hush tends to fall on those who enter. If the US legal system is a kind of religion to its practitioners, then the local county courthouses are neighborhood churches. Federal courthouses are the cathedrals, meant to inspire and awe even the most skeptical.

Of the ninety-four federal judicial districts in the United States, the crown jewel is the Southern District of New York, or SDNY. Its jurisdiction encompasses the New York City boroughs of Manhattan and the Bronx as well as the city's northern suburbs. SDNY has established itself as home to the biggest trials, the worst defendants, and the boldest lawyers and judges. Rudy Giuliani's political career was propelled largely by his five years in the 1980s as the US attorney for SDNY. Before him, Robert Morgenthau parlayed eight years as US attorney into a twenty-five-year stretch as the Manhattan district attorney. The SDNY courthouse has handled every type of high-profile criminal case imaginable—from Russian spies to mob bosses, from terrorists to billion-dollar con artists.

The lawyers filing into the courtroom that day in 2002 were not in the mood to be quiet. Defense lawyers are an argumentative lot by training and experience, and sometimes by nature. On this particular day, they were incensed. Blocks away, the fires in the belly of the debris pile of the World Trade Center had finally been extinguished, but the awful stench still lingered. The collapsed wreckage of the Twin Towers had burned for more than three months following the 9/11 attacks. Nearly three thousand had been killed, and the medical examiner was still trying to sort through massive quantities of remains, hoping to identify through DNA some scrap of loved ones for burial.

No one in the courtroom needed a reminder of what had happened. But the defense lawyers were angry and worried about how the government was responding to the attacks. Federal law enforcement, in its hunt to identify anyone who might have aided the nineteen hijackers who brought down four airliners, had taken hundreds of people into custody. Many were detained for having overstayed their visas. A small number of individuals were locked up as material witnesses—a rarely used authority to detain someone who might have critical information on an investigation and might flee to parts unknown if left to their own devices. But in the exceptional circumstances, around the country, roughly twelve hundred citizens and aliens had been detained for questioning. Most were held at the request of the Immigration and Naturalization Service. At the federal jail in Brooklyn known as the Metropolitan Detention Center, dozens of men were being held on suspicion of having broken immigration laws. In nearby Passaic, New Jersey, a county jail held four hundred aliens arrested by federal agents in the wake of the attacks.

Some of the lawyers in the ceremonial courtroom represented those locked-up men. Being defense lawyers, many in the group were deeply suspicious that the government had engaged in a breathtaking violation of civil rights—a roundup of the stereotypical "usual suspects." They came to hear an explanation from President George W. Bush's new US attorney, James B. Comey.

Most people have the same reaction upon meeting Comey for the first time, and it usually goes something like this: "I knew he was tall, but I had no idea he was *that* tall." Often they say it to his face. At six feet eight inches, Comey is the kind of tall person who instinctively ducks his head walking into almost any room. Even if the doorjamb in question is high enough to accommodate him, his muscle memory does not trust doorways. The second thing people notice about Comey is that he is an exceptionally compelling and charismatic speaker. It's a skill he honed over years of questioning witnesses, imploring juries, and arguing in front of judges. But there are thousands of lawyers with similar experience and résumés—Comey's power of persuasion is unmatched by all but an infinitesimally small number of them.

In the ceremonial courtroom, Comey knew he would be speaking to a skeptical, possibly hostile audience. Many government officials approach such situations in something of a rhetorical crouch, expecting a trap or an angry outburst in every question. Comey took the opposite tack. "It's hard to hate up close," he liked to say, meaning that if you got in a room with someone who distrusted or disliked you, you could often convince them that you were, if not right, then at least not evil. It was an approach that worked far better for Comey than many of his contemporaries. Waving his long arms wide out before him, Comey at times appeared to be reaching out to the entire room; he embraced his audience both rhetorically and physically, as he gave a short introduction of himself, explained his past work in the US Attorney's Office, and his enthusiasm for his new job, and offered a self-deprecating description of how he worked. He also offered a defense of what the Justice Department was doing in its quest to prevent the next terrorist attack and investigate the last one.

The defense attorneys began asking questions—how did he justify holding people in custody for weeks or even months at a time, without telling those individuals what they were suspected of? Holding people without charge was antithetical to American justice. How could he keep so many matters under seal that in some cases their lawyers felt hamstrung to even represent their clients against some ill-defined suspicion?

As the lawyers' questions came hotter and faster, Comey decided it was time to make his central point. Imagine a scenario, he said, in which you have been told by a foreign government that a particular person is going to drive a bomb to New York City in two days, and you don't know the route, and you don't know the car, but you have a name or part of a name, and you have forty-eight hours to stop it. He presented this scenario, he said, not as a scary work of fiction, but as a real-world example of the kind of intelligence the FBI was being asked to act on immediately. "What would you do if you were in my situation?" Comey asked the crowd. "Just think for a minute, how should we proceed?"

The question seemed to stump his audience. There were follow-up questions and criticism, but Comey had shifted the momentum in the room, and everyone felt it. In the wake of 9/11, even seasoned defense lawyers were alarmed at the prospect of the next attack. Eventually, the meeting broke up and the defense lawyers filed out of the room. It was the end of the day and many of them were heading home from the courthouse. They bid a respectful good-bye to Comey, who was gracious and smiling in a reassuring way. The new US attorney had displayed all of the skills that would come to define Comey as he rose higher in government. He commanded the room. He was eloquent without being emotional. He was convincing without being condescending. And in his lawyerly way, he had just sold sand in the Sahara.

In politics and government, there are rare officials who have such a mastery of public speaking that they are, in effect, their own best spokesman. Comey was one of those people. In 2002, the Bush administration often struggled to explain how their antiterrorism efforts did not run afoul of civil liberties laws dating back to the country's founding. In part, that was because senior officials like Vice President Dick Cheney made civil libertarians suspect they were deliberately trying to exceed the law. "We also have to work, sort of, the dark side, if you will," Cheney said on *Meet the Press* the Sunday after the 9/11 attacks. He was speaking largely about US intelligence activities overseas, but as horror stories emerged about mistreatment in the United States of people wrongly suspected of terrorism, defense lawyers, civil rights groups, and citizens began to question if the Bush administration had curtailed the Constitution in the name of security.

Comey, on the other hand, talked about the war on terror in a way that conveyed a sense of urgency and worry, without cheap fear-mongering. Amid heated arguments about federal trials versus military tribunals at Guantanamo Bay, Cuba, Comey seemed to have a deft touch at discussing the issue in a calm and comforting manner, arguing that each venue had merits for prosecuting terrorists, depending on the facts of the case.

The Bush administration noticed. After less than two years in New York as the US attorney, Comey became the deputy attorney general—or in the lingo of the Justice Department, the "DAG." As the US attorney in Manhattan, Comey already had one of the highest-profile jobs in the Justice Department. But as the DAG, he would be one of the most powerful. The DAG's job is to oversee day-to-day operations at Justice and its component agencies—the FBI, the Drug Enforcement Administration, the Bureau of Alcohol, Tobacco, Firearms and Explosives (ATF), the US Marshals, and the Bureau of Prisons. Inside the building, it is often the DAG who makes key decisions, or at least takes responsibility for them.

The DAG works out of a fourth-floor office of Justice Department headquarters, in a small, wood-paneled office that sits directly underneath the attorney general's small, wood-paneled office on the fifth floor. The top two positions at Main Justice (the term used most by Justice Department employees to describe their headquarters in downtown

Washington, across Pennsylvania Avenue from FBI headquarters) are situated within about twenty vertical feet of each other, but depending on the relationship of the two people in those jobs, it can feel like twenty inches, or twenty miles.

As the DAG, Comey worked well with his boss, Attorney General John Ashcroft. But Comey's biggest test in the job would come in just the first few months. In March 2004, Comey began making waves inside the Bush administration about a top-secret program called Stellar Wind. The program was launched after the 2001 terror attacks, and it involved warrantless surveillance on suspects and citizens. Justice Department lawyers working under Comey had come to the conclusion that the legal foundation of the program was shaky at best, and the amount of information the National Security Agency was scooping up under the program was in practice far beyond what the legal rationale supported.

In the wake of 9/11, and the subsequent 9/11 Commission to find out what mistakes had been made and how to make sure they did not happen again, the government was obsessed with "connecting the dots" to find terror plots. Stellar Wind was part of the government's dot-connecting efforts, but a small number of Republican lawyers inside the Bush administration had decided it was collecting, rather than connecting, too many dots, and those lawyers had convinced Comey they were right.

As Comey was figuring out exactly what Stellar Wind did and why that was a problem, Ashcroft was suddenly stricken with acute pancreatitis, and rushed to George Washington University Hospital in downtown DC. His health was so frail that he could not perform the functions of the attorney general, and Comey became the acting head of the department.

Ashcroft's illness came just as the Stellar Wind conflict between Justice and the White House was coming to a head. Comey was summoned to a meeting at the White House where he was told that thousands of people could die if Comey, as acting head of the Justice Department, didn't sign paperwork renewing Stellar Wind. To Comey, this was symptomatic of the post-9/11 era. As he liked to tell colleagues, "People in government aren't worried about the next 9/11. They're worried about the next 9/11 Commission," meaning senior officials worried too much about bureaucratic and political blame games that might follow any successful terror attack.

In a tense standoff with Vice President Cheney and others over Stellar Wind, Comey did not relent. The following day, he heard that two senior Bush officials—chief of staff Andy Card and White House counsel Alberto Gonzales—were going to see Ashcroft in the hospital. To Comey, it was clear the White House was trying to go above and around him and get a sick Ashcroft to reauthorize the program because Comey wouldn't.

Comey raced to the hospital, while summoning reinforcements on the phone, in the form of FBI director Robert Mueller and Justice Department lawyers. Comey got to Ashcroft's room shortly before Card and Gonzales. The two White House officials told Ashcroft they were there to discuss an important national security program that needed to continue.

Ashcroft, however, surprised everyone by rising in his hospital bed to give a detailed criticism of the program, then ending the debate by saying his opinion didn't matter anyway, since legally speaking, Comey was the attorney general at the time. Card and Gonzales retreated without a signed document. In that moment, "I felt like crying," Comey later wrote. "The law had held."

But the fight was not over. As the White House prepared to reauthorize the program without Justice Department approval, Comey and others at the department prepared to resign. After some tense discussions between President Bush and Comey, then Bush and Mueller, the president ordered Justice to craft changes that would make Stellar Wind legally acceptable to the Justice Department. Comey had won his showdown, but in early 2005 Alberto Gonzales became attorney general. Comey was already tired from long hours, and Gonzales's arrival as his boss meant the writing was on the wall. Later that year, he would leave the department for a job in the private sector.

Comey's successor as deputy attorney general was Paul McNulty, who had once been Comey's boss in the federal prosecutors' office in Virginia. Comey's intelligence, charm, and savvy had catapulted him above

McNulty, and now McNulty was following his footsteps into the number two position at Main Justice.

When McNulty came to see Comey in 2005 to talk about the job, Comey offered him some advice. "Paul, remember they're paying you for your judgment," Comey told him. "That's the bottom line, and it doesn't matter really where you are physically, a lot of things can be in flux but at the end of the day, it's your judgment that is the distinctive thing you're bringing to the situation."

It was good advice, but to McNulty the full import of Comey's words changed over time, after the hospital confrontation became public knowledge, and Comey took on an almost mythical air of the righteous superhero battling craven politicians.

"Jim is one of the most impressive people that anyone is likely to meet," McNulty said. "It's hard to have any contact with Jim and not really be struck by what an extraordinary type of person he is, in the truest sense of that word. But that also carries a risk of overconfidence."

After leaving the DAG job in August 2005, Comey went to work for defense contractor Lockheed Martin, where he generally kept out of the limelight, with one notable exception that would redefine his public image and set him on a path toward eventually running the FBI.

In 2007, Comey testified before Congress, revealing for the first time the details of the confrontation in Ashcroft's hospital room. That testimony elevated Comey's stature in official Washington as a government do-gooder, rather than the dime-a-dozen former official he'd been when he left the department.

Comey's testimony had a second, more immediate impact, one that wasn't lost on those who knew him well: he'd hurt Alberto Gonzales badly. Comey was called to testify right as Senate Democrats were attacking the attorney general over the alleged politicization of the Justice Department. Comey testifying against his former boss contributed to the domino-like effect of revelations that forced Gonzales's resignation announcement several months later. The dramatic account had greatly enhanced Comey's reputation, and badly damaged his former boss's.

Comey took another important step in his private-sector life in 2010, when he went to work for Bridgewater Associates, a wildly successful hedge fund run by its founder, Ray Dalio. Comey's new job confused a lot of his former friends and colleagues at the Justice Department. In the aftermath of the collapse of the housing market, the financial markets, and the economy, going to work for a billionaire's hedge fund seemed like political suicide for anyone who might entertain the notion of someday becoming the attorney general or FBI director. Comey told friends he wasn't interested in the FBI job anyway. He'd been the DAG, and the FBI director reports to the DAG, so why would he take a demotion? Many of his friends didn't accept that explanation at face value, but working at a hedge fund seemed to them a clear signal that he had written off the idea of returning to government.

Bridgewater was famous in the financial world for its adherence to founder Dalio's principles, which included a commitment to what he called "radical transparency" and "radical open-mindedness." Dalio's philosophy is laid out in the 567-page book *Principles*, which argues that success in life and business is dependent upon a devotion to transparency and honesty, even if that means social pain, personal embarrassment, and temporary loss of status among colleagues. Such pain, Dalio argues, is good because it forces people to face reality as it is, not as they wish it would be. Dalio's business is structured around these principles, and he has used them to great effect. Bridgewater is generally considered the largest hedge fund in the world, and he credits his principles with teaching a sprawling workforce to learn quicker than their competitors what forces will shape global markets, and how.

"Being radically transparent and radically open-minded accelerates this learning process. It can also be difficult because being radically transparent rather than more guarded exposes one to criticism," Dalio wrote in his book. "It's natural to fear that. Yet if you don't put yourself out there with your radical transparency, you won't learn." Dalio's principles envision an individual's personality as essentially a struggle between their "higher level" self—their emotion-free intellect—and their "lower level" self—their emotional ego.

"Radical open-mindedness allows you to escape from the control of your lower-level you and ensures your upper-level you sees and considers all the good choices and makes the best possible decisions," Dalio wrote. To some former Bridgewater employees, and to some of his competitors, the Dalio approach comes across as cultlike, a sublimation of the ego in the quest for higher consciousness.

Comey found Dalio's formula attractive, if occasionally confusing. It offered a structure and framework for a lot of ideas Comey already had about life and work. The former DAG came to Bridgewater with a firm belief that people in positions of power should explain themselves fully, and tackle tough problems not just privately but publicly as well. He also felt he had struggled all his life to manage his ego. Coworkers knew Comey thought very highly of himself, and Comey worked hard to tamp down that trait when he interacted with others. He didn't always succeed, in part because wherever he went he developed a following—devoted fans who fed that same ego he was trying to rein in.

Given his instincts, Dalio's mantra struck a chord deep within Comey. "Most of my friends think I am having a midlife crisis," Comey told the *New Yorker* in 2011. "The mind control is working," he joked. "I've come to believe that all the probing actually reduces inefficiencies over the long run, because it prevents bad decisions from being made." Of Dalio, Comey said, "He's tough and he's demanding and sometimes he talks too much, but, God, is he a smart bastard."

In 2013, Comey left Bridgewater and later that year told President Obama that, yes, he would serve as his next FBI director. At his confirmation hearing, Comey held up his Bridgewater experience as the kind of transparency he wanted to see more of in the Bureau. "I went to Bridgewater in part because of that culture of transparency," Comey said. "It's something that's long been a part of me. I think it's incumbent upon every leader to foster an atmosphere where people will speak truth to power. Bridgewater and the FBI are two different institutions, but I promise I will carry those values with me and try to spread them as far as I can within the institution."

The Rise of Andy McCabe

BEFORE DECIDING TO PICK Comey as the next FBI director, the Obama administration had struggled for two years to come up with a worthy successor to Robert S. Mueller III. A dour, gray-haired government lifer sometimes referred to as "Bobby Three Sticks" behind his back for the patrician suffix at the end of his name, Mueller had overseen a sweeping transformation of the Bureau. FBI agents often talk of the Bureau as two organizations—the one that existed before September 11, 2001, and the one built following those attacks.

From his earliest days running the FBI, J. Edgar Hoover envisioned his agency would investigate and arrest radicals who threatened national security. When he was twenty-nine, Hoover took over what was then known as the Bureau of Investigation, and set out to professionalize, modernize, and grow the organization. As a young man, Hoover hunted radical anarchists. In middle age, he pursued communists and their feared fifth column—those communist sympathizers and spies lurking inside the government and American society who would betray the nation and compromise its security. In his later years, he hunted subversives, a dangerously broad category that came to include opponents of the Vietnam War and civil rights leaders. But Hoover, whose tenure as FBI director lasted forty-eight years, also knew that the Bureau's best

selling point was crime fighting. Whether it was kidnappers, bank rob-
bers, or gangsters, the public judged the FBI on its ability to take down
Public Enemy No. 1.

For decades, that enemy was crime. In the post–World War II peck-
ing order inside the Bureau, the top G-men, as FBI agents were often
called, were the ones who put handcuffs on dangerous killers. Criminal
cases were also the surest path to promotions and plum assignments.
Intelligence work and national security cases were important, but they
tended to take a backseat to the G-men who made splashy, front-page
arrests.

Through the latter half of the twentieth century, the FBI's counterterrorism work grew gradually as a piece of their larger crime-fighting
mission. Terrorism investigations started as a subset of criminal cases,
then over time grew to be a larger part of the FBI's workload. They were
concentrated in certain cities like New York, where the first Joint Terrorism Task Force was launched in 1980 with ten FBI agents and ten
New York Police Department detectives. In Washington, both FBI headquarters and its field office did a significant amount of counterterrorism
work, but there were plenty of cities around the country where terrorism
was a tiny fraction of the FBI workload.

Robert Mueller had been the director of the FBI for all of a week
on the Tuesday morning in 2001 when the World Trade Center collapsed, the Pentagon was struck by a hijacked passenger jet, and Flight
93 crashed into a field in Shanksville, Pennsylvania. Days after the attack,
Mueller was briefing President Bush on all the information his agents
had gathered about the nineteen dead hijackers. Mueller had barely begun speaking, describing what the FBI had learned about the hijackers,
when Bush interrupted him with a question: "What are you doing to
prevent the next attack?"

"I did not have an answer," Mueller would later say. Bush's question
would radically change how the FBI operated. Mueller didn't like to call
it a transformation; he preferred the term "augmentation." But within
the Bureau, it was perfectly clear how drastic the difference was. "The

mission changed, literally in a moment," said John Pistole, who under Mueller would become the longest-serving deputy director in the FBI's history. At the time of the 2001 terror attacks, the FBI had roughly ten thousand special agents. Two thousand of them would be moved from criminal investigative work to national security cases. And that was just the beginning.

Mueller embarked on a years-long overhaul of the FBI, turning its primary focus from crime fighting to one whose round-the-clock responsibility was preventing terror attacks. It's hard to overstate how significant those changes were for people inside the J. Edgar Hoover Building and within the fifty-six FBI field offices around the country. The priorities for an entire generation of federal agents changed overnight, as nearly every FBI agent dropped what they were doing to assist in the 9/11 investigation known as PENTTBOM. Over the months that followed, many of those agents would gradually return to the nonterrorism cases they had before the attacks. But as an organization, the FBI would never return to the agency it was before 9/11. From that moment on, the criminal work would take a backseat to national security priorities.

At the time, the vast majority of FBI agents bought into the change immediately. The nation was under attack and needed saving. For the most part, everyone accepted the new mission. It would be years before some agents, particularly those who'd built their careers on criminal cases, began complaining about the FBI's priorities. Some agents who had spent their careers working criminal cases chafed at the new importance of the national security guys, particularly those who worked in counterintelligence, mocking them as "the no-headlights crew" because they supposedly came into work after the sun was up and left before it went down.

There was another dynamic to Mueller's changes. For most of its history, FBI agents liked to say that the best place to work was in a field office, where the bosses, known as "special agents in charge" (SAC), largely operated as rulers of their own fiefdoms, guiding their own cases with minimal interference from headquarters. "The career ambition for many agents seeking advancement was to become an SAC, and you pretty much got to run your own show, but that completely changed after 9/11, and there was a sense of loss about that. But it was necessary and prudent to ensure all the intelligence gathered across all the field offices was synthesized, analyzed, and disseminated," said John Pistole. "That didn't happen prior to 9/11."

Andrew McCabe had joined the FBI in 1996, starting in the New York field office, where he was eventually assigned to Russian organized crime cases. When the 2001 attacks happened, like most of his fellow agents, McCabe was immediately tasked with helping on the PENTTBOM case, and he would leave the world of gangsters almost entirely. McCabe went to work in counterterrorism and rose rapidly up the ranks of the FBI, thanks to a work ethic that stood out even in squads full of driven agents. He also developed a knack for briefing superiors in ways that won him attention and praise, according to those who worked with him.

In 2009, Mueller showed how much he had come to trust McCabe by putting him in charge of a new program called the High-Value Detainee Interrogation Group, or HIG. The HIG was the Obama administration's answer to the contentious political debate over how terror suspects should be detained and questioned, after the detainee abuse scandals of the Bush administration. Once Obama was president, Republicans accused his administration of being soft on terror suspects, a charge that ignored the relative track records of the criminal justice system and military tribunals. The HIG was created to be a rapid-response group of interrogation experts who could apply the full breadth of US intelligence resources to questioning suspects, in a way that could preserve, if senior officials chose, the possibility of charging the suspects in federal court. The HIG was an attempt to create best practices in the war on terror, but it was also a bureaucratic answer to a political problem.

Led by McCabe, the HIG proceeded to do by and large what the FBI had done for decades—question suspects, win their trust, get them to wittingly or unwittingly provide important evidence, then arrest them on charges that would earn them decades in prison.

McCabe was part of a new generation of FBI executives whose counterterrorism work fueled their rise up the organizational chart. Among ambitious FBI agents, it was well understood that after 2001, you probably needed at least one significant counterterrorism assignment to move up into important jobs. McCabe did many. He played a key role supervising the investigation and manhunt after the Boston Marathon bombing in 2013.

Along the way, that rapid rise by a relatively young agent rankled some of his contemporaries. For one thing, McCabe could be tough on people he thought were not living up to his expectations, and to some in the Bureau, he seemed to be toughest on the FBI agents who worked on the criminal side of the shop. At high-level meetings, it seemed at times the criminal agents could do nothing right in McCabe's eyes, and the national security agents could do no wrong. For some of the agents working criminal cases, McCabe embodied what they didn't like about the new FBI. Counterterrorism guys got promotions and criminal guys got punished, some complained. "McCabe and most of those guys couldn't make a white collar fraud case if their life depended on it," grumbled one veteran.

Irrespective of the critical muttering, McCabe was a "blue flamer," the term used by generations of law enforcement agents for a highly ambitious official rocketing up the organizational chart. In September of 2014, he became the assistant director in charge of the FBI's Washington field office—an important position in its own right, but in the Mueller era especially, a launching pad to the inner circle of FBI leadership at headquarters.

■■■■■■■■■

Andrew McCabe's rise in the FBI came at the same time his wife, Jill, was also gaining some public recognition. A medical doctor, Jill McCabe had weighed into the debate about health care in the United States during a tour of the hospital where she worked in Loudon County for Virginia's governor, Terry McAuliffe. In her role as a hospital doctor, she had given an interview to the *Washington Post* about the importance of Medicaid expansion, a signature Obama issue, in the state.

"I think expanding care for the folks who need it has to be part of the solution," Dr. McCabe told the *Post* in February 2014. Expanding Medicaid, she argued, would mean that kids with asthma would be on medication and get immunization shots, rather than show up in her emergency room. "They end up in here because they have complications that aren't being addressed."

A year later, McAuliffe's deputy and Virginia's lieutenant governor, Ralph Northam, called Jill McCabe to feel her out about running for the state senate. Northam, raised on Virginia's eastern shore, a sparsely populated finger of land that cradles the Chesapeake Bay, was a doctor-turned-Democrat politician, and he wanted Jill McCabe to follow the same course. McAuliffe and other Virginia Democrats were looking for a fresh face to challenge the aging Republican lawmaker Dick Black, who represented McCabe's area in the state senate. Black, the Democrats felt, was beatable.

Jill and Andrew McCabe were invited to a Democratic caucus meeting in Richmond so that she could talk to other state politicians about the possibility of running for office. Democrats also told the McCabes they might be able to meet McAuliffe, depending on the demands on his schedule that day.

A day before their trip to Richmond, McCabe had reached out to the head of the FBI's office in Richmond, Adam Lee. McCabe outranked Lee, but the two worked closely and had cases that overlapped. McCabe asked Lee for his thoughts about his wife running for office, and asked if Jill McCabe meeting with the state legislators would create any issues for investigations being worked by the FBI in Richmond. Lee told him there were no cases complicated by such a meeting, but warned McCabe that if he met with McAuliffe, he'd be "tethered to the Clintons forever," and that could have consequences for his career in the government.

Lee's advice was based on the fact that Terry McAuliffe had worked closely with Bill and Hillary Clinton for decades. He'd been a key fundraiser, a party boss, run Hillary Clinton's 2008 presidential campaign, and before becoming governor, sat on the board of the Clinton Foundation.

In political circles, McAuliffe's name was virtually synonymous with the Clintons. Conservatives liked to call him the Clintons' "bag man." Lee tried to impress upon McCabe that if his wife became publicly aligned with McAuliffe, it could dampen his prospects for promotion if a Republican administration went looking for someone to put at the top of an agency.

When the McCabes got to Richmond, they were invited to the governor's mansion to meet McAuliffe. The governor had a straightforward pitch for Dr. McCabe—he wanted to expand Medicaid, and felt a key way of making that happen in Virginia was to target a few state senate seats, including the district in which the McCabes lived. The Democratic Party, McAuliffe told them, would support McCabe's run for office if she decided to jump in. If she and a few other Democratic challengers were successful, the party could take control of the state senate, putting Medicaid expansion and a host of other policy goals suddenly within reach. The meeting took place less than one week after the *New York Times* had reported Hillary Clinton had used a private email server for her work as secretary of state, but four months before the FBI would open its investigation into the emails. Nonetheless, two unconnected issues had suddenly drifted into dangerous and potentially explosive proximity.

After talking for more than thirty minutes, Jill and Andrew McCabe got into McAuliffe's official vehicle and the trio rode to a nearby hotel where the governor gave a speech. After the speech, the McCabes rode back to the governor's mansion with McAuliffe, spent time at another event there, and then left. On the drive home, McCabe called Lee again, and described McAuliffe's forceful, gregarious personality.

Over the next week, Andy McCabe had a number of conversations with FBI officials about the ethical implications of his wife running for elected office. The FBI's then deputy director Mark Giuliano later told investigators that he warned McCabe that his wife running for office was a "bad idea." According to Giuliano, when he voiced reservations about McCabe's wife getting into politics, McCabe replied, "She's supported me for all these years; I need to support her." McCabe also talked to Comey's then chief of staff, Chuck Rosenberg, who told him the director had no concerns with his wife running for office. "He's totally comfortable with it," Rosenberg told McCabe.

Four days after the McCabes' trip to Richmond, Andrew McCabe sat down with Patrick Kelley, the FBI's chief ethics officer, and James Baker, the FBI's top lawyer and a close friend of Comey, to talk about the potential ethics issues raised by his wife's run for office.

The main topic of the meeting was to lay out what McCabe couldn't do—violate the 1939 Hatch Act, which among other things bars federal employees from using their government positions or time to advocate for a political candidate. They also discussed the possibility of recusing McCabe from certain cases involving Virginia politicians, if such cases arose, but those would be addressed as needed. A month later, an FBI lawyer formally entered into the computer system a document spelling out that McCabe would recuse from "all public corruption investigations arising out of or otherwise connected to the Commonwealth of Virginia," due to his wife's campaign. "Therefore, out of an abundance of caution, [McCabe] will be excluded from any involvement in all such cases." The day after the meeting, Dr. Jill McCabe announced her candidacy for the Virginia state senate.

Two months later, the FBI received a request to investigate Hillary Clinton over the Clinton Foundation and her use of a private email server. The suspicions fueled by right-wing radio and Fox News would blossom into a central line of attack on Clinton as she ran for president—that her husband's charitable foundation, by raising millions of dollars from corporations and wealthy individuals around the globe, was an unethical and possibly illegal enterprise trading donations for access to State Department officials. The request for an investigation was forwarded to the Washington field office, where McCabe directed a subordinate to "conduct a standard assessment." He later followed up with more specific instructions, pulling back on his previous instruction: "To be clear, we are info gathering at this point. Please do not open a case or assessment until we have the chance to discuss further."

McCabe's subordinate forwarded the email conversation to a supervisory agent in the Criminal Division, who replied that McCabe "s recuse himself from this matter in my opinion." This was the first known expression of an opinion that would be increasingly voiced inside the FBI in the months ahead.

The concerns were raised again to Kelley, the FBI's chief ethics officer who had previously drawn up a template for McCabe's possible recusal. He considered the question, and felt there was no need for McCabe to recuse himself from any Clinton cases at that time. The connection between McAuliffe and Clinton was too tangential, he thought.

When, in July 2015, the FBI formally opened an investigation into Hillary Clinton's use of a private email server, to determine if she or any of her staff had broken the law when it came to the handling and sharing of classified information, the investigation was run out of FBI headquarters, with staff support from the Washington field office, which was overseen by McCabe. No one then reexamined the recusal question surrounding McCabe.

In October 2015, Jill McCabe's campaign for state senator in Virginia received donations of $467,500 from Common Good VA, McAuliffe's political action committee. Her campaign also got $207,788 from the Virginia Democratic Party, an entity over which McAuliffe held significant sway. Together it amounted to $675,288, or about 40 percent of the total contributions Dr. McCabe received during her campaign. Among Virginia state senate candidates, she was the third-largest recipient of money from McAuliffe's PAC that year.

That same month she picked up the endorsement of the *Washington Post*, but on Election Day 2015, she lost to Black, who garnered 52.4 percent of the vote. Her husband, though he didn't yet know it, would lose a great deal more.

But Their Emails

THURSDAY, MARCH 10, 2016

For months, the FBI agents working the Clinton email case had grown increasingly skeptical they would end up charging anyone with a crime. They had spent months talking to the IT staffers who set up and maintained the Clinton email accounts, searching old servers for stray bits of data, and creating a timeline of her digital data. Now it was time to start working up the ladder of a different set of witnesses—the ones who had written some of the key emails. Cameron Munter, the former US ambassador to Pakistan, had retired from the State Department. For his interview, he entered a nondescript FBI building in Manhattan's Chelsea neighborhood, across the street from a labyrinthine indoor food market. He was escorted into a SCIF, a sensitive compartmented information facility, where US government secrets can be discussed without fear of listening devices. Per standard procedure, he surrendered his phone before entering the room.

The FBI agents wanted to talk to Munter about emails. Specifically, emails he'd been sent, emails he'd forwarded, in chains that years earlier had made their way to Hillary Clinton's inbox, meaning they lived on her private server in the basement of her Chappaqua home.

As the US ambassador to Pakistan, Munter played a critical role in CIA drone strikes—they did not fire without his approval. He also had to make sure his superiors in Washington knew immediately of important developments in that part of the world. Munter would send messages to the office of the special representative to Afghanistan and Pakistan, or SRAP, and assumed that people there would decide whether or not to tell Secretary Clinton.

The agents had printed out a series of email chains that included Munter and began showing them to him. He declined to discuss a number of them, which frustrated the agents and made them think their concerns about careless handling of classified secrets were justified. But Munter was also being cautious, feeling that the priorities of the police and the priorities of diplomats were suddenly, awkwardly at odds. The FBI didn't have the same worries about keeping an open channel with Pakistan, or keeping supply routes open for NATO troops.

Agents showed Munter an email chain that began with a message he had sent on the morning of Friday, December 23, 2011, the last official workday before the Christmas holiday. For a subject line, Munter wrote "(SBU)," the government acronym for "sensitive but unclassified." The body of the email was a cryptic, one-line heads-up that there was a drone strike in Pakistan expected shortly. Munter was careful to use euphemisms when writing unclassified emails, like writing "bird" instead of "drone," to ensure no one but the recipients would know what he was talking about.

But this particular email chain had an unintended side effect. Munter's heads-up had been sent first to his boss Dan Feldman at State, who relayed it to two top Clinton advisers, Cheryl Mills and Jake Sullivan. When there was no public reporting of a drone strike around the holiday, Mills sent a follow-up message on December 27, asking what had happened. Feldman responded in two separate emails.

To the FBI, that kind of conversation was particularly alarming and infuriating. It's one thing to discuss on an insecure channel a drone strike that just happened. That was bad, senior FBI officials thought. But to have that kind of discussion about a drone strike that hadn't happened yet was unconscionable. What if someone could look at those messages in real time? Would a high-value terror target get a warning and sneak away?

█████████████

<u>Agents questioned</u> Munter again more than a month later, in Washington. In that session, Munter explained some of the context behind the Christmastime email—the US bombing of Pakistan soldiers had taken place about a month earlier, leading to major problems for the United States both in Pakistan and the war effort in Afghanistan. State Department officials were particularly focused at that time on knowing if some new complication was about to make the bad times even worse.

Munter was also asked about the email chain surrounding the July 6, 2012, drone strike at Zowi Sidgi, the one that allegedly killed the fourteen-year-old boy, though the agents didn't ask about the boy's death. He read the messages, and told the agents he didn't see how anything he had written had jeopardized anyone involved.

Part of the FBI's concern—and the CIA's, for that matter—was not the contents of any particular email. While Munter's December heads-up had been very brief, it was followed by a series of messages that made it far easier for anyone who might access Clinton's inbox to figure out what they were discussing; euphemisms and "talking around" classified subjects didn't work very well if the participants kept talking, and talking, and talking. In some of the conversations, it was the chain, not any individual piece of it, that was the problem, the FBI agents thought.

TUESDAY, MARCH 15, 2016

Munter's deputy for a time in Pakistan was Richard Hoagland, a career diplomat. Before serving as the deputy ambassador in Pakistan, Hoagland served as the US ambassador to Kazakhstan, and before that Tajikistan. In the late 1990s, he was the press spokesman for the US embassy in Moscow.

Hoagland became the deputy ambassador to Pakistan in 2011, at a time when relations between the two countries were under constant strain, in no small part because of the drone program. Munter and Hoagland were under instruction to flag to their superiors in Washington any developments that could pose new problems for that relationship. They did a lot of flagging.

Three years after his time in Pakistan, the FBI scheduled an interview with Hoagland at the Washington field office, a modern sandstone building on the edge of the city's quickly gentrifying Chinatown neighborhood. Hoagland entered the building and was ushered into a secure office room with three agents. An agent behind a desk had printouts of some of his old emails from Pakistan, and handed them to him one by one to read.

In one of the messages, Hoagland had written "my high side is down, so I'm summarizing this on this system," using government vernacular to distinguish between his classified and unclassified email systems. FBI agents use similar nomenclature, but also have a color-coded set of terms to describe classification levels. Hoagland's "high side" sentence encapsulated much of the challenge Clinton's inbox presented to investigators. Many of the messages the FBI viewed as most problematic were sent around times when the senders, or recipients, or both, were unlikely to have access to their classified systems because they were away from work or on vacation. To State Department personnel it was a sign of professionalism that they would find words to "talk around" classified matters in a safe way. To the FBI inspectors the habit was akin to reckless driving—an accident waiting to happen.

In his interview, Hoagland conceded that the email in his hands was "getting close to the line, obviously." But after decades in the foreign service he was confident he knew how not to cross it. "If you are a professional," he told the agents, "you know how to do it and how much to do." It had not occurred to him until the Clinton email case that the FBI would come back years later and decide the line could be drawn elsewhere, and the agents could decide he was on the wrong side of it.

To some degree, the disagreement was generational. Older diplomats and government employees whose careers predated the 2001 terror attacks found that the younger generation was often more cautious.
Some senior officials thought the younger generation was surprisingly,
depressingly rigid in their thinking. In the years since September 11, 2001,
the government as a whole became stricter about classified information,
both in categorizing more information as classified and enforcing the
controls on it. The training of everyone from FBI agents to postal inspectors included more ominous warnings about the possible criminal
consequences of talking, even to other employees, about government secrets. "They put the fear of God in them from the start," said one former
official. "It's a little sad, and at times it can feel a little silly."

As the interview went on, the FBI agents handed Hoagland printouts
of more emails, including the Christmastime discussion of a planned
drone strike that ended up not taking place. They also showed him the
email chain that began with a news story about the July 6, 2012, drone
strike in Zowi Sidgi. He again explained why he did what was necessary
and safe to get important, time-sensitive information to his bosses. As
the interview wound down, Hoagland felt he'd done a good job explaining the difficulties and intricacies of diplomacy in a far-off country.

WEDNESDAY, MARCH 16, 2016

Not everyone was content to let the FBI handle the Clinton email case
on its own, behind closed doors. Julian Assange, the founder of the anti-
secrecy group WikiLeaks, had been sharply at odds with Hillary Clinton
since her days as secretary of state, and he wanted to publicize the Clinton email controversy. Assange had made his personal dislike of Clinton
clear; to him, she was part of a war-mongering ruling class whose liberal
credentials made her that much more likely to use military force around
the world. Assange had risen to global prominence in 2010 by releasing thousands of internal files of the US military and State Department,

given to him by then US Army intelligence analyst Bradley Manning (now Chelsea Manning). Clinton had spent months trying to contain the diplomatic fallout from those releases.

In late 2010, Sweden issued an arrest warrant for Assange on suspicion of sexual assault. The activist called the case a pretext to get him in handcuffs and eventually turned over to the United States. In 2012, he sought and was granted asylum in Ecuador's embassy in London, where he would remain for nearly seven years living in the basement and getting his message out via webcam interviews and tweets, and encouraging others to follow Manning's example.

In mid-March, Assange released in a more searchable form repackaged versions of the Clinton emails being made public by the State Department. The State Department releases were presented online in such a reader-unfriendly way that reporters and anyone else curious enough to sift through them had to navigate a clunky computer format. Assange realized that if he made a more user-friendly version of the same data, people would be drawn to the WikiLeaks website, and some portion of those people might credit WikiLeaks with the emails' discovery.

The WikiLeaks version of the Clinton email archive was posted with a political cartoon of the former secretary of state sitting at a laptop, typing messages about bombs and money. With the publication, Assange amplified the email controversy for those who didn't necessarily understand the nuances of government records laws, and at the same time, advertised his site as a home for more Clinton documents. In a matter of months, Assange's gambit would pay off handsomely.

Loretta and Jim

APRIL 2016

By the spring of 2016, James Comey and Loretta Lynch had been work-ing together as FBI director and attorney general, respectively, for a year. Comey reported to Lynch's deputy, Deputy Attorney General Sally Yates, but in the real world of Washington power, the FBI director often held more sway than his bosses. In part, that's because the FBI can possess more cachet in Congress and the White House than the Justice Depart-ment. The other factor at play in 2016 was that by then Comey had been FBI director for several years and would probably continue to be so for years to come. Yates and Lynch, by comparison, were relative newcom-ers in their jobs, and short-timers at that. At White House meetings in 2016, officials would sometimes tease Comey that he alone among them would still be dealing with these issues the next year. But the power dy-namic between Lynch and Comey wasn't all about bureaucracy and ten-ure. They had similar résumés, but different backgrounds, and different personalities.

Comey and Lynch liked each other. They had first worked together in 1990, when they were young prosecutors in New York. At the time, Lynch was the lead prosecutor on a case in which a Staten Island bread-truck driver had concocted a scheme to sell cocaine along his delivery route. After he and his alleged coconspirators were arrested, one of the defendants was caught on jailhouse tape talking about killing the federal judge assigned to the case, Reena Raggi. It was a Brooklyn case, but as it happened, Raggi was married to a federal prosecutor in Manhattan, so SDNY wanted one of their people to join the threat investigation. They assigned Jim Comey.

The future FBI director and future attorney general investigated the threats before ultimately deciding it wasn't worth adding fresh charges. Instead, one of the senior Brooklyn prosecutors, Charles Rose, called the defendant and his lawyer into his office, played them the tapes, and told them in blunt language to knock it off. The first Lynch-Comey professional pairing hadn't led to an indictment, but everyone walked away satisfied with the outcome. Twenty-five years later they were back together, and on the surface, got along fine.

To some senior Justice Department officials, however, it seemed gender, and sometimes race, affected how Comey interacted with them. When the staffs of the attorney general and FBI director would meet, the FBI side of the table would be overwhelmingly white men, looking across a conference table at a collection of women, some of them minorities. "You couldn't help but notice it the moment you sat down with them," said one of the former senior Justice Department officials.

The issue of policing and race sometimes raised tensions between the FBI and Justice Department. At a speech in late 2015 to police officials in Chicago, Comey spelled out his concern that anger at police was causing officers to be more reticent, which might explain sudden increases in violence in some US cities.

"We can't lose sight of the fact that there really are bad guys standing on corners in America's cities with guns. The young men dying on those street corners in all those cities are not committing suicide or being shot by cops, they are being shot by other young men," Comey said.

Lives are saved, Comey said, when police officers are out of their police cars and asking those men, "What are you guys doing standing on a street corner at 1 am?"

At the end of his speech, the law enforcement officials seated on stage with Comey all stood to applaud him, except for one: the Justice Department's Ron Davis, Director of the Office of Community Oriented Policing Services.

To Davis, Comey's speech offered a dangerous kind of nostalgia for the era of high-volume arrests to clear the streets in poor neighborhoods, a strategy that Davis had carried out earlier in his career as a cop, but that he, Lynch, and many others had come to see as short-sighted. To Davis, that approach had been shown over time to disproportionately arrest young men of color.

After the speech, Davis approached Comey and said, "we need to talk." When they were both back in Washington, Davis went to Comey's office at the FBI to explain his concerns.

"Here's the problem, Jim: You're not identifying with the young men," said Davis. If white men hang out on the street in Georgetown at night, they are far less likely to be stopped and questioned by police, Davis pointed out.

Comey offered an analogy: In the same way a baseball pitcher needs to be able to throw inside near the batter in order to get strikeouts, police officers need to be active on the streets. Davis replied, "If the pitcher is hitting the batter, that's a problem. How about you train the pitcher to throw a strike and not hit the batter?"

Comey wasn't convinced, but he listened carefully to the points made by Davis, who also spoke to Loretta Lynch about his concerns that Comey's public statements on the issue were both out of date and out of synch with the Obama administration. Differences of opinion over policing and race would continue to drive a wedge between the FBI and Justice Department in 2015 and 2016, but it wasn't the only divisive topic. At times, gender politics also seemed in play.

At the end of one security meeting about encryption, Comey began telling Lynch how much he'd enjoyed reading the book *Lean In* by Facebook's chief operating officer, Sheryl Sandberg. Comey told his bosses he was struck by a description in the book of how women sometimes make a point in meetings that is ignored, and then when a man makes the same point minutes later, the idea is embraced. Comey said since reading the book, he had started to notice that behavior. Lynch burst out laughing at the fact that this was some kind of revelation to Comey.

"What? What?" Comey asked good-naturedly.

"How old are you?" Lynch teased him. (Comey was in his mid-fifties).

At the time, Lynch viewed such instances as insignificant. She essentially liked Comey and thought the feeling was mutual. Comey liked Lynch personally and kept any criticisms of her management style—he thought she was not a forceful leader—within the walls of the FBI.

Yates was more frustrated with the FBI director. If there was a case or an issue on which Yates already had many of the facts, Comey was willing to share details of what the FBI knew and was doing. If Yates was in the dark, Comey was often reluctant to fill her in. "It's like pulling teeth," Yates complained to colleagues more than once. She also feared that the man whose national reputation was made largely from a confrontation with his superiors over a secret surveillance program was primed to have a similar confrontation again at some point in his career. Despite such misgivings, Lynch still believed there was a basically good relationship between Comey and her, and the FBI and the Bureau. She was wrong.

On the surface, things were fine. FBI officials were generally solicitous and respectful of their Justice Department bosses. Inside the Hoover building, however, Bureau officials complained frequently about what they felt was feckless or politically focused leadership from Justice. Comey liked Lynch, but felt she lacked a commanding presence that inspired loyalty, respect, and, when necessary, fear. Others in Comey's circle felt the same: they saw themselves as major league players who excelled in the spotlight and under pressure, but they thought Lynch's team did not.

Whether in front of a live television camera or squirreled away inside a top-secret SCIF, Lynch was an understated, calm presence who rarely raised her voice in anger or excitement. As a young trial prosecutor in Brooklyn federal court, she had worked her way up the Justice Department hierarchy—a world of predominantly white, male prosecutors and federal agents—by not looking for drama or confrontations and focusing instead on the cases and the criminals. But in New York, as in Washington, Lynch's even keel and southern manners could sometimes be mistaken for a lack of willpower or leadership.

Sometimes Lynch didn't help herself. She did not generally like doing media interviews, but in late February agreed to a sit-down interview with Bret Baier of Fox News Channel. Fox was far from Lynch's favorite news source, but the department was trying to drum up public support for the idea that the government should be able to require Apple and other tech companies to help federal agents look at the data inside a cell phone, with a valid order from a judge. From Lynch's point of view, sitting down with Fox held some risks, but Baier was generally regarded around town as a serious guy who did not engage in the histrionics and truth-warping seen on Fox's early morning or nighttime broadcasts.

The issue with encrypted phones, Lynch told Baier, was "the government's need to access evidence as we do in every single case that may be found on an electronic device." Not surprisingly, Baier asked about the Clinton investigation, which the attorney general said was being handled "like any other review," using that term instead of "investigation," a move that irked Comey. She also pledged there would be no "artificial deadline" imposed on the case.

Lynch had chosen her words carefully throughout the interview, but when it was over she and Baier kept chatting while the television crew disassembled their gear. At one point, Lynch referred to the Clinton email investigation as "a big nothing-burger." For a brief moment, Lynch staffers held their breath, afraid their boss's slip of the tongue could be turned into a screaming headline. But Baier apparently didn't hear the phrase, and the conversation kept moving. Crisis averted. For now.

From the start of the Clinton case, Comey had eyed Justice Department leadership warily, not trusting them entirely. He and some of his senior advisers were concerned about how it looked to have the appointee of a Democratic president overseeing the investigation of the Democratic candidate for president. He largely kept his own counsel, not sharing these suspicions outside his small circle of senior advisers. There was another factor that had nothing to do with politics: senior FBI officials often chafed at the Justice Department telling them how to run their cases. Throughout 2016, some senior FBI officials simply felt they knew better than their bosses at the Justice Department about the best way to run a case.

If Lynch's remark had been noticed and reported, it would have undoubtedly fed Comey's reservations about Justice Department leadership being in the tank for Clinton. But to Lynch, everyone, including the FBI, was making too big a deal out of the Clinton email case. On the facts alone, it was something that could be handled by any midlevel prosecutor in any of a number of US attorneys' offices, she thought. In the mindset of a prosecutor who had spent her career handling mob and terrorism cases involving all manner of murder and mayhem, the Clinton case was minor. No one had died; no one was going to die. Of course Lynch knew that in the wider world, the email case had major political implications. Still, sometimes she wished there were a way for the Justice Department and the FBI to treat it like a regular piece of business.

Comey, Yates, and Lynch regularly attended meetings together about three times a week, but most of the day-to-day discussion between Justice Department leadership and FBI bosses was conducted by the principal associate deputy attorney general, or PADAG (pronounced *pay-dag*). The PADAG is an incredibly important position inside the Justice Department, but one that is largely unknown to the outside world. In 2016, the PADAG was Matt Axelrod, a former federal prosecutor from Florida who had long admired Comey and used to give new assistant US attorneys a copy of one of Comey's speeches to read. Like Lynch, he too thought he had a good relationship with his FBI counterparts. But like the attorney general, he was wrong.

"The relationship was bad before Clinton and the summer of 2016," said one former senior FBI official. "Most of the FBI-DoJ [Department of Justice] conversations were happening with Axelrod. We didn't have a good feeling about most of the senior officials there."

In the spring of 2016, those tensions remained largely hidden, including from the Justice Department. But an indication of how at odds the two departments could be came from a conversation that may have taken place around that time—one side said it did, the other said it didn't. According to Lynch, she was attending a national security meeting at FBI headquarters. After the meeting, Comey and McCabe asked to speak with her about a national security issue and the three went into her nearby office inside the FBI building. There, Comey and McCabe told Lynch about an investigation into a young businessman named Carter Page, who had once worked for an investment bank in Moscow; he had more recently been working in New York, where he engaged in a number of business conversations with Russian spies posing as diplomats and a businessman. Specifically, they told her that intelligence had picked up chatter of Russians discussing their interest in using Page. In early 2016, Donald Trump had named Page as a foreign policy adviser to his presidential campaign. The FBI officials didn't ask for authority to do anything; they were just letting Lynch know it was something they were interested in. According to Loretta Lynch, for the FBI, Carter Page was a concern long before the larger worries about the general election campaign came into view. The conversation lasted about twenty minutes, she recalled.

When asked about Lynch's memory of the conversation, though, both Comey and McCabe would later tell internal investigators that they didn't remember it, and they doubted it happened. Both men said they didn't recall even hearing Carter Page's name until later that year. It's an astonishing divergence, reflecting a profound disconnect between the events of 2016 as described by FBI officials, and the way they were described by others, including their bosses at the Justice Department. Carter Page may have been a long-winded oddball, a low-level adviser tacked on to the Trump campaign in 2016 as a bit of window dressing for a candidate who had no foreign policy experience. But Carter Page and his pro-Russia worldview would loom large in the minds of senior federal law enforcement officials.

There is one piece of documentary evidence that seems to support Lynch's account. According to internal FBI emails, in late April the FBI's New York field office sent a summary of the information it had on Carter Page that had led them to open their counterintelligence investigation of him earlier that month. Those records show that the information was to be used for a briefing of the FBI director on April 27.

But by the time the Justice Department inspector general began asking Comey and McCabe about Lynch's recollection of that meeting, the Carter Page case had become deeply problematic and embarrassing for the Bureau. The pursuit of Page, everyone came to realize, was riddled with errors, omissions, and misjudgments so serious that internal investigators would come to doubt the "human error" explanations they were given. By 2018 and 2019, senior law enforcement officials were distancing themselves from the Carter Page investigation, arguing that the core of the FBI's work on Trump-Russia connections was other suspects, like a low-level Trump campaign aide named George Papadopoulos.

In April 2016, however, the conversation—which did or didn't happen depending on who was speaking—proved one thing for sure: the FBI and the Justice Department were having trouble agreeing on anything of substance, a situation that would get progressively worse as the election year ground on.

MONDAY, MAY 2, 2016

In May of 2016, Ray Dalio's book *Principles* was making itself felt in James Comey's mind: Comey had been working on something over the weekend and wanted to share it with some of his inner circle. In an email to his chief of staff, James Rybicki, deputy director Andrew McCabe, and the head of the FBI's legal shop, James Baker, Comey described the document as a "straw person" outline of what he should say if he decided to unilaterally announce the end of the Clinton email investigation. The vast majority of the interviews had been conducted and had not discovered the kind of evidence that would show an intent to break the law.

There was, of course, one very critical interview still to conduct—Clinton herself. But FBI and Justice Department officials were skeptical that a smart politician with the best lawyers money could buy would suddenly crack under pressure and confess. They also doubted she would be so foolish as to commit a new crime of lying to them in an interview.

In the meantime, the FBI director was mapping out a plan for some radical transparency and a leading role for one James B. Comey. "In my imagination, I don't see myself taking any questions," he wrote. "Here is what it might look like."

Over the next two months, senior FBI officials would edit and refine Comey's words, expanding the group of senior officials who consulted on it. They included Andy McCabe, James Baker, Bill Priestap, Peter Strzok, and Lisa Page. It was made clear to everyone as they debated the precise wording that no one at the Justice Department was to know about it.

Baker was the FBI's general counsel, its top lawyer who oversaw hundreds of lawyers at the Bureau. He was not a high-powered manager so much as a kind of wise man on national security law. He'd spent years at the Justice Department overseeing sensitive terrorism and espionage investigations before the Foreign Intelligence Surveillance Court, and had developed a reputation as something of a stickler for the Justice Department rules and procedures that had grown up around those cases. By 2016, he had written a lot of them.

Priestap, one of the more senior officials in the discussion, had been an assistant football coach at the University of Michigan in the 1990s, when he was so impressed by a visiting FBI agent's pitch to the football players to steer clear of gambling and other vices that he decided to apply to become an agent. Priestap's early years in the Bureau were primarily spent on criminal cases, but after the 2001 terror attacks, he switched over to national security cases and never looked back. By 2016, he had spent more than a decade doing counterterrorism and counterintelligence work. Inside the Hoover building, people often referred to Priestap as a boy scout; sometimes they meant it as a compliment, sometimes not.

Peter Strzok, the case agent, was a rising star in the FBI's counterintelligence ranks. As a child, Strzok had traveled the world as the son of an army officer who became an international development worker. In college in the early 1990s, Strzok joined ROTC, where fellow students remembered him as a young man of quiet intensity. Strzok had joined the FBI in 1996, first as an analyst on terrorism cases, before becoming a special agent in Boston and Washington. Gradually, he developed an expertise in espionage and counterintelligence work. "He was beloved by the agents on his squad, and you could tell he was going places," said Ryan Fayhee, a former Justice Department prosecutor who worked with him. "He was by far the best leader that I'd met in the FBI, and he had the most success of any counterintelligence agent."

After the 9/11 attacks, Strzok located the rental car abandoned by three of the 9/11 hijackers. In 2010, he helped arrest Russian spies who had been living a secret life as "illegals," pretending to be non-Russians living and working as everyday Americans while quietly trying to be-friend Americans with positions of influence.

In his cases, Strzok showed a knack for following leads and marshal-ing the bureaucratic machinery of the FBI—a talent that eludes even some of the best investigators in the bureau. He also seemed to have a gift for the hardest part of counterintelligence work: turning intelligence evidence into a prosecutable case. That kind of transformation can be an arduous task because intelligence agencies often decide that, rather than air out dirty laundry in a courtroom, they would rather settle for a quieter victory, like a resignation or a firing. But Strzok was at times able to turn a seemingly hopeless case into a conviction. His bosses noticed and put him on the Clinton email case.

Lisa Page had come to the FBI after a stint in the deputy attorney general's office. While short on prosecutorial experience, Page brought intensity to the work, and impressed an FBI official then rocketing up the ranks: Andy McCabe. When McCabe became deputy director, he asked Page to join him as his legal adviser. She jumped at the chance, but debated what her job title should be, before deciding on special counsel. At the FBI, senior leadership was dominated by middle-aged men, but Page stood out as a forceful, some argued too forceful, voice in meetings. And it was clear to almost everyone in the building that she served as

McCabe's eyes and ears. McCabe was the building's top disciplinarian, and Page was his right hand. That degree of influence in someone so young who was neither an agent nor a man rankled some of the others, but even her critics conceded she was an expert on national security law and a hard worker.

This was the team Comey had assembled to work the Clinton case, sometimes called a "skinny" group because it was a leaner version of his senior staff meetings. Together the members brought decades of combined expertise in national security cases. But like in many organizations, their greatest strength could also be a weakness. Steeped in the cloistered, bureaucratic world of US intelligence, the FBI officials overseeing the Clinton email case carried far less knowledge about white-collar and public integrity investigations—the type of work that before 9/11 had been the FBI's bread and butter. To Page, Strzok, and others, Congress was a hopeless mess dominated by petty ignoramuses who understood far too little about how the FBI worked.

At the same time Comey's skinny group was having private discussions about Comey's planned statement to close the investigation, many of those same FBI officials were engaged in a dissembling dance with their bosses at the Justice Department—Sally Yates, her deputy Matt Axelrod, and others. The FBI had simply not found anything in the emails or witness interviews to justify a criminal prosecution. At the Justice Department, officials hoped Comey would be party to a joint announcement, and as Yates put it, they would all "hold hands and jump off the bridge together." At the Justice Department, most saw a clear benefit to having Comey be part of the public announcement; he was a Republican-appointed former deputy attorney general, one of the best-known public faces of the Obama administration, and had a reputation as being highly ethical. His presence at any such moment would help Lynch, Yates, and others show they had not let politics play a part in deciding against prosecuting Hillary Clinton.

Comey would later say that when he sent the May 2 email to his inner team (but not to Justice), it was a hypothetical announcement, and did not reflect a firm decision he'd made. But as his staff debated and edited the decision over the subsequent weeks, it became more apparent to many of them what he aimed to do, as long as his Justice Department bosses didn't stop him. For that, it was critical that Lynch, Yates, and their staff not know what the FBI was up to.

But Comey did tell one person outside the FBI—his former chief of staff Chuck Rosenberg, who at that point was running the Drug Enforcement Administration. There was no drug angle to the email case; Comey simply trusted Rosenberg and wanted his feedback, and knew Chuck would not tell Yates or Lynch, even though they were also Rosenberg's bosses.

Comey showed Rosenberg a copy of the draft statement. Over the course of three conversations with Rosenberg, Comey raised no particular ethical concerns about Lynch, other than her being a Democratic appointee overseeing the investigation of a Democratic presidential candidate. Rosenberg told Comey it was a "52-48" call, and went back and forth on which side had the slight edge.

Comey was clear in his mind why he wasn't going to tell his Justice Department bosses of his plans: they might order him to cancel his moment of drama. Comey thought if he was still the deputy attorney general, he'd have ordered any FBI director not to make such a statement without coordinating it with the Justice Department. Comey would later tell internal investigators that if they had given such an order, he would have followed it; Lynch and Yates would later say they were certain he would not have.

During this same time period, Lynch and Yates were developing their own theory of how to announce the end of the Clinton email case. Lynch in particular thought it should probably be something similar to how they had ended a probe into whether an IRS official named Lois Lerner had illegally targeted Tea Party groups for additional scrutiny. That case too had unleashed a political firestorm among conservatives, and when it ended with no charges, the Justice Department sent a lengthy letter to Congress outlining its findings—that the IRS had been sloppy and misguided, but not engaged in criminal conduct. She thought a similar type of white paper, paired with a public announcement, might be called for in the Clinton case.

To some Justice Department veterans, using the Lerner case as a template was worrisome in itself. Earlier in the Obama administration, the Lerner case had been a cause célèbre on Fox News and in the conservative press, as Republican members of Congress pushed the FBI to investigate harder and longer, with an eye toward charging Lerner with crimes. Lerner's lawyer insisted for years that she did nothing wrong, and when the FBI declined to seek such charges, the department gave lawmakers an unprecedented amount of access to the underlying findings, on the theory that giving Congress some of what they wanted would settle the issue. The events of 2016 and the following years suggest Republicans learned the opposite lesson from the Lerner case—that the FBI and the Justice Department could be bullied.

It would be many months before senior Justice Department lawyers found out Comey and his aides had secretly planned in April, May, and June of 2016 to make a solo statement announcing the end of the Clinton case. When they learned of it, many of them were apoplectic.

"They sat in those meetings, looked in our eyes, and lied to us," said one former Justice Department official. Said another: "It's infuriating to realize that people you thought were your colleagues were sitting with you, and by misdirection and omission, were lying to your face."

Comey would later say that he hadn't made up his mind about giving a solo press conference, and the final factor that tipped the scales for him was a chance meeting in late June between Lynch and former President Bill Clinton.

To Lynch, the notion that FBI lawyers and agents spent weeks formulating a legal theory of the Clinton email case, without input from the actual prosecutors assigned to the case, felt like the worst kind of betrayal. Comey and his deputies had created an undisclosed group of lawyers inside the FBI to make decisions normally left to prosecutors. It was equivalent to a bureaucratic end run around the actual Justice Department lawyers assigned to the case. It sounded, she thought, like a secret special counsel.

THURSDAY, JUNE 9, 2016

British music promoter Rob Goldstone arrived at Trump Tower hoping to impress the candidate's oldest son, Donald Trump Jr. Goldstone had reached out earlier by email, saying that a Russian prosecutor might have "some official documents and information that would incriminate Hillary and her dealings with Russia." The candidate's son had replied, "If it's what you say I love it especially later in the summer."

Trump Jr. agreed to arrange a meeting, and invited campaign chairman Paul Manafort and Trump's son in law, Jared Kushner, to attend as well. The main speaker at the meeting was a Russian lawyer named Natalia Veselnitskaya, who though not a prosecutor herself has claimed connections to a top Russian prosecutor.

"I believe you have some information for us," Don Jr. encouraged Veselnitskaya as the meeting began. But instead of dirt on Clinton, Veselnitskaya offered a presentation on the unfairness of the Magnitsky Act, a law that barred eighteen Russian officials and businessmen from coming to the United States.

From the Trump campaign's point of view, the meeting was a bust, and Goldstone, the man who set it up, was embarrassed, thinking he had squandered some of his credibility. But the meeting's existence would remain a secret until the following year, around the time it was reported by the *New York Times*.

An Already Big Fire

TUESDAY, JUNE 14, 2016

As the FBI was trying to extricate itself from presidential politics, at least as far as the Clinton email investigation went, another headache was brewing for the country, for the election, and for the Bureau. On a sunny Tuesday in June, a *Washington Post* headline introduced a subject that would also preoccupy the FBI in the run-up to the November election. The implications of the story were clear: the FBI might be nearly done with the Clinton email case, but the election was not done with the FBI.

"Russian Government Hackers Penetrated DNC, Stole Opposition Research on Trump," declared the headline. It was a shocking story, and a case that would reverberate through the two presidential campaigns. "The intruders so thoroughly compromised the DNC's system that they also were able to read all email and chat traffic, said DNC and the security experts," read the story by Ellen Nakashima. Some of the hackers had been inside the Democratic National Convention network since last year, it continued. A Russian government spokesman said it was not possible that any part of his government was involved.

The announcement came as a shock to the outside world, but its timing was part of a complex and costly plan by the DNC to flush the invaders out of their computer network by completely overhauling the software and hardware the party relied on to communicate. The FBI was hot on the hackers' trail, which led back to two separate arms of Russian intelligence, which appeared to be operating independently of each other to exfiltrate large amounts of data from the DNC.

Cybersecurity experts were quick to point out that it was not that unusual for governments to gather information on their adversaries. So far, the Russian efforts did not seem to point to a public campaign of disclosing the stolen files. But two months earlier, on April 19, the Russian intelligence agency GRU had done something that suggested it contemplated making the stolen files public. On that date, Unit 26165 of the GRU registered the internet domain DCleaks.com, according to US investigators. As early as April 2016, it seemed, the Russians had contemplated turning the cache of hacked files into a PR campaign against Clinton.

And on the day that the hacking efforts were exposed in mid-June, the DCLeaks Twitter account sent a private message to WikiLeaks: "You announced your organization was preparing to publish more Hillary's emails. We are ready to support you. We have some sensitive information too, in particular, her financial documents. Let's do it together. What do you think about publishing our info at the same moment? Thank you." Russian intelligence, it seemed, was gearing up to go well beyond what US intelligence agencies considered the tolerable norms of hacking spycraft. Stealing data from foreign governments was one thing; many governments engaged in that behavior. But the GRU was about to launch an ambitious and far-reaching public campaign to try to harm the election prospects of a US presidential candidate.

Russian intelligence was actively taking sides against Clinton's candidacy, though the breadth and intensity of that effort would take months to show itself. And along the way, the FBI would move closer and closer to center stage in American politics.

WEDNESDAY, JUNE 15, 2016

The day after the *Post* story, Russia's leak campaign kicked into high gear. US investigators would later conclude that the GRU created an online persona called Guccifer 2.0, a name designed to suggest a second iteration of a Romanian hacker who'd made a name for himself in criminal and law enforcement circles in 2013, by publicizing the hacked emails of celebrities and US and Romanian politicians.

Guccifer 2.0 would go on to engage with numerous reporters at different news organizations, dangling different slices of purloined files, all while insisting he was definitely not Russian. US intelligence officials, on the other hand, were quite certain Guccifer 2.0 was a phony online persona, managed by a team of GRU hackers, as "he" began blogging and releasing some of the documents stolen from the DNC and Democratic Congressional Campaign Committee systems.

MONDAY, JUNE 27, 2016

"'That's something new," began the email from Guccifer 2.0 to William Bastone, a reporter for the Smoking Gun website. Many things about the email were odd—from the use of a French AOL account, to the account name "Stephan Orphan," to the strained syntax of the offer.

"Specially for you. This's the inside for you. This's a part of the big archive that includes Hillary Clinton's staff correspondence. I asked the DCleaks, the Wikileaks sub project, to release a part with a closed access. I can send you a link and a pass. You'll have a couple of days to study the mails until it becomes available for public access. But DCLeaks asked me not to make any announcements yet. So I ask you not to make links to my blog. Ok?"

The outreach to Bastone was the first of what would become a pattern in which Guccifer 2.0 offered leaked emails to specific reporters. It's telling that in the email to Bastone, Guccifer 2.0 described DCLeaks as a "sub project" of WikiLeaks, and that the persona had a plan to generate news stories based on the hacked emails of DNC staffers. It would take several more steps before the full implications of the offer became clear.

That afternoon, Loretta Lynch boarded a plane for a weeklong swing to the west of the country. She was making a series of stops to talk about community policing—a major policy goal of the Obama Justice Department following the police shooting of Michael Brown in Ferguson, Missouri, and the fatal injuries sustained by Freddie Gray while in the custody of Baltimore police.

Lynch was heading to Arizona, then the West Coast and a few other stops. The attorney general of the United States does not fly on commercial airlines. Whoever is serving as the attorney general flies in a government plane with a security detail and the gear to enable highly secure communications with other senior government officials. Often the attorney general flies on an FBI plane, because the Bureau has more aircraft at its disposal than the Justice Department.

Around seven in the evening, the attorney general's plane touched down at the Phoenix Sky Harbor Airport. Lynch's staff got off the plane and into the staff van, as the detail prepared Lynch for her ride in a more secure SUV. About twenty-five yards away sat another private plane—one carrying former president Bill Clinton, who'd been golfing and was about to depart. All former presidents travel with a Secret Service detail. The Secret Service agents told Clinton that the attorney general was alongside on the tarmac. He looked out the window, saw her staff coming off the plane, and decided to greet her.

"I thought, she's about to get off and I'll just go shake hands with her when she gets off," Clinton told investigators later. "I just wanted to say hello to her."

As Lynch stood up to walk off the plane, the head of her security detail told her that President Clinton wanted to speak to her. Lynch was confused at first, so she had the FBI agent repeat himself. Once she agreed to see him, Bill Clinton immediately appeared at the door of the plane.

The two had met once or twice before, but were not what anyone would call friends even though Clinton had nominated Lynch in 1999 to be the

US attorney for Brooklyn. Lynch introduced the president to her husband, who was traveling with her. The resulting conversation lasted nearly a half hour: Clinton lived up to his reputation as a gregarious, long-winded politician. He talked about Brexit, the political issue roiling British politics at the time. He also opined on coal mining in West Virginia, and then segued into a discussion of how he and Hillary were enjoying being grandparents.

What both Clinton and Lynch had initially thought would be a quick hello was turning into something much longer. The three of them were standing, but eventually Clinton moved some bags off a nearby seat and sat down. That prompted Lynch and her husband to also sit down while they kept talking, with Clinton, as was his style, doing most of it.

Sitting in the van by the plane, Lynch's staff had spotted Clinton boarding the plane, and after five minutes started getting nervous. Kevin Lewis, the press spokesman traveling with Lynch, called his boss Melanie Newman at Justice Department headquarters and told him Bill Clinton had dropped by. At Newman's urging, Lewis got out of the van and asked one of the agents outside the plane to tell the head of the security detail inside the plane that Lynch needed to end the meeting. The agent didn't seem interested in conveying that kind of order to his boss, Lewis later recalled. Lewis got back in the van.

Another Lynch staffer, Uma Amuluru, was unsure of what exactly was happening on the plane, but she had a bad feeling about it. Amuluru walked into the cabin and stood over the group, with the quiet impatience of a staffer trying to signal their boss that it was time to go.

"We do have to go," Lynch said, finally acknowledging the signal. "We have a pretty busy schedule." She had got the hint. So had Clinton, but he didn't care. Clinton joked that one of Lynch's staffers was "mad at me, because I've been on the plane too long."

███████████

After five more minutes of talking, Lynch stood up.

"It was very nice of you to come," said the attorney general. "Thank you so much."

As Amuluru and Lynch left the plane, the staffer said, "That was not great."

"Yeah," said Lynch. They got into separate vehicles and drove to their hotel. Among Lynch's staffers, there was a sinking feeling that they had been too passive and too polite in the face of a former president.

It is not possible to hermetically seal a cabinet official off from the outside world, particularly when they are traveling for the express purpose of meeting people and giving speeches. But any veteran political hand will agree it is the staff's responsibility to act as gatekeepers, deciding who does and who doesn't get to meet the attorney general. None of the people traveling with Lynch that day had contemplated having to play gatekeeper to a former president who just popped up out of nowhere from the next plane.

"Some people were a bit starstruck, some were just too deferential," said one Justice Department official. "It's President Clinton, right? He's the president. It's easy to say, thinking about it later, 'Go say no to the president,' but when you're in that situation, someone has to actually say no. To the president. And they didn't do it soon enough. And they should have done it much sooner."

TUESDAY, JUNE 28, 2016

Lynch was speaking to local Phoenix reporters, about her work on police relations, when she got the question she had been expecting about her conversation with Clinton.

"I did see President Clinton at the Phoenix airport as I was leaving, and he spoke to myself and my husband on the plane. Our conversation was a great deal about his grandchildren. It was primarily social and about our travels. He mentioned the golf he played in Phoenix, and he mentioned travels he'd had in West Virginia," Lynch said. "There was no discussion of any matter pending before the Department, or any matter pending before any other body. There was no discussion of Benghazi, no discussion of the State Department emails, by way of example. I would say the current news of the day was the Brexit decision, and what that might mean. And again, the Department's not involved in that or implicated in that."

The lack of any follow-up questions at the press conference gave Lynch's team some hope they might have dodged a PR nightmare. Back in DC, her spokeswoman had prepared a statement, but no one asked for one. Officials began to hope that just maybe the strange rendezvous would go unnoticed.

At FBI headquarters, Justice Department officials were pressing the FBI to explain their plan for the expected announcement that no charges would be filed in the Clinton case. By late June, the planning for an announcement was taking on greater urgency, because the FBI had scheduled its interview with Hillary Clinton for the July 4 holiday weekend. The interview would be the capper, and assuming she did not crack, lie, or confess, the case would then be shut down.

But as they got closer and closer to the day of the Clinton interview, the FBI was still being cagey with their Justice Department bosses about how exactly they planned to make an announcement. Everyone understood that unless Clinton flagrantly lied in her interview, they were headed for what government lawyers called a "declination," a formal decision to decline to seek charges.

David Laufman, a senior lawyer in the Justice Department's National Security Division, wanted to know from Peter Strzok what the FBI planned to send the prosecution team after the interview, what their schedule might be, how they envisioned the wind-down. "God I am getting GRILLED by Laufman right now," Strzok texted Page shortly after noon.

WEDNESDAY, JUNE 29, 2016

The tarmac meeting would not blow over. The Justice Department beat-reporters, and their bosses, had gotten wind of the story from the local Phoenix ABC affiliate and started to ask questions. What began as a trickle in the afternoon by nighttime had become a flood.

Congressional Republicans also jumped in, criticizing the attorney general and questioning her account of the conversation. The more paranoid corners of the internet connected it not just to the Clinton email case, but to the question of whether Lynch might have been promised something, like an extension of her time as attorney general, or a seat on the Supreme Court. The conspiracy theories were flying faster than the news.

"I don't know whether I'm more offended that they think I'm crooked or that they think I'm stupid," Bill Clinton would say later, mocking the scenario floated by his critics that he would engage in rampantly unethical or even illegal conduct in front of scads of witnesses. "I've got an idea, I'll do all these things they accuse me of doing in broad daylight in an airport in Phoenix when the whole world can see it," he scoffed.

The public criticism of Lynch had a secondary effect: it heightened the distrust between the Justice Department and the FBI. Lynch staffers griped to each other that the security detail, consisting of FBI agents, should have been more proactive in keeping Clinton away. They also worried that the FBI might be leaking embarrassing details to the press. The FBI, for their part, felt they were being blamed for what was squarely a failure of the political staff to protect their principal from embarrassment. They thought the Justice staffers had made the mess.

Coming right as Comey and his aides were trying to put together their final plan for closing the Clinton email case, the Lynch tarmac incident only seemed to increase the pressure on everyone.

"Not a big deal, just ASTOUNDINGLY bad optic," Strzok texted Page.

"Yup. Stupid stupid stupid. And if we had done it, we'd never be hearing the end of it," she replied. To Peter Strzok, the Lynch screwup only underscored how annoying the Justice Department's attempts at micromanaging them were "when they randomly bitch about what the D [Comey] wants, or our timetable."

Inside the Justice Department, there was also anger at the press for what some felt was overhyping the issue. "This is such BS," groused one senior Justice Department official in a late-night venting session to me. "You're telling me that if I run into someone at the airport and say hello, it's an ethics problem? That's completely absurd and unfair."

Lynch's own staff did not share that view. Privately, the attorney general conceded the mistake, and immediately after the Clinton meeting her staff decided that, from now on, the most senior aide traveling with the attorney general would stay with her from the plane all the way to her vehicle, so that another Clinton-type meeting could not happen.

THURSDAY, JUNE 30, 2016

It had felt like pulling teeth sometimes, but the Justice Department had gotten an answer from the FBI about how the announcement of the decision to close the Clinton case was likely to go: the Justice Department would be briefed the following Wednesday or Thursday, and the public announcement would be made on Friday, July 8. And with that, the giant headache of a case could be over.

FRIDAY, JULY 1, 2016

"What on earth were you thinking?" seated on stage at the Aspen Ideas Festival in Colorado, *Washington Post* columnist Jonathan Capehart asked Lynch.

Originally envisioned as a way for Lynch to showcase her role in police reform efforts, her long-scheduled appearance at the event had become a full-tilt effort at damage control. Republicans were attacking her, and Democrats weren't defending her. So she would have to defend herself. Lynch's plan was to take the blame and promise not to interfere with whatever the career staff at the Justice Department recommended be done with the Clinton case.

"I think that's a perfectly reasonable question," she told Capehart. "Certainly my meeting with him raises questions and concerns. Believe me, I completely get that question."

To try to calm the concern, Lynch offered a public pledge: when it came to the Clinton email case, she would follow the recommendation of the career prosecutors and federal agents. At first blush, what she was saying almost sounded like she was recusing herself from the case. But she wasn't. Rather, she was vowing to keep control of the case, but publicly stating she would not try to overrule or modify the recommendation made by the prosecutors assigned to the case.

Beset by criticism, Lynch's offer was an attempt to give something to Republicans, without relinquishing her actual authority in the case. Within the Justice Department and the FBI, it was viewed mostly as a PR play and a somewhat cynical attempt to squelch the public criticism. "Yeah, it's a real profile in courage, since she knows no charges will be brought," Page texted Strzok.

Lynch emphasized that she had already decided to accept the prosecutors' recommendation even before the tarmac meeting with Clinton, but that only seemed to underscore the self-serving nature of the announcement. Very few people in the Justice Department expected Lynch to overrule the career personnel on such a politically sensitive case—she would have been pilloried for it. So in effect she was promising to do the very thing she had been planning to do all along.

Lynch told the crowd at Aspen that she knew the controversy could "cast a shadow" over the Justice Department. "It's painful to me," she said.

SATURDAY, JULY 2, 2016

Hillary Clinton arrived at FBI headquarters for what would be a three-and-a-half-hour interview, flanked by five lawyers: David E. Kendall, Cheryl Mills, Heather Samuelson, and two others. Most FBI interviews are conducted by two agents. This one had so many agents, prosecutors, and private lawyers that between the two sides, they could have fielded a baseball team.

The agents were particularly annoyed at the presence of Cheryl Mills, and had debated whether to try to keep her and Heather Samuelson out of the interview; they were also witnesses to facts in the investigation, and therefore should not be present for the interview of another witness, Hillary Clinton. There was another, lingering reason for resentment of Mills by some of the older FBI officials—she had been a White House lawyer during the Monica Lewinsky investigation, and in that bruising fight, some in the FBI came to dislike Mills in particular.

For an interview that had been built up for months and months, both in public and inside the FBI, the actual event was somewhat anti-climactic. In general, Clinton insisted she was not a close observer of technical issues relating to emails, didn't know much about them, and trusted her staff to take care of such matters.

When Peter Strzok and the other FBI agents pressed her about the types of information found in some of the messages, and whether that information was classified, Clinton said she did not consider it classified, in part because the first messages were sent by experienced diplomatic professionals who knew where the lines were and followed them.

One of the agents handed her an email, dated December 27, 2011, with the subject line "FW: (SBU)." This was an email from Mills to Clinton, re-capping a conversation over that Christmas break about a planned drone strike in Pakistan. It was the same email chain that began with Ambassador Cameron Munter giving his superiors a brief, cryptically worded heads-up about an expected strike.

Clinton said she did not have any concerns about the email, and did not believe it contained classified information. She couldn't imagine how that particular email, had it become known publicly, "would have added more fuel to an already big fire."

The very subject line, the acronym for sensitive but unclassified, showed that the information was not classified, she said. Clinton's hours-long FBI interview rehearsed the same argument that had been going on for months about her emails, leading to the same nowhere.

The question-and-answer session provided no seismic new informa-tion, and as far as the onlookers could tell there was no obvious discrep-ancy in Hillary Clinton's answers. She had not attempted to mislead or deceive; no one had caught her in a bold-faced lie. The investigation into the pile of years-old emails foolishly stored on a nongovernmental server logically should have fizzled out. Clinton was eager to put it behind her, and Comey's FBI was ready to be done with it. But the Clinton email case, propelled by the furor of the election season, would not simply sputter out. Once launched, it seemed that no one could completely control or defuse it.

PART 2
BRAVERY

Radical Transparency

TUESDAY, JULY 5, 2016

Sarah Schweit's first day as an intern in the FBI press office was not like any other Tuesday. "They told me that it was going to be a busy day, but they were a bit vague as to why," said Schweit, a twenty-one-year-old student at James Madison University in Virginia, who had spent a couple of weeks interning at a different part of the Bureau before being told to report that day to the FBI's National Press Office.

"I remember having a lot of responsibility for someone's first day on the job," she said. Her first task was to take reporters waiting in the lobby of the Hoover building up to the room where Comey planned to make an announcement. Every reporter going into FBI headquarters has to check in twice, pass through metal detectors, and then be escorted to whatever office they are visiting. The room filled as it got closer to the scheduled start time of 11:00 A.M., until there were about fifty people inside. Some FBI staff stood in the back of the room.

FBI employees, including Schweit and other interns, started getting written copies of Comey's planned speech as reporters were still trickling into the room. The text was written on thick sheets of paper, giving it heft in the FBI staffers' hands as they held it. "Everyone pored over it for a second, because nobody had seen it yet," said Schweit. "Everyone was very careful. People kept their thoughts to themselves. That's something the FBI prides themselves on: just not being opinionated. You could tell there was some worry, hesitation, wariness."

Reporters kept arriving in the room, and anxiety built for the people who knew what Comey was about to say, and those who didn't. "It was *quiet*," said Schweit. "There was almost no murmuring, and the energy was very high, because everyone had inferred what was coming," she said.

At that moment, across the street at the Justice Department, Attorney General Loretta Lynch, her deputy Sally Yates, and their senior staffers were all in the dark. On a gut level, they knew there would be no charges coming against Clinton, but they didn't have any sense of what the director of the FBI was going to say. They could only watch television like everyone else. As everyone waited, an intern on her first day in the FBI press shop knew more than the nation's top law enforcement official, her deputy, and their staffs. Comey had spent weeks planning it this way.

According to the game plan he had crafted, the press was notified at 8:00 A.M. that the FBI would be holding a press conference. He would tell Yates at 8:30, and Lynch at 8:35. But when reporters saw the email at 8:00 A.M., they immediately began calling the Justice Department for some clue about what was happening. Was it Clinton?

Loretta Lynch's spokeswoman, Melanie Newman, got a call from a reporter and started scrambling to figure out what was going on. Newman called her counterpart at the FBI, Mike Kortan, who told her the director had called Yates, which wasn't the case yet. Minutes later, Comey picked up the phone to Yates.

In the call, Comey told Yates he was holding a press conference to announce the completion of the "Midyear Exam" investigation, the name given to the Clinton email server investigation by the FBI. Sometimes in conversation or texts, FBI and Justice personnel would refer to the case by initials, MYE or MYR. "I'm not going to tell you anything about what I will say, for reasons I hope you will understand," Comey said. He said he thought it was important that the FBI speak before telling the Justice Department, and that when the announcement was finished, the FBI would be back in touch.

Yates was annoyed at how emphatic Comey was that he would not reveal anything to her. But she held her tongue. "Thanks for letting me know," she said before hanging up and immediately calling Axelrod to try to find out more.

Melanie Newman was furious. She'd been frustrated before with the FBI keeping her in the dark, but this was unprecedented in her experience and, as she later told investigators, "absolutely ridiculous."

Comey walked over to the desk of his chief of staff, James Rybicki, to call Loretta Lynch. He informed her he would be making a statement "very soon" about the email investigation, but wouldn't tell her what it was. "I hope someday you'll understand why, but I can't answer any of your questions," Comey told her.

By 8:28, Comey had finished his call with Lynch, which, according to his plan, meant it was time for his deputy Andrew McCabe to notify George Toscas, a senior lawyer at the Justice Department's National Security Division, and for the lead case agent, Pete Strzok, to notify Toscas's colleague, David Laufman.

McCabe couldn't immediately reach Toscas by phone, so he sent him an email: "The Director just informed the DAG that at 1100 this morning he has convened a press conference to announce the completion of our investigation and the referral to DOJ. He will not tell her what he is going to say. It is important that he not coordinate his statement in any way. He will not take questions at the conference. His next call is to the AG."

"I wanted you to hear this from me," McCabe continued. "I understand that this will be troubling to the team and I very much regret that. I want to talk to you after the PC [Principals Committee] and am happy to bring my folks over to DOJ this afternoon to discuss next steps."

The Justice Department officials were as confused as they were angry. For Axelrod, the main concern was that the FBI seemed to have decided to go forward alone with announcing the end of the Clinton investigation, after they had spent weeks discussing ways in which the Bureau and the DOJ would announce it together. Until that morning, Axelrod had thought it unlikely the FBI would finish its work so quickly. The Clinton interview over the holiday weekend was just a few days ago. He had assumed it would be days, if not weeks, before an announcement.

But in all the calls between Justice and the Bureau, no one ordered Comey to stop. No one ran, or even walked, across the street to try to speak to someone face-to-face about what was coming. They stayed in their offices and waited.

At eleven o'clock, Comey walked into the briefing room and strode behind the lectern, standing almost as tall as the four flags behind him. Wearing a blue dress shirt and a yellow tie, he began:

> Good morning. I'm here to give you an update on the FBI's investigation of Secretary Clinton's use of a personal email system during her time as Secretary of State. After a tremendous amount of work over the last year, the FBI is completing its investigation and referring the matter to the Department of Justice for a prosecutive decision. What I would like to do today is tell you three things: what we did; what we found; and what we are recommending to the Department of Justice.
>
> This is going to be an unusual statement in at least a couple of ways. First, I am going to include more detail about our process than I ordinarily would, because I think the American people deserve those details in a case of intense public interest. Second, I have not coordinated this statement in any way with the Department of Justice or any other part of the government. They do not know what I am about to say.
>
> But I want to start by thanking the FBI employees who did remarkable work in this case. Once you have a better sense of how much we have done, you will understand why I am so grateful and proud of their work.

In the room, there was rapt attention and strained silence. Comey commanded everyone's attention. He had set the stage and was about to bring on the show.

So first, what we have done: The investigation began as a referral from the intelligence community inspector general in connection with Secretary Clinton's use of a personal email server during her time as secretary of state. The referral focused on whether classified information was transmitted on that personal system.

Our investigation looked at whether there is evidence that classified information was improperly stored or transmitted on that personal system, in violation of a federal statute that makes it a felony to mishandle classified information either intentionally or in a grossly negligent way, or a second statute making it a misdemeanor to knowingly remove classified information from appropriate systems or storage facilities.

And consistent with our counterintelligence responsibilities, we have also investigated to determine if there is evidence of computer intrusion by nation states or by hostile actors of any kind.

Comey then detailed what he meant by email servers and how many devices the FBI had examined. He made it sound like a classic piece of detective work conducted over complex digital terrain.

FBI investigators have also read all of the approximately thirty thousand emails that Secretary Clinton provided to the State Department in 2014. Where an email was assessed as possibly containing classified information, the FBI referred that email to any government agency that might be an "owner" of that information, so that agency could make a determination as to whether the email contained classified information at the time it was sent or received, or whether there was reason to classify it now, even if the content had not been classified when it was first sent or received, and that's the process sometimes referred to as "up-classifying."

From the group of 30,000 emails returned to the State Department, 110 emails in 52 email chains have been determined by the owning agency to contain classified information at the time they were sent or received. Eight of those chains contained information that was Top Secret at the time they were sent; 36 of those chains contained Secret information at the time; and 8 contained Confidential information at the time. That's the lowest level of classification. Separate from those, about 2,000 additional emails were "up-classified" to make them Confidential; those emails had not been classified at the time that they were sent or received.

Never afraid to take risks or grab the spotlight, Comey did both at once. Whether the public would like or dislike his announcement, he was packing it with specifics and technical findings. The reporters in the room were scribbling the figures and details as fast as they could, but part of the challenge Comey posed for his audience that day was asking them to follow along with him through a dense thicket of classification, data storage, and math. He had a lot to say, about twenty-seven hundred words' worth. Live television was, at best, a clunky format in which to pepper the American people with so many weedy details stacked on top of each other. But he was in full flow, describing a painstaking investigation:

The FBI also discovered several thousand work-related emails that were not among the group of thirty thousand emails returned by Secretary Clinton to State in 2014. We found those emails in a variety of ways. Some had been deleted over the years and we found traces of them on servers or devices that had been connected to the private email domain. Others we found by reviewing the archived government accounts of people who had been government employees at the same time as Secretary Clinton, including high-ranking officials at other agencies, folks with whom a Secretary of State might normally correspond.

This helped us recover work-related emails that were not among the thirty thousand that were produced to State. Still others we recovered from that painstaking review of the millions of email fragments dumped into the slack space of the server that was decommissioned in 2013.

With respect to the thousands of emails we found that were not among those produced to the State Department, agencies have concluded that three of those were classified at the time they were sent or received, one at the Secret level, and two at the Confidential level. There were no additional Top Secret emails found. And finally, none of those we found have since been "up-classified."

I should add here that we found no evidence that any of the additional work-related emails were intentionally deleted in an effort to conceal them in some way. Our assessment is that, like many email users, Secretary Clinton periodically deleted emails or emails were purged from her system when devices were changed. Because she was not using a government account—or even a commercial account like Gmail—there was no archiving at all of her emails, so it's not surprising that we discovered emails that were not on Secretary Clinton's system in 2014, when she produced those thirty-thousand-some emails to State.

It could also be that some of the additional work-related emails that we've recovered were among those deleted as "personal" by her lawyers when they reviewed and sorted her emails for production in late 2014.

Comey then delved deeper into the search process, expressing some doubt about how watertight it was. In this he was almost certainly not entirely aware of the impression he was conveying—Comey was not a data specialist, however confident he sounded. The details were probably as obscure to him as they were to the reporters struggling to keep up with him and to evaluate what was significant from what was routine.

———

The lawyers doing the sorting for Secretary Clinton in 2014 did not individually read the content of all of her emails, as we did for those available to us; instead they relied on header information and they used search terms to try to find all work-related emails among the reportedly more than sixty thousand that were remaining on her system at the end of 2014. It's highly likely that their search missed some work-related emails, and that we later found them, for example, in the mailboxes of other officials or in the slack space of a server. It's also likely that there are other work-related emails that they did not produce to State and that we did not find elsewhere, and that are now gone because they deleted all emails they did not produce to State, and the lawyers then cleaned their devices in such a way as to preclude complete forensic recovery.

We have conducted interviews and done technical examination to attempt to understand exactly how that sorting was done by her attorneys. Although we do not have complete visibility because we are not able to fully reconstruct the electronic record of that sorting, we believe our investigation has been sufficient to give us reasonable confidence there was no intentional misconduct in connection with that sorting effort.

And, of course, in addition to our technical work, we interviewed many people, from those involved in setting up the personal email system and maintaining the various iterations of Secretary Clinton's server, to staff members with whom she corresponded on email, to those involved in the email production to State, and finally, Secretary Clinton herself.

Last, we have done extensive work to try to understand what indications there might be of compromise by hostile actors in connection with that personal email system.

Comey's voice was getting raspy; he'd been speaking for ten minutes and counting.

So that's what we have done. Now let me tell you what we found. Although we did not find clear evidence that Secretary Clinton or her colleagues intended to violate laws governing the handling of classified information, there is evidence that they were extremely careless in their handling of very sensitive, highly classified information.

This sentence, after a long preamble of technical detail, set many viewers on edge. Was Comey about to say she should be charged? That seemed inconceivable to the lawyers at the Justice Department who had worked the case, but Comey's language sounded accusatory. And he continued in a prosecutorial tone:

> For example, seven email chains concerned matters that were classified at the Top Secret/Special Access Program at the time when they were sent and received. Those chains involved Secretary Clinton both sending emails about those matters and receiving emails from others about the same matters. There is evidence to support a conclusion that any reasonable person in Secretary Clinton's position, or in the position of those with whom she was corresponding about those matters, should have known that an unclassified system was no place for that conversation.

Here, then, Comey was accusing Clinton and her deputies. If any reasonable person had known better, was he saying Clinton or her staff had committed a crime to send emails about those subjects on an unclassified system?

> In addition to this highly sensitive information, we also found information that was properly classified as Secret by the U.S. Intelligence Community at the time it was discussed on email (that is excluding the later "up-classified" emails).
>
> None of these emails should have been on any kind of unclassified system, but their presence is especially concerning because all of these emails were housed on unclassified personal servers not even supported by full-time security staff, like those found at agencies and departments of the US government—or even with a commercial email service like Gmail.
>
> I think it's also important to say something about the marking of classified information. Only a very small number of the emails here containing classified information bore markings indicating the

presence of classified information. But even if information is not marked "classified" in an email, participants who know or should know that the subject matter is classified are still obligated to protect it.

This was another public shot at Clinton and her staff, followed by a sentence that meant a great deal to the bureaucracy, but was almost certainly lost on the vast majority of the public watching then or later:

While not the focus of our investigation, we also developed evidence that the security culture of the State Department in general, and with respect to the use of unclassified systems in particular, was generally lacking in the kind of care for classified information that's found elsewhere in the US government.

As he delivered that line, Comey subtly shook his head. And inside the FBI, a significant number of counterintelligence agents quietly cheered his words. To the public, the Clinton email case was largely about politics, the Clintons, and the presidential election. But in the cloistered world of FBI employees, it was very much also about the Bureau's long-building frustration with what they viewed as the cavalier and sloppy attitude of the State Department.

Earlier that year, the FBI had abandoned its pursuit of Robin Raphel, a veteran State Department official who'd spent decades developing relationships with senior Pakistan officials. She had come under investigation for possibly sharing classified information with one of those contacts; FBI agents had also found a dusty classified document in her basement. But in the end, she was not the secret agent that FBI agents had suspected. Raphel had insisted she'd done nothing wrong, and the end of the case frustrated the FBI, as many agents who'd dealt with it felt her State Department colleagues had circled the wagons to protect her from being punished. Raphel's colleagues in the State Department, by contrast, pushed back hard against the suggestion that she had broken the law. The FBI agents, the diplomats argued, did not understand the complexity of navigating relations with a country like Pakistan, and thought the Bureau's approach risked "criminalizing diplomacy," as one of them put it.

To many FBI counterintelligence agents, the Raphel case fed a general sense of frustration that the diplomats just didn't get it. To the FBI, the problem was the State Department's work culture. Some agents were incredulous that many State employees still didn't have to take polygraph exams to get a job or a sensitive position at the department. At the FBI, even summer interns were polygraphed. The State Department's lack of a general practice of polygraphing employees showed just how unserious they were about safeguarding government secrets, some FBI officials felt.

"It's cultural," a former official said. "The FBI is very structured about communications. Agents see things as binary—on or off, authorized or unauthorized, black and white. State has a bunch of informal communications channels. Things are gray. It's just the way State is."

By the time the FBI dropped the Raphel case, it had already been investigating Clinton's use of a private email server for nearly a year. But those weren't the only two State Department women under investigation around that time.

Another, previously undisclosed case involved Nisha Biswal, who had served as an assistant secretary of state for the Bureau of South and Central Asian Affairs. In that role, Biswal had dealt with the fallout in US-India relations stemming from the arrest, in New York in December 2013, of Indian foreign service officer Devyani Khobragade on charges of visa fraud and underpaying her maid; this was a case that enraged the Indian government, which insisted she'd done nothing wrong and had been mistreated by US investigators.

The Khobragade controversy would eventually go away, but months later, FBI agents questioned Biswal about whether she had promised to tell the Indians if a criminal case was being built against any other Indian diplomats. Biswal insisted the only thing she had told the Indian government was exactly where the legal lines were drawn, in order to ensure their diplomats stayed on the right side of them. The FBI eventually closed its investigation, but the suspicion and distrust remained.

Between Clinton, Raphel, and Biswal, the FBI was busy in 2014 and 2015 investigating a number of senior officials at the State Department, all of them women. And by 2016, some of the Bureau's most senior counterintelligence officials felt the diplomats were long overdue for a stern lesson in how to treat classified information. All of which meant that by the time Comey stepped to the podium in early July, relations between State and the FBI were at a low ebb.

"The counter-intelligence guys, they can be a bit dogmatic about some of this stuff," said one senior law enforcement official. "At the same time, if you are operating a work culture where people are freewheeling or cavalier about classified information, that is a problem, and it becomes our problem."

Comey's line about State Department practices, and his shake of the head, may not have meant much to the voting public, but it meant a great deal to some of his workforce. Comey, McCabe, and other FBI leaders were keenly focused on explaining their decision in a way that would satisfy, or at least not anger, their own agents.

After castigating the State Department, Comey's performance was building to its crescendo. Like the trial prosecutor he used to be, Comey had marshaled the key facts and was walking the jury through his summation argument toward the final, damning flourish.

With respect to potential computer intrusion by hostile actors [the FBI's term for hackers], we did not find direct evidence that Secretary Clinton's personal email domain, in its various configurations since 2009, was hacked successfully. But given the nature of the system and of the actors potentially involved, we assess we would be unlikely to see such direct evidence. We do assess that hostile actors gained access to the private commercial email accounts of people with whom Secretary Clinton was in regular contact from her personal account. We also assess that Secretary Clinton's use of a personal email domain was both known by a large number of people and readily apparent. She also used her personal email extensively while outside the United States, including sending and receiving work-related emails in the territory of sophisticated adversaries. Given that combination of factors, we assess it is possible that hostile actors gained access to Secretary Clinton's personal email account.

This was in some ways the most aggressive statement Comey made that day. By his own admission, there was no evidence of a computer intrusion on Clinton's servers. Yet Comey made the case that there could have been such an intrusion, because hackers in places like Russia and China are good at covering their tracks, and because Clinton used her email while traveling to at least one of those countries. But Comey was speculating.

"So that's what we found," Comey said. By this point, viewers and listeners could be forgiven for thinking he was about to accuse Clinton of a crime. Yet all that buildup, all that prosecutorial summation, was not driving toward a conviction. It was driving toward nothing.

Finally, with respect to our recommendation to the Department of Justice: In our system, the prosecutors make the decisions about whether charges are appropriate based on evidence that the FBI helps collect. Although we don't normally make public our recommendations to the prosecutors, we frequently make recommendations and engage in productive conversations with prosecutors about what resolution may be appropriate, given the evidence. In this case, given the importance of the matter, I think unusual transparency is in order.

Comey's use of the phrase "unusual transparency" was a clear echo of Ray Dalio's "radical transparency." Those close to Comey felt his use of the phrase at that moment was a subtle nod to how working for Dalio had influenced Comey's approach to law enforcement. Since his days as a prosecutor in Virginia and New York, Comey had always been more outspoken than most of his fellow law enforcement officials. But Dalio's philosophy had resonated with Comey, amplifying and cementing an impulse he'd always had. Here, in his most high-profile moment at the

FBI, Comey was trying to broadcast a bit of the Bridgewater mindset to his employees, and to the country.

> Although there is evidence of potential violations of the statutes regarding the handling of classified information, our judgment is that no reasonable prosecutor would bring such a case. Prosecutors necessarily weigh a number of factors before deciding whether to bring charges. There are obvious considerations, like the strength of the evidence, especially regarding intent. Responsible decisions also consider the context of a person's actions, and how similar situations have been handled in the past.
>
> In looking back at our investigations into the mishandling or removal of classified information, we cannot find a case that would support bringing criminal charges on these facts. All the cases prosecuted involved some combination of clearly intentional and willful mishandling of classified information, or vast quantities of information exposed in such a way as to support an inference of intentional misconduct, or indications of disloyalty to the United States, or efforts to obstruct justice. We do not see those things here.

More than thirteen minutes after he began speaking, Comey was getting to the point.

> To be clear, this is not to suggest that in similar circumstances, a person who engaged in this activity would face no consequences. [Comey thumped his hand on the lectern.] To the contrary, those individuals are often subject to security or administrative sanctions. But that's not what we are deciding now. As a result, although the Department of Justice makes final decisions on matters like this, we are expressing to Justice our view that no charges are appropriate in this case.

The prosecutor's closing argument—probably as dramatic a telling as one could possibly make of a case about old computer servers, slack space, and data retention—was that there'd been no crime at all.

I know there will be intense public debate in the wake of this recommendation, as there was throughout the investigation." [Comey was wrapping up.] What I can assure the American people is that this investigation was done honestly, competently, and independently. No outside influence of any kind was brought to bear.

He had one last point to make, and it was to the FBI's critics:

I know there were many opinions expressed by people who were not part of the investigation—including people in government—but none of that mattered to us. [Comey thumped his hand again.] Opinions are irrelevant, and they were all uninformed by insight into our investigation, because we did our investigation the right way. Only facts matter, and the FBI found them here in an entirely apolitical and professional way. I couldn't be prouder to be part of this organization. Thank you very much.

With that, he closed the black binder at the lectern and exited, stage left, from the room. Comey had commanded the room, the city, and the country. But even in his own building, some struggled to understand why he had done it this way.

There are more than ten thousand FBI agents in the country, and they are far from uniform in their political views. As a group, they do lean conservative, much the same way Justice Department lawyers tend to lean liberal. Most days, in most cases, those distinctions are completely irrelevant and never even mentioned. When politics do bubble up in a case, the FBI's tendencies and the Justice Department's often balance each other out.

After Comey's announcement, even some agents who intensely disliked Hillary Clinton and had hoped she would be charged with a crime struggled to process what the director had done. No one at the Bureau had ever seen this kind of press conference before. "He just kept talking about all the bad things she did. But he wasn't charging her. That's . . . not . . . what . . . we . . . do," said one agent, drawing out the words to emphasize the point. "I don't care who she is, or what I or anyone else thinks of her. We don't do this to people. And I can't understand it."

━━━━━━━━━

Comey justified the extraordinary step he'd just taken—cutting out not just the attorney general but the entire Justice Department from the most important case they had—as not just a once-in-a-lifetime oddity, but something so rare that it would be a hundred or five hundred years before another FBI director would face tough decisions about investigating a presidential candidate during their campaign. In this his assessment was wildly off. In fact, that very day, at a meeting in London, a veteran special agent was being handed the first set of allegations that would eventually feed an FBI probe into the other presidential campaign.

Christopher Steele, a former British intelligence officer with expertise on Russia, had left Her Majesty's Secret Service in 2009 and started a firm called Orbis Business Intelligence. The following year, he started providing information to the FBI on organized crime in Russia and Eastern Europe.

Steele was friends with a Justice Department official named Bruce Ohr. Now that Steele was in the private sector, he started sending Ohr reports he wrote for his business clients that he thought might also be of interest to the US government. At the time, Ohr worked as chief of the Organized Crime and Racketeering Section at the Justice Department.

As Steele was getting his business up and running, Ohr introduced him to Mike Gaeta, an FBI agent based in New York who pursued Eastern European organized crime suspects. Gaeta thought highly enough of Ohr to think well of Steele. After their first meeting, every couple of months Steele would send Gaeta a report. From Gaeta's point of view, it was a useful relationship, but not so important that it warranted filling out the paperwork to declare Steele a confidential human source of the Bureau's.

But the FBI has an insatiable appetite for intelligence on the internal workings of the Kremlin and the Russian oligarchs who moved in

President Vladimir Putin's orbit. Steele offered insights on some of those oligarchs, including some Gaeta viewed as quite valuable.

After Steele steered the FBI in 2013 to a valuable witness about corruption in the Soccer World Cup, Gaeta decided he should formalize the FBI's relationship with the ex-spy, and put him on the books as a confidential human source. That would mean Steele would be paid for information, and Gaeta tasked him with digging for more details on the oligarchs. Since Gaeta was also about to move from New York to Rome, Italy, it would be easier to keep working with Steele, Gaeta thought, if he registered him as a source.

To Steele, the new, more formal arrangement was a business relationship between the FBI and his firm, Orbis. He was not an informant; he was a contractor, and the FBI was one of his clients. The distinction was important to Steele, because as a former British intelligence officer he could not casually work for a foreign government. To the FBI, Steele was an informant with his own code name. Each side was willing to let the other believe what it wanted.

Over the next two years, Steele provided Gaeta with reports. During this time, the FBI hoped Steele could put them in touch with oligarchs who might be willing to talk to FBI agents. Russian oligarchs were big fish, and in this regard Steele was at least partly successful, because he did some work for a lawyer who represented Oleg Deripaska. Steele helped Gaeta and Ohr meet with Deripaska's lawyer.

In Steele's mind, his work fell into two categories. One stream was the work he did for business clients, and if some of that information might be valuable to the FBI, he would share it with Gaeta at no cost. The other stream was work he was specifically asked by the FBI to do, and he charged the Bureau for that. To Steele, this distinction allowed him to keep his ethical obligations to all of his clients.

In June 2016, one of Steele's clients, a Washington, DC–based research firm named Fusion GPS, reached out with a new assignment. Fusion's founder, former *Wall Street Journal* writer Glenn Simpson, wanted him to see if he could find out if Donald Trump had any personal or business ties to Russia, and if so, what they were. Fusion had begun looking at

Trump's business history in late 2015 for the Free Beacon, a conservative online publication funded by Paul Singer, a hedge fund billionaire and major GOP donor who backed Senator Marco Rubio in the Republican presidential primaries. When Trump secured the Republican nomination, Fusion lost its client, and offered its services to Perkins Coie, the law firm representing both the Clinton campaign and the Democratic Party. The law firm hired Fusion, which in turn hired Steele's firm, Orbis. With that fateful sequence of events, Fusion found itself at the center of the bizarre triangle of Clinton, Trump, and Russia that would define the 2016 presidential election.

By early July, Steele's initial lines of inquiry had returned alarming allegations. He wrote up "Company Intelligence Report 2016/080," using the bureaucratic memo style of his intelligence agency training. Steele was alarmed by what he had heard in just a few weeks of nosing around about Trump, so he called Gaeta and asked to meet.

So on the same day that Comey was announcing the end of the investigation into Hillary Clinton, an FBI agent sat in Steele's office, where he was given allegations against her opponent, Donald Trump, provided by an investigator who was hired, indirectly through a series of intermediaries, by Clinton. Steele's first report claimed the Russian government had been "cultivating, supporting, and assisting" Trump for at least five years, and that his inner circle had "accepted a regular flow of intelligence from the Kremlin," including information about Democrats. The document also claimed Trump had engaged in "perverted sexual acts" in a visit years earlier to Moscow, making him vulnerable to Russian blackmail. Almost as an aside, the report claimed Russian intelligence operatives had collected kompromat on Clinton.

Steele didn't tell Gaeta who his ultimate client was, but it was clear enough to Gaeta that senior Democrats close to Clinton were the end user. Gaeta thought the FBI had to be wary, given the involvement of a politically minded client and a law firm. But it was hardly the first time political opposition research had been offered to the FBI in the midst of a heated election season; they just had to be careful. He told Steele this work for Fusion GPS was not being done at the Bureau's request. "We are not asking you to do it and I'm not tasking you to do it," Gaeta said.

Steele understood Gaeta's concern and gave him a set of reports—one on Trump, and others on his more standard fare of Russian-centered criminal activities, including cyber activity, athletic doping, and interference in European politics.

Worried about the sensitivity of the information, Gaeta was reluctant to send it stateside in a way that might be broadcast even inside the confines of the FBI. Steele, on the other hand, was alarmed by what he'd found and wanted to be reassured it was being acted on. A week after their meeting he called Gaeta to find out what was going on, and Gaeta put him off. "I'll get back to you," the agent replied.

Gaeta called one of the bosses he knew from his time at the FBI's New York field office and explained in general detail what he had. But he did not call FBI headquarters or the Bureau's counterintelligence units.

8

Asymmetrical Politics

For the second morning in a row, Comey was in front of a camera, but this time it was not for broadcast television, just for a video conference with FBI offices around the country. Comey's tone was apologetic over the previous day's events—not for the substance of what he said, but because the shroud of secrecy had left the field offices scrambling to deal with the fallout. Typically at the FBI, if big news is coming, headquarters will give the field some kind of heads-up so they can deal with any questions from local press or officials; Comey had not done that here because he'd wanted to maintain maximum secrecy until the news was official.

Comey thanked the field offices for sticking with him through the turmoil. He knew he'd put an extra burden on their press offices, knew they'd get tough questions and would not have much to say, at least in the initial hours. He also knew there were plenty of questions and some doubts within his own workforce about what he'd done.

"He was trying to be appreciative of the fact that we didn't get a lot of lead time to prepare for what was coming," said Sarah Schweit, describing her second day with the director. Comey spoke for about ten minutes, and then was gone, as he had to prepare to defend his decision to Congress.

Comey had never expected explaining the investigation to Congress would be easy, but he was starting to realize it was going to be harder than he'd thought. There was one thing in particular in his announcement that was generating significant heat and criticism, both from the usual conservative critics on the Hill and from some quarters inside the FBI and Justice Department.

The first draft Comey had written of his announcement described Clinton's conduct as "gross negligence." As Comey's skinny group on the Clinton case kicked around drafts, Sally Moyer, a senior national security lawyer at the FBI, realized that sounded like the language from the criminal statute they were considering. It wouldn't make a ton of sense, Moyer reasoned, to clear Clinton of a crime and then describe her conduct using the very legal definition of that crime. So Comey's team deleted the term "gross negligence" from his statement and called the conduct "extremely careless" instead.

But the change didn't go far enough for a lot of people. Inside the FBI, as Comey prepared to face hostile conservative politicians, people questioned how they would explain the difference between gross negligence and extreme carelessness without sounding like a pointy-headed professor. Moyer's boss, Trisha Anderson, had warned Comey beforehand about this potential problem, but Comey had felt strongly that "extremely careless" was the right description of what Clinton had done, and he wanted it to stay in the script. Moyer would come to regret she hadn't pushed for a different term entirely.

THURSDAY, JULY 7, 2016

Comey knew he was in for a bruising from the Republicans on the House Committee on Oversight and Government Reform, but he was still confident he could earn the begrudging respect of most of his critics.

"Hillary Clinton created this mess," said Rep. Jason Chaffetz, the Republican committee chairman from Utah, before pivoting to Comey. "We believe that you have set a precedent and it's a dangerous one. The precedent is, if you sloppily deal with classified information, if you're cavalier about it—and it wasn't just an innocent mistake, this went on for years—that there's going to be no consequence," Chaffetz said. "I have defended your integrity, but I am mystified, and I am confused."

Setting the pattern for the hearing, the top Democrat on the panel defended Comey.

"I want to begin by commending you and the public servants at the FBI for the independent investigation that you conducted. You had a thankless task," said Rep. Elijah Cummings of Maryland. "Amazingly, some Republicans who were praising you just days ago for your independence, your integrity, and your honesty just days ago . . . in their eyes you had one job, and one job only: To prosecute Hillary Clinton. But you refused to do so, so now you are being summoned here to answer for your alleged transgressions, and in a sense, Mr. Director, you're on trial . . . I firmly believe that your decision was based not on convenience but on conviction."

Those opening notes would echo again and again through the hearing, as angry Republicans berated the director and tried to get him to acknowledge flaws or misjudgments in the Clinton investigation, while Democrats defended Comey and accused conservatives of trying to politicize the FBI.

Comey kept his cool for much of the day, offering the kind of earnest answers he hoped would show the sincerity of the effort. He also tried to avoid getting dragged into discussing new areas to investigate. Through the spring, Republicans had increasingly argued that the Clinton Foundation, the charity created by former president Bill Clinton during his post–White House life, was ripe for an investigation into ethical conflicts. The foundation took in millions of dollars, many from corporations or individuals who also had issues before the State Department, and Republicans charged, often with little or no evidence, that the entire operation was a "pay to play" scheme.

At the hearing, Comey stiff-armed a question about whether the FBI was investigating the foundation, saying he was "not going to comment on the existence or nonexistence" of such an investigation. In fact, the FBI was investigating the Clinton Foundation, albeit in a meandering, unfocused kind of way. Comey was unwilling to discuss it publicly for plenty of valid reasons—there was no need to do so, it had not been confirmed through any official channels or investigative activity like interviews or subpoenas, and Justice Department officials had made clear they did not intend to approve subpoenas unless the agents, working out of offices in New York, Washington, Los Angeles, and Little Rock, Arkansas, could find more meaningful evidence of possible crimes. But as Comey spoke to the committee, all that history and all that tension lay hidden under the surface.

The hearing quickly switched back to the more pressing matter: the closing of the email investigation. Throughout the case, it was unclear what, exactly, was the nature of the classified material that had been on her private server. Conservative media talked again and again about Clinton or her staff stripping classified markings from documents before sending them.

In response to a question from Republican Ron DeSantis of Florida, Comey tried to make clear that "stripping headers," as it's described by government workers, did not happen in the Clinton case.

"How did classified information get on her email?" DeSantis asked.

"By people talking about a top secret subject in an email conversation," said Comey. "It's not about forwarding a top secret document, it's about having a conversation about a matter that is top secret."

In most cases, Comey said, the classified conversations were initiated by State Department officials lower down the chain, and the replies and forwards eventually reached up to Clinton, who sometimes responded. He didn't mention Pakistan or drone strikes, or the US embassy in Islamabad, but that was in large part what he was talking about.

As lawmakers argued repeatedly about how voters would react to Comey's decision, he pointed out more than once that he was more focused on a different audience, the federal employees who had been told, again and again and again, that violating classification rules could lead to criminal charges.

"My primary concern is the impact on what other employees might think in the federal government," said Comey. Asked why no one at the State Department steered or shoved Clinton away from using a private server, the director replied, "That's an important question that goes to the culture of the State Department that's worth asking."

Ted Lieu, a California Democrat, invoked *Macbeth*, comparing the hearing to "sound and fury, signifying nothing." The congressman then proceeded to strut and fret his hour upon the stage, as he argued that none of the lawmakers could be objective on the Clinton question. "I can't be objective, I've endorsed Hillary Clinton for president, as have the Democratic members of this committee. My Republican colleagues can't be objective, they oppose Hillary Clinton for president," said Lieu. "Which is why we have you. You are a non-partisan career public servant that's served our nation with distinction and honor."

Comey seemed to welcome the point. "I care about the FBI's reputation, I care about the Justice Department. I care about the whole system deeply. And so I decided I'm going to do something no director's ever done before," he said. "I offered extraordinary transparency, which I'm sure confused and bugged a lot of people."

Comey's word choice was a conscious echo of Ray Dalio. He was acknowledging how much confusion and anger that approach had caused, also a hallmark of Dalio's philosophy. To Dalio and those who adopted his worldview, the "pain" caused by radical transparency was ultimately positive, because it forced people to accept reality—not the reality they wanted to believe in, but the whole, unvarnished truth.

Comey conceded his actions might make life harder for some future FBI director, but suggested that would be a long way off. "Now, the next Director who is criminally investigating one of the two candidates for president may find him- or herself bound by my precedent," he said. "Okay, if that happens in the next 100 years, they will have to deal with what I did. I decided it was worth doing." It wouldn't be a hundred years.

In a month, Comey's agents would be opening investigations into four advisers to presidential candidate Donald Trump.

The back-and-forth continued. While Republicans publicly excoriated Comey, congressional Democrats praised him. Whatever private doubts they may have had about Comey's methods, they were pleased the Clinton email case was finally over, freeing her of the ugly baggage of a criminal investigation that could trip her up on the way to the White House.

Not every Democrat was so optimistic. Matthew Miller had served as the top Justice Department spokesman early in the Obama administration. A political operative who had learned a great deal about the Justice Department in his time there, Miller thought the hearing was a disaster for Democrats. The Republicans had berated Comey as if they, not the Democrats, were the aggrieved party. "He had taken a case that was never going to yield charges, where there was a unanimous conclusion by career officials that there shouldn't be charges, and somehow come up with a press conference in which he savaged the Democratic nominee for president in total violation of DoJ's rules," said Miller.

Furious over what he felt was the Democrats' signaling that Comey could keep trying to appease Republicans and keep attacking Democrats, Miller was sharply, publicly critical of Comey. About two dozen of his former Justice Department colleagues reached out to congratulate and agree with him. Miller told some of those friends that it would be good if other Justice Department veterans also spoke publicly. Each of them declined, saying they had to maintain their professional relationships with the FBI.

Comey, Miller said, "was given a free pass by the Democratic party that he didn't deserve. When you're only getting criticized by one side, you only worry about that side, and that has an impact on your decision-making."

Russia Was Listening

TUESDAY, JULY 19, 2016

At the same moment that to all outward appearances the FBI was step-ping back from its prominent role in the election—the Clinton email in-vestigation was over—inside the FBI a steady drip of incoming material had started to pull the Bureau back into the campaign.

The Clinton email case had moved in more or less a straight line, demanding attention at all times to a single, shouted question. That changed sharply in July, when fast-moving developments on multiple fronts pulled the FBI in multiple directions, all of them deeper into a political morass. "Company Intelligence Report 2016/94" arrived in FBI agent Mike Gaeta's inbox, declaring "Secret Kremlin Meetings Attended by Trump Adviser Carter Page in Moscow (July 2016)." Steele's report described an allegedly secret meeting the Trump campaign adviser at-tended just days earlier on his trip to the New Economic School in Mos-cow. The report asserted Page had met with the chairman of the giant Russian energy company Rosneft, Igor Sechin. The two discussed the possible lifting of sanctions against Russia, the report said. In a separate meeting, according to Steele's sources, a key staffer of the Putin administration named Igor Divyekin told Carter Page of the existence of kompromat on Hillary Clinton.

Gaeta recognized Sechin's name, but not Page's, and generally felt he didn't have the right background to make a judgment call on the information. For a few days he kept the report to himself; he didn't feel he needed to act upon it.

TUESDAY, JULY 26, 2016

Stories connecting Trump and Russia weren't only coming from Steele. In London, Australian diplomat Alexander Downer reached out to an associate at the US embassy. Something that had happened months earlier seemed suddenly important, and he felt he should tell the Americans. In early May, Downer had gotten drinks with a young Trump campaign staffer named George Papadopoulos. Over gin and tonics at the Kensington Wine Rooms, they chatted about politics and diplomacy. The meeting had been set up by a junior Australian diplomat, Erika Thompson, who had met Papadopoulos before.

Downer now wanted the Americans to know that during that May conversation, Papadopoulos had mentioned the Russians had "dirt" on Hillary Clinton. Though Papadopoulos spoke vaguely, the implication seemed to be that the Russians might release information to damage Clinton's election chances. At the time, Downer thought it an interesting tidbit, but hardly earth shaking. Back then the public didn't know Russian intelligence had hacked Democratic National Committee (DNC) servers, and DCLeaks had not released any stolen files. In a diplomatic cable back to his bosses in the Australian capital of Canberra, Downer mentioned the Papadopoulos conversation, but only in passing and toward the end of his dispatch.

Papadopoulos "suggested the Trump team had received some kind of suggestion from Russia that it could assist this process with the anonymous release of information during the campaign that would be damaging to Mrs. Clinton (and President Obama)," the cable said. "It was unclear whether he or the Russians were referring to material acquired publicly or through other means. It was also unclear how Mr. Trump's team reacted to the offer. We note the Trump team's reaction could, in the end, have little bearing on what Russia decides to do, with or without Mr. Trump's cooperation."

But the diplomat's thinking on the matter suddenly changed in late July, given recent events in America. Four days earlier, WikiLeaks had released nearly twenty thousand emails on the eve of the Democrats' national convention in Philadelphia. Downer now viewed his conversation with Papadopoulos in a potentially more sinister light. Along with the United States, Australia is part of the intelligence-sharing alliance known as "Five Eyes" (Britain, Canada, and New Zealand are the others) and, to him, there was little question that if there was meaningful information, it should be shared with the Americans and possibly the FBI.

Downer would later insist he had not intended to pry any secrets out of the young American. "I didn't go to the meeting thinking he was even going to mention Russia in the context of the election campaign," Downer said in a television interview three years after his meeting with Papadopoulos. "I had no idea what he would say."

Downer also said he never meant to imply the Trump campaign was colluding with the Russians. "There was no suggestion from Papadopoulos nor in the record of the meeting that we sent back to Canberra, there was no suggestion that there was collusion between Donald Trump or Donald Trump's campaign and the Russians," he said. "All we did is report what Papadopoulos said, and that was that he thought that the Russians may release information, might release information, that could be damaging to Hillary Clinton's campaign at some stage before the election."

Officials in the US embassy in London would spend more than a day discussing among themselves how to handle the information from Downer while, in Washington, James Comey was still trying to shore up any lingering doubts among the FBI workforce about how he had handled the Clinton email case. He was clearly still annoyed by the criticism, particularly when it came from current or former agents. "What I don't have patience for," he said in a video message to employees, "is people suggesting that the FBI did it in some way that was anything other than apolitical and independent, because that's just not true, and anybody who knows the FBI should know better."

That same night in Philadelphia, Hillary Clinton was formally nominated for president at the Democratic National Convention. In a bit of scripted symbolism, the Vermont delegation voted last in the state-by-state roll call, giving her primary rival, Senator Bernie Sanders, the role of calling for the party to unite behind Clinton.

As they often liked to do, Peter Strzok and Lisa Page texted each other about the politics of the evening. "Chills, just because I'm a homer for American democracy that way," Strzok texted. "If they played patriotic music or did something with the flag and an honor guard, I probably would have teared up."

"Yeah, it is pretty cool," Page replied. "She just has to win now. I'm not going to lie, I got a flash of nervousness yesterday about trump. The sandernistas have the potential to make a very big mistake here."

Strzok did not share her concern. "I'm more worried about the anarchist Assanges who will take fed information and disclose it to disrupt," he texted.

WEDNESDAY, JULY 27, 2016

"Russia, if you're listening, I hope you're able to find the 30,000 emails that are missing. I think you will probably be rewarded mightily by our press," Donald Trump declared at a press conference in Florida. The former reality television star's penchant for drama was never more evident than when he invited foreign hackers to dig up the emails Hillary Clinton's lawyers had deleted. There was plenty that was unconventional about the Republican presidential candidate and his campaign, but the public suggestion that others go find—or did he mean steal?—his opponent's files was remarkable for its sheer brazenness.

The "if you're listening" line was an ad lib, Trump's deputy campaign chairman, Rick Gates, would later tell investigators, though it reflected a genuine obsession inside the campaign with finding those deleted Clinton emails. The Trump campaign saw the potential in them. The number varied. Sometimes it was thirty thousand; usually it was thirty-three thousand. But time and again, Trump and those close to him would privately share their hope that someone—anyone—could find the deleted emails and publish them before Election Day. They had convinced themselves that the cache of discarded data contained something momentous and could be fatal to Clinton's candidacy.

The deleted emails were a blank slate upon which Clinton's critics liked to draw. In their absence, Trump staffers and supporters imagined the emails held evidence of all manner of misconduct. Or some dirty secrets of the Clinton Foundation. Or details about her personal health, which they speculated was failing. Trump thought the deleted emails could explain what Clinton did or knew regarding Uranium One, a complex corporate acquisition Republicans suggested sold out American national security interests for the personal benefit of the Clintons. Clinton has long denied any wrongdoing related to Uranium One, saying it was all handled at a level well below her. Since no one knew what was in the emails, people were free to imagine they contained almost anything. And many Republicans' imaginations were running wild in 2016.

In fact, there was even less left to the imagination than the Trump campaign understood. In the course of the FBI's investigation, agents had found about 14,900 emails and documents that Clinton's lawyers had not turned over to the State Department. So the elusive cache of 33,000 vanished emails that conservatives liked to talk about was probably more like half that number. But such distinctions were lost in heated political debates—about as memorable as Comey's televised primer on slack space and data storage.

While Rudy Giuliani and other Trump backers talked endlessly on Fox News about a vast criminal conspiracy with Clinton at its center, Trump and his staff envisioned the emails were out there somewhere, like a pirate's buried treasure.

Within five hours of Trump's audacious statement at the press conference came a signal that Russia was indeed listening. Unit 26165 of the GRU sent spear-phishing messages with malicious links to fifteen email accounts used by Clinton's personal office. Earlier in July, Comey had publicly speculated about the possibility that hackers had penetrated her server previously but left no trace. The attempts to hack Clinton-related email accounts on July 27 was not speculation—they were spotted by US investigators. It was the first time the FBI saw evidence of the GRU targeting Clinton's personal office. The Russians had come to play.

THURSDAY, JULY 28, 2016

Nine days after FBI agent Mike Gaeta received Chris Steele's second Trump report, and twenty-three days after receiving the first one, Gaeta sent them both to an FBI supervisor in New York. Officials there told Gaeta they would confer with higher-ups and figure out what to do next.

That same day, an FBI official in London sent the Philadelphia office and FBI headquarters a report describing the tip from Australian ambassador Downer about Papadopoulos's comments back in May. The Downer tip immediately got the attention of the higher ups at the FBI, who briefed McCabe about it immediately, setting off several days of intense discussions among senior officials on how to proceed.

Meanwhile, the Steele reports still went nowhere, according to FBI officials.

SUNDAY, JULY 31, 2016

Pete Strzok drove into the office on a Sunday, after being told by his boss, Bill Priestap, to open a counterintelligence investigation into George Papadopoulos. The senior leadership of the Bureau was all on board. The Russian hacking activity was already under investigation; now they would try to determine if someone on the Trump campaign was involved, or being groomed by the Russians for a role in the election interference efforts.

One of the enduring ironies of the 2016 election is that the FBI, as it investigated the digital security and communications discipline of the State Department, would suffer significant consequences for its own communication habits—primarily the tens of thousands of texts exchanged between Lisa Page and Peter Strzok.

The case agent and the high-level lawyer used their work phones to communicate in order to hide their chat from their spouses, a decision that would have enormous consequences for them personally and the Bureau. Their texts offer a stream of real-time commentary on the thinking of key players in the FBI's decision making. As a historical record, the texts are constant but incomplete, frequently veering into their political and personal views. Their more caustic remarks sounded at times like Statler and Waldorf, the irascible old men on *The Muppets* who heckle the performers from the balcony. Like those wisecracking coots, Strzok and Page often amused each other with their put-downs of others, but their heckling was never meant to be heard by anyone but themselves.

As the FBI prepared for the momentous step of opening the investigation they would name "Crossfire Hurricane" into Papadopoulos and, by extension, the Trump campaign, Peter Strzok and Lisa Page vented to each other about their intense dislike for Russia.

"Very little I find redeeming about this. Even in history. Couple of good writers and artists I guess," Page texted.

Strzok answered: "f*cking conniving cheating savages. At statecraft, athletics, you name it. I'm glad I'm on Team USA."

That evening, after he'd formally opened the investigation on the FBI's computer system, Strzok shared his sense of satisfaction that he was embarking on a case even bigger than the Clinton emails, texting Page: "Damn this feels momentous. Because this matters. The other one did, too, but that was to ensure we didn't F something up. This matters because this MATTERS. So super glad to be on this voyage with you."

Strzok got the name for Crossfire Hurricane from a line from a Rolling Stones song. He was right about the importance of the moment.

Strzok's bosses made another decision at that time that was almost as important, choosing not to warn the Trump campaign or national GOP officials about possible Russian efforts to recruit and use them.

In some cases, the FBI will provide what's called a "defensive briefing" to people they think are being targeted or recruited by crooks or spies. Defensive briefings can serve many purposes besides being an obvious warning. A defensive briefing can also give agents important new details that help an FBI investigation, or they can help build rapport with the person being warned. In the best-case scenario, a defensive briefing can short-circuit a criminal conspiracy before it goes any further. Here, though, the FBI, and principally Priestap, decided not to give a defensive briefing to anyone at the Trump campaign or the Republican National Committee (RNC).

Priestap felt defensive briefings were only justified when there was zero indication that the person being briefed might be working with the bad guys. Just days earlier during a press conference, the presidential candidate had explicitly encouraged the Russians to release more hacked emails. If the person at the top of the campaign was publicly embracing such behavior, how could the FBI justify warning anyone who worked under him?

One of the other challenges, in Priestap's mind, of giving a defensive briefing to a Republican official was that Papadopoulos's alleged statement to Downer was so vague that it was completely unclear to the FBI which Americans might be conspiring with the Russians, or being groomed by them. Not knowing whom to trust at the top of the Republican Party, the FBI trusted no one.

It was a momentous choice, and one that stood in contrast to decades of FBI practice in other areas, particularly criminal cases. When in 2000 the FBI was tipped off to a criminal fraud conspiracy to cheat at the popular prize-winning games offered by McDonald's—the kind of games based on collecting game pieces named after Monopoly properties—the agents decided to notify the company's leadership, even though at the time the FBI was unsure if McDonald's employees were in on the scam (they weren't). Yet in 2016, facing questions about Russian influence seeping into a major presidential candidate's campaign, Priestap and his colleagues decided there was in essence no Republican who could be trusted to work with them to determine what the Russians might be up to. It was another instance of how the upper ranks of the FBI had come to be dominated by the generally more tight-lipped and more suspicious intelligence agents.

The next day, Strzok and Supervisory Special Agent Joe Pientka boarded a flight to London to interview the Australian diplomats.

MONDAY, AUGUST 8, 2016

"I can't wait to hear what I have to say," Roger Stone declared as he began speaking to the Southwest Broward Republican Organization. Stone, wearing a light suit, dark tie, and a button-down shirt that had already taken a beating from the Florida heat, chuckled at his own joke, standing in front of a large wooden barrel that served as the group's lectern.

In political circles, Stone was a loud, strange blend of conspiracy theorist, consultant, and agent provocateur. In his sixties, Stone had worked for a variety of third-party long shots, but now he was backing a major party candidate in the biggest race in the country: his longtime friend Donald Trump.

This election, Stone declared, was "not Republicans versus Democrats. It's the insiders versus the outsiders." Stone talked a lot, and most of it flew under the radar because he was generally considered a fringe character. But something he said while standing in front of that wooden barrel would have huge repercussions for the 2016 election. An audience member asked Stone: "With regard to the October Surprise, what would be your forecast on that, given what Julian Assange has intimated he's going to do?"

"Well," Stone replied, "it could be any number of things. I actually have communicated with Assange. I believe the next tranche of his documents pertain to the Clinton Foundation, but there's no telling what the October Surprise may be."

It was a shocking answer in many ways. At that moment, public re-porting indicated that Russia had hacked the Democrats, and Assange had already published DNC documents. Trump had publicly asked for Russia to find the elusive thirty-three thousand emails he and others hoped held Clinton's dirty secrets about the foundation. Now, here was Stone, a person with a close, decades-long relationship with Trump, indi-cating he was talking to Julian Assange about his planned releases.

In the days, months, and years to come, this claim by Stone would be-come a central data point of the Russia investigation, fueling much of the suspicion that Trump's team conspired with a foreign adversary. But by the time Stone uttered those words, he had spent nearly an hour making wild, false claims on a wide range of topics. He falsely claimed Hillary wore blackface at a college party. He falsely claimed a Gold Star father, a lawyer whose son had been killed in Iraq and who criticized Trump at the Democratic convention, had received hundreds of thousands of dollars from the Clinton Foundation. He called the foundation a "Ponzi scheme" that never distributed any real AIDS medicine in Africa. And his message was warmly received. As he spoke, a man in the audience declared, "RICO Act," referring to a federal law used to prosecute the Mafia.

Stone also spoke at length about his certainty that Vice President Lyn-don B. Johnson had arranged the murder of President John F. Kennedy. None of those outrageous statements, steeped in the conspiracy-infested corners of the internet, raised as much as a ripple in the wider world. But there would be tremendous consequences for his claim about As-sange, particularly after it emerged that Stone exchanged election-year messages with both WikiLeaks and Guccifer 2.0. If Stone was telling the truth that day in Florida, there appeared to be a global conspiracy to un-dermine American democracy. If he wasn't, he was just a crackpot with a microphone.

Predicate

WEDNESDAY, AUGUST 10, 2016

Peter Strzok was back from London, and his team had been culling intelligence and law enforcement databases for any indications that other Trump associates beyond Papadopoulos had ties to Russia worth investigating. Paul Manafort, Trump's campaign chairman, was already under Justice Department scrutiny for his work in Ukraine, though it was the kind of investigation under a law called the Foreign Agents Registration Act that often went nowhere. Manafort had made millions as a campaign consultant to a host of foreign candidates, but Ukraine had become his cash cow. Carter Page, whose interactions with Russian diplomats years earlier had been investigated by the FBI, was also already under investigation by FBI agents in New York, so Strzok's team decided to fold him into the Crossfire Hurricane umbrella. The subcases would get their own Crossfire codenames, some replacing "Hurricane" with different types of extreme weather. The Papadopoulos investigation was named "Crossfire Typhoon." Former lieutenant general Michael Flynn, on whom the FBI opened a case a week later, would become "Crossfire Razor." The Crossfire group of cases were counterintelligence investigations, designed to see if any of the four were secretly acting at the behest of foreign governments, principally Russia.

As the Crossfire cases expanded, Andy McCabe went to see the attorney general, Loretta Lynch, to give her a warning about a Russian intelligence document they'd received back in March that had claimed Lynch planned to protect Clinton from the email investigation. McCabe described, in general terms, the document alleging an email existed in which Lynch had assured a senior Clinton campaign staffer, Amanda Renteria, that Clinton did not have to worry about the email probe, because she would keep the FBI in check.

"Just so you know, I don't know this person and have never communicated with her," Lynch told McCabe, according to one person's account of the meeting. McCabe told her the defensive briefing was not a formal interview and the document "didn't have investigative value"—the Bureau's way of saying they had not pursued it. Lynch was also told there were possible "translation issues," a vague reference that wasn't explained further to her. She told McCabe the FBI was welcome to speak to her staff and to conduct a formal interview of her if they wanted, according to one person familiar with the exchange. The Bureau declined.

McCabe walked back across the street and told his boss about the conversation, but in his telling, Lynch's reserved demeanor was worrisome. He told Comey he would feel better if she had made some kind of forceful denial. But she just said "thank you," McCabe told Comey.

The incident was noteworthy mostly for what it said about the continually deteriorating relationship between Comey and Lynch, and between the FBI and the Justice Department. It also pointed to one of the quirks of the FBI's defensive briefings. They are meant to be what they sound like: a warning and a heads-up to officials, companies, or private citizens about a potential issue that could cause them harm. In Lynch's case, the ostensible purpose of the briefing was to let her know that, at some point, this document could become public, causing people to question her motives or ethics. McCabe told Lynch he had no reason to think it would become public, but wanted her to know the contents in case it ever did. But FBI agents don't just talk in defensive briefings; they also listen, and notice any reactions. By scrutinizing those reactions, FBI agents sometimes draw inferences about the underlying information—whether the person being briefed is worried, defensive, angry, or calm. McCabe certainly did so with Lynch. By that unspoken measure, the briefing went badly for Lynch, without her realizing it.

The backstory of the Russian intelligence document was bizarre. On its face, it was the kind of espionage information the FBI craved. Relayed to the FBI by hackers associated with Dutch intelligence, the Russian document claimed knowledge of a secret understanding between the Clinton campaign and the Justice Department.

Lynch, the document claimed, had privately assured a Clinton campaign official, Amanda Renteria, that the ongoing FBI investigation into Clinton's use of a private server would not dig too deep. The Russian intelligence document didn't attach the purported email, just described it. Even so, the accusation was potentially explosive, suggesting corruption at the highest level of the Justice Department. But the document didn't make a ton of sense—it also claimed that Comey planned to hurt Clinton's election chances by prolonging the email investigation. Inside the FBI, people didn't believe either allegation.

The document claimed that, in an email from then Democratic National Committee chairwoman Deborah Wasserman Schultz to a man named Leonard Benardo, she claimed Lynch had been in private communication with Renteria and had assured Renteria that she, Lynch, would keep Clinton safe from the email probe.

When the FBI first obtained the document, agents asked the Dutch to try to get them the underlying email described in it, but were told that was not possible. Inside the FBI, there was some debate about the document's importance, but a consensus quickly developed that the allegation was simply untrue. Some in the FBI came to suspect the document itself may have been bogus, a particularly nefarious trick to make the Americans more suspicious of each other, but most FBI officials, and all of the senior FBI officials, believed the document itself was a legitimate piece of Russian intelligence, even if the allegations were bogus.

The FBI never interviewed the people named in the document, so in 2017 I called them and asked about the accusations. "Wow, that's kind of weird and out of left field," said Renteria. "I don't know Loretta Lynch, the attorney general. I haven't spoken to her."

Renteria said she did know a different woman named Loretta Lynch, a fellow Californian who was a lawyer specializing in utility company issues. The Loretta Lynch in California had done some work years earlier for the Clintons involving the Whitewater investigation. When Lynch was nominated in late 2014 to become attorney general, some initially confused the two women.

Wasserman Schultz was equally adamant that the claims in the document were untrue. "Not only do I not know him [Bernado]," Wasserman Schultz said, "I've never heard of him. I don't know who this is. There's no truth to this whatsoever. I have never sent an email remotely like what you're describing."

Benardo said much the same of Wasserman Schultz: "I've never met her. I've only read about her. I've never in my lifetime received any correspondence of any variety—correspondence, fax, telephone—from Debbie Wasserman Schultz. If such documentation exists, it's of course made up."

The far-fetched allegation in the document made little sense to American eyes, but to those aware of Russian propaganda, it seemed familiar, particularly given Benardo's job at Open Society Foundations, an organization founded by billionaire George Soros to promote democracy around the world. The Kremlin has long regarded both Clinton and Soros as political enemies trying to undermine and unseat Russian president Vladimir Putin.

Even without any FBI interviews of the people named in the document, there was another, simpler reason to doubt its claims. A month or two earlier, the FBI had received a different Russian intelligence document from the same source, and US intelligence officials were certain the allegations in that second document were untrue. But the issue would not burst into the public eye until 2017, when the FBI was under tremendous pressure from all sides.

THURSDAY, AUGUST 11, 2016

FBI officials were trying to shift their focus off of Clinton and onto Trump, but the controversies surrounding their work on Clinton refused to die. CNN had a new report on a riddle that had perplexed Justice Department reporters for months. Senior officials, the cable news station reported, had blocked the FBI from investigating the Clinton Foundation.

"First on CNN: Inside the Debate over Probing the Clinton Foundation," the headline read. In a meeting months earlier, the report said, FBI officials had pressed to open an investigation into the foundation, based on a suspicious bank transaction. "DOJ officials pushed back against opening a case during the meeting earlier this year," the report asserted. "Some also expressed concern the request seemed more political than substantive, especially given the timing of it coinciding with the investigation into the private email server and Clinton's presidential campaign."

Hours later, the Daily Caller, a conservative website, published a very different piece on the same topic. "EXCLUSIVE: Joint FBI-US Attorney Probe of Clinton Foundation Is Underway," the headline declared. "Multiple FBI investigations are underway involving potential corruption charges against the Clinton Foundation, according to a former senior law enforcement official," the story said. The investigation, according to the website, was being spearheaded by Preet Bharara, the US attorney for the Southern District of New York, whose "prosecutorial aggressiveness has resulted in a large number of convictions of banks, hedge funds, and Wall Street insiders."

Although the two stories contradicted each other in many ways, it's notable how much they got right. There had, in fact, been a meeting in February in which FBI agents eager to more aggressively investigate the Clinton Foundation had been shot down by their Justice Department bosses.

The Clinton Foundation case was something of a muddle in late 2015, when four FBI field offices—New York, Los Angeles, Washington, and Little Rock—were searching for evidence that might show financial crimes or influence peddling.

The Los Angeles office had issued a subpoena for bank records grow-ing out of a separate public corruption case, but FBI headquarters didn't even find out about the subpoena until later. Separately, the Washing-ton field office was looking at financial relationships involving Terry McAuliffe when he was active with the foundation. And FBI agents in the financial capital of New York had done a significant amount of work examining financial records to look for signs of criminal wrongdoing.

In early 2016, the agents on the foundation case sat down with Leslie Caldwell, the head of the Justice Department's Criminal Division, and public integrity prosecutors. The case, the prosecutors thought, seemed based principally on a book, *Clinton Cash*, and a *New York Times* story drawn largely from the book. The agents, in turn, didn't understand why the prosecutors seemed so uninterested in looking at the questions raised by the book.

The Justice Department officials told the agents they would not be getting approvals for subpoenas or a grand jury. "Frankly, I was embar-rassed for them," said one former Justice Department official. Through-out the meeting, prosecutors mostly stared silently at the agents as they spoke. "That was one of the weirdest meetings I've ever been to," said one participant. The feeling was mutual.

The Justice Department had not ended the investigations, but simply reduced them to a low-level project for which they authorized no overt investigative measures. The CNN and Daily Caller stories that appeared in August, by and large, did not capture the public's attention. But they hinted at a degree of subterranean grumbling inside the Justice Depart-ment and FBI, while on the surface, reporters strove to understand what, if anything, the FBI was investigating when it came to Clinton.

The eleventh of August was also a pivotal day in the nascent Crossfire Hurricane case. Supervisory Special Agent Joe Pientka had approved the use of Stefan Halper as a confidential human source for the investigation. Halper was perfect for the job. He'd been involved with Republican polit-ical campaigns dating back to the 1970s. He was an emeritus professor at Cambridge University, but had spent years secretly providing informa-tion to the FBI for money.

Halper's relationship with the FBI was sometimes erratic, and in 2011 he had been shut down as a source for "aggressiveness" toward agents, due to his complaints about not getting paid enough and a concern by his handling agent about Halper's possible loyalty to targets of his intelligence gathering, according to internal FBI documents. The breakup was short-lived, though, and Halper was reinstated as an FBI source two months later. In 2012, Halper picked up a new source of income, according to federal records. A Pentagon think tank called the Office of Net Assessment paid him more than $1 million over the years for research and development in social sciences and humanities. Some of those funds were used to hire academics and experts to conduct research, according to US officials. In 2015, Halper took the title of honorary senior fellow of the Centre of International Studies.

Halper had married into the world of US intelligence. His first wife was the daughter of the former CIA analyst Ray Cline, who worked under President John F. Kennedy during the Cuban missile crisis in 1962. Associates say Cline mentored Halper and introduced him to those he knew in politics and intelligence. As a young man, Halper served on President Richard M. Nixon's domestic policy council, and later became an assistant to President Gerald Ford's chief of staff. He would go on to work on George H. W. Bush's 1980 presidential campaign, and, when Bush was picked by Ronald Reagan to join the ticket, worked for the Reagan-Bush campaign.

That race brought Halper's first brush with accusations of political spying. Halper was one of several Reagan aides accused of spying on then president Jimmy Carter's campaign and obtaining private documents Carter was using to prepare for a debate with Reagan. Some Reagan White House officials later claimed Halper had used former CIA agents to run an operation against Carter, a charge Halper called "absolutely false." Halper has long denied any wrongdoing during the 1980 presidential campaign.

By 2016, Halper was known in GOP circles as a moderate, old-school Republican whose foreign policy focus had in recent years turned to sounding alarms over the growing power of China. That put him out of step with many of the neoconservatives who populated the administration of George W. Bush, and Halper cowrote a book critical of that president's handling of the Iraq War. To his students at Cambridge, Stefan Halper was the host of friendly wine and cheese parties full of friendly political debates.

The agent who dealt with Halper in 2016 had come to think of him as a bit of a hothead. When the agent reactivated the relationship, he gave Halper a warning: this was his last chance to work with the FBI, and the Bureau would not allow the kind of conflict that had emerged with the last handler. Halper seemed to mellow. He was willing to engage "without any hesitation" when asked, his new handler would later tell investigators.

When the FBI decided they needed someone to sidle up to Trump campaign staff, Halper seemed like a perfect fit. Though his relationships tended to be with GOP establishment figures who were on the outs with the Trump crew, Halper still knew how campaigns and foreign policy aides operated. So when agents in Washington drove to meet with Halper on August 11 to broach the issue of Russian election interference, they did not tell him exactly what their suspicions were.

Asked about George Papadopoulos, Halper told the agents he'd never heard of him, but agreed to reach out to him. Halper then told them that in mid-July, Carter Page had attended a three-day conference at Cambridge, during which he had approached Halper and asked him to be a foreign policy adviser for the Trump campaign. Halper told the agents he was noncommittal on joining the campaign. Halper said he expected a more senior member of the Trump campaign would reach out to him soon about possibly joining the campaign.

Halper offered another interesting tidbit, saying he'd known Trump's then campaign chairman, Paul Manafort, and had also interacted before with General Michael Flynn. The agents couldn't believe their luck that Halper had already been in contact with three of the four targets of the Crossfire investigations. "Quite honestly," said one, "we kind of stumbled upon him knowing these folks." When the FBI agents drove back to headquarters, though, their bosses thought Halper's connections were so good, they might be a problem.

If the professor was thinking about taking a position on Team Trump, Pientka, Strzok, and Priestap reasoned, it could put their informant "too close" to the campaign. In the minds of senior FBI officials, they wanted someone who could connect with people in the campaign, talk to them in confidence, but not be one of them. If the FBI had wanted to place an informant inside the campaign itself, they could probably have done so, but it was a bad idea in the minds of Peter Strzok and others.

"No, no, no, no, no," Strzok thought. "God no. Absolutely not." If Halper was even considering joining the Trump campaign, the FBI investigation should leave him out of it, Strzok reasoned. FBI lawyers felt the same. "No freaking way," they responded when asked about the possibility of Halper joining the campaign.

Fortunately or unfortunately for the bosses and lawyers at the FBI, Halper assured them he wasn't really interested in being part of the Trump campaign. He would turn down Carter Page's offer, opening the door for him to do highly sensitive work for the FBI as it investigated that campaign.

While the FBI was pursuing the possibility of a sinister conspiracy between Americans and Russians to influence the election, other parts of the Russian interference apparatus were brazenly out in the open.

"North Carolina finds 2,214 voters over the age of 110 #VoterFraud," the Twitter account of @TEN_GOP posted that day, warping an old story about the state's outdated voter rolls into something that sounded far more sinister than the truth. It was a popular twitter account, amassing more than a hundred thousand followers over the course of the campaign, including high-profile Trump advisers. The account, though, was not connected to Tennessee Republicans, but rather run by operatives at the Internet Research Agency, a sophisticated online troll farm based in

St. Petersburg, Russia, that, according to a later indictment, spent years preparing for an ambitious effort to pump out election-focused propaganda in the United States. The Internet Research Agency ran a multi-million-dollar operation targeting the internal politics of other countries besides the United States, but in 2016, at the Kremlin's direction, it devoted much of its resources to messing with American voters' heads, US officials have said.

Facebook, Twitter, and other social media sites had created a golden opportunity for the kind of divisive fear mongering and division sowing that Russia and the Soviet Union deployed against the United States over the decades. Online outrage could make an accusation go viral in a matter of hours, long before anyone stopped to wonder if the person making the accusation was accurate, or if they were who they claimed to be.

In a sea of false personas and bots, the Internet Research Agency found a huge audience, though the presence of Russian disinformation in US politics was only dimly understood at the time. By the time the fake Tennessee GOP account was tweeting spurious and dated allegations of voter fraud, the group behind it had been engaged in a years'-long campaign. On February 10, according to an indictment filed in federal court, Internet Research Agency workers were instructed by their bosses on the points they should hit. Focus on US politics, they were told, and "use any opportunity to criticize Hillary and the rest (except Sanders and Trump—we support them)."

The Russian propaganda efforts targeted racial issues above almost all others to try to drive political wedges into the public debate. Black Lives Matter, police shootings, and border policy all got angry amplification, thanks to the Russian trolls. In 2016, US intelligence officials dealing with the WikiLeaks email dumps and Russian interference marveled at the Russians' apparent understanding of the subtleties of American society and culture, and how that impacted its politics.

"I don't see how Russia could have this sophisticated an understanding of our politics and our media," one senior law enforcement official said to me at the time, mentioning the email releases and the apparent focus on internal disagreements among Democrats. "Someone in America must be helping them figure out how to do this," the official reasoned. But the Internet Research Agency case, when it was unveiled later by special counsel Robert S. Mueller III, would show Russian operatives in fact had worked for years to understand American society, in order to better manipulate it.

The @TEN_GOP account would be shut down about a year after its August tweets, and by that time officials would have a far better picture of how widespread the Russian election disinformation campaign had been. Facebook would later estimate that roughly 29 million people were delivered content directly from the IRA, and after sharing among users, roughly 126 million Americans may have seen it.

August 11 was a significant day at the FBI for other reasons. Around lunchtime, Lisa Page texted Peter Strzok with news. "Congratulations," she wrote. "You're the new DAD of the Counterintelligence Division"— using the acronym for Strzok's new promotion to deputy assistant director. "Don't tell," she added. As McCabe's right hand, Lisa Page knew about a lot of personnel moves inside the Bureau before most others.

Strzok aspired to bigger things at the Bureau, and his promotion was a major step up. By 2016, he was starting to worry he was being pigeon-holed by superiors as a great agent, but not management material. A deputy assistant director was another rung closer to senior management, but in Strzok's case, he was still very much an agent. He was managing Cross-fire Hurricane, which was quickly becoming the Bureau's most import-ant case now that the Clinton email saga had ended. The investigation would be a chance to prove he was executive material.

But around the seventh floor, there were whispers of concern about Strzok, or to be more precise, about his close relationship with Lisa Page. Strzok's boss, Bill Priestap, wanted to assign Crossfire Hurricane to some-one else. He liked and trusted Pete, but he had concerns about his rela-tionship with Page. That feeling was shared by Priestap's boss, Michael Steinbach. The issue, as the two of them saw it, was that they seemed to back-channel information between themselves. There were suspicions in the building—correct, as it turned out—that the two were having an af-fair, but for Steinbach and Priestap this was not the main concern.

The FBI is a very hierarchical organization adhering to a military-like chain of command, abhorring anyone who goes around their boss to try to get what they want. In plenty of offices, this kind of behavior is called "doing an end run," or going over someone's head. FBI agents use those terms, but there is another, more crass phrase agents use to describe this specific conduct: motherfuck. They use it as a verb. To motherfuck someone is to go outside normal channels.

Strzok and Page had gotten a reputation in some quarters as a duo who frequently motherfucked people. Strzok back-channeled information to Page, and she did the same for him. That often frustrated Steinbach, Priestap, and others, who wanted information to flow through regular channels before it got to Andrew McCabe's desk, the director's desk, or moved down to the case agents.

Inside the FBI, a workspace dominated by (mostly male) agents, Lisa Page bore the brunt of this whispered criticism. She was young, she was not an agent, and she was not a man. Executives complained to McCabe more than once about Page, but she was his eyes and ears in the Bureau, she was his legal adviser, and he trusted her. He would not shut her down or shunt her aside.

Back in March, she had vented to Strzok about how angry and embarrassed she was that her boss had to field those sorts of complaints about her. "I am so goddamn pissed," she texted him. "And now I want to curl up in a ball and die. Yet again, It's lisa out of her lane." She speculated about just quitting. "Why the fuck am I working my tail off and missing my family just to have people criticize my involvement in things?"

More than many of her colleagues, Page had a fairly clear-eyed view of how she was viewed inside the FBI, and it was not a pretty picture. Her reputation was that she had "sharp elbows" and fought with people unnecessarily. Some executives considered her a toxic presence in meetings, willing to profanely disagree with a senior official if she thought he was wrong. "When I'm on their side, everyone loves Lisa," she vented to Strzok at one point. "But God forbid I disagree." Strzok encouraged her to stick to her guns and get McCabe to tell any critical executives to back off. Which McCabe generally did when such complaints reached his desk.

Priestap and Steinbach would later tell internal investigators that they tried to get Strzok taken off of Crossfire Hurricane primarily because of his close relationship with Page, but they were overruled by McCabe. McCabe would tell the same investigators he did not overrule anything, and Steinbach had offered a much softer, less compelling reason to remove Strzok—that he should get more traditional management experience in his new deputy assistant director job. McCabe told investigators he never interceded on Strzok's behalf, and Strzok simply continued to run the investigation. McCabe said he did talk to Lisa Page about spending less time with Strzok.

None of the FBI executives would learn until much later that a separate, worse problem lurked inside the Strzok-Page relationship. Three days before Page congratulated Strzok on his new promotion, she sent him an explicitly political text about candidate Donald Trump.

"He's not ever going to become president, right? Right?!" Page asked him.

"No. No he won't. We'll stop it," Strzok replied.

The exchange, coming less than two weeks after the opening of Crossfire Hurricane, would outrage Republicans when they learned of it more than two years later. To conservatives this was smoking-gun proof that, from the very beginning of the investigation into Trump campaign figures, the investigators were determined to stop him from becoming president. Strzok and Page would defend themselves by saying all they ever meant by "We'll stop it" was that voters would not elect Trump president. Republicans scoffed at that explanation, as they would at another text between the two in mid-August.

"I want to believe the path you threw out for consideration in Andy's office—that there's no way he gets elected—but I'm afraid we can't take that risk," Strzok texted Page. "It's like an insurance policy in the unlikely event you die before 40."

When that message surfaced much later, Strzok would insist all he meant was the FBI had to ensure that, even if the chances of Trump being elected president were slim, as many pundits kept saying, the FBI still had an obligation to figure out if Russia was trying to manipulate or otherwise influence the Trump campaign. Conservatives read it much more darkly—that at the highest levels of the FBI, officials were so biased against Trump they were willing to use their investigative powers to hobble him.

FRIDAY, AUGUST 12, 2016

The FBI was eager for Halper to get started on the investigation, and the agents visited him again the very next day, urging him to set up a meeting with Carter Page. Halper said he would.

While the pieces seemed to be quickly falling into place for the FBI's Russia-Trump probe, things were falling apart when it came to the Justice Department, the FBI, and Hillary Clinton. Robert Capers, the US attorney in Brooklyn, called Matt Axelrod at Justice with a problem. The FBI agents were pushing for a Clinton Foundation subpoena, even though the Justice Department's instructions from February hadn't changed: no subpoenas, no grand juries, and—especially since there was a full-throated presidential election campaign under way—no investigative moves that could be noticed by the outside world and make it into news stories. In other words, no noise.

It wasn't just that the agents were trying to do an end run around what they were told at the beginning of the year. It was now much closer to the election, and the Justice Department had a rule about avoiding making any moves that could be seen by the public as picking sides in an election. Many Justice Department officials thought of it as a "sixty-day rule," meaning there should be no overt activity on politically sensitive cases sixty days before an election. But there was no such formal timeline for the practice.

When Axelrod heard Capers describe what the FBI agents were doing to try to get a subpoena issued, he was furious. Almost immediately after he hung up with the US attorney, he called the FBI's deputy director, Andrew McCabe. Axelrod came in hot, angrily insisting the FBI agents were out of line and needed to be reined in. Axelrod "was very pissed off," according to a person close to McCabe. The deputy director was taken aback and began defending his people, although he wasn't entirely sure what he was defending them against; he didn't know of any recent developments.

"Are you telling me I need to shut down a validly predicated investigation?" McCabe asked, meeting Axelrod's anger with his own. "Of course not," Axelrod said, but the two continued to argue. As their back-and-forth continued, it seemed to Axelrod that McCabe was unfamiliar with the particulars of the February meeting in which the Justice Department had told FBI agents it would not authorize any subpoenas or grand juries until they had more incriminating evidence.

As Axelrod relayed the history of the case, both men calmed down a little, and reached a temporary truce. To McCabe's defenders at the FBI, his angry exchange with Axelrod highlighted the difficult position the Bureau remained in, even after the Clinton email case had ended. *Any* Clinton investigation, even a dormant, meandering, zombie of a case like the Clinton Foundation case, still was a kind of kryptonite to those who touched it.

After the call, the head of the FBI's Criminal Investigative Division, Assistant Director Stephen Richardson, was summoned upstairs by a superior. Richardson looked like a throwback to a 1960s FBI agent, complete with a blond buzzcut and a southern accent. After McCabe's angry phone call, he went back down to the Criminal Investigative Division offices with an instruction. "Tell your guys in New York they've got to knock it off," Richardson said, according to someone familiar with the conversation. "The deputy is pissed—he got a call from across the street and they're pissed that these guys were trying to shop it," Richardson said, referring to the agents' efforts to get a subpoena approved by one prosecutor's office after it had been rejected by another. "Tell them to stand down."

As Richardson described it to others, the Justice Department was angry that since the US attorney in Manhattan had already rejected subpoenaing financial records regarding the Clinton Foundation, the agents had pitched it to Capers, the US attorney in Brooklyn. It's not uncommon for FBI agents in New York who get a case rejected by either the Brooklyn or Manhattan US attorney's office to pitch it to the other one. That kind of "prosecutor shopping" can tick off Justice Department lawyers, but it gives the FBI a bit of a tactical advantage on close-call cases.

After receiving the order to stand down and knock it off, it was not clear to some of the agents involved in the Clinton Foundation probe whether or not the instruction was a temporary stay until the election was over. To some, it felt like the foundation case was being ordered shelved for good.

But Clinton cases had an effect on the Bureau like almost no other. Concern, suspicion, and distrust crept into many exchanges that would otherwise be considered part of the back-and-forth inside an extremely rigid and hierarchical organization that made something of a fetish of following orders and keeping quiet. When it came to anything involving Clinton, some agents worried they would be hauled before Congress someday to explain it. Those doubts were somewhat justified. By 2016, Republicans in Congress had spent years pushing the FBI on the Lois Lerner case involving IRS scrutiny of conservative groups, and the Justice Department had provided a startling degree of information about that investigation and the reasons why charges were not pursued. Before the Lerner case, there was Fast and Furious, a botched gunrunning investigation by the ATF that led to years of congressional conservative claims of Justice Department malfeasance. In 2012, another presidential election year, the Republican-controlled House of Representatives voted to hold Attorney General Eric Holder in contempt for withholding some documents related to Fast and Furious. By 2016, the fear of wrathful members of Congress—and it was really Republicans, not Democrats, that made the FBI wince—had been internalized to such a degree by the FBI that following orders to drop matters related to Clinton caused some agents to immediately fear personal consequences on Capitol Hill. Some agents felt they could justify their own decisions, but still at times felt nagging doubts about whether they could say the same for colleagues or supervisors.

Some of the agents involved in the Clinton Foundation discussions wondered if they should start memorializing the conversations related to

Clinton, so they would later have something to defend themselves with to a congressional committee. In the coming months, many other law enforcement officials would wrestle with the same fear.

Inside the FBI, the instruction to "knock it off" and "stand down" meant vastly different things to different people. "If I thought someone was acting for political reasons, I would resign," Richardson said, trying to dispel any doubts among his team. It did not have the desired effect, as some agents who had long been frustrated by what they viewed as a lack of interest from supervisors in the Clinton Foundation stewed over McCabe's role in the case. Why was someone whose wife had taken hundreds of thousands of dollars from a former member of the Clinton Foundation board making decisions about which offices would handle which parts of the case? Why was McCabe working on Clinton issues at all, given McAuliffe's decades-old history with the Clintons, and McAuliffe's donations to McCabe's wife? And why did the bosses at FBI and Justice stomp down agents' concerns when they were raised? And what would the agents say for themselves if Congress asked them later?

Dangle

WEDNESDAY, AUGUST 17, 2016

Supervisory Special Agent Joe Pientka sat down with Donald Trump, retired lieutenant general Michael Flynn, and New Jersey governor Chris Christie. The purpose of the meeting was to give the Republican candidate and two of his senior advisers an intelligence briefing: explain to the candidate and those closest to him how foreign intelligence services try to target US officials, and warn them that Russian and Chinese agents pose the greatest threats in such matters.

Pientka had been well prepped for the meeting, practicing in a mock setting with Peter Strzok, Lisa Page, and others. The briefing wasn't the FBI's alone—the Office of the Director of National Intelligence (ODNI) was in charge, and the plan was for the FBI briefer, Pientka, to talk for about ten minutes of the two-hour session.

But since the new Crossfire Hurricane investigation was ongoing—a case with a number of branches, including the one for Flynn dubbed Crossfire Razor—senior FBI officials decided the intelligence briefing, a long-held practice for presidential candidates, could be a useful way to gauge how Trump and Flynn thought about Russia. If nothing else, Pientka might learn a little bit about their personalities and interests. There was little concern inside the FBI that they might be crossing any ethical lines by using an intelligence briefing meant to deliver intelligence to a presidential candidate to passively gather some as well.

James Baker, the FBI's top lawyer, later told investigators he didn't raise any concerns about the plan because Pientka wasn't being sent to "induce anybody to say anything . . . He was not there to do an undercover operation." Pientka was sent, Baker said, "on the off chance that somebody said something that might be useful."

For his part, Pientka viewed his job as making an assessment and gaining some familiarity with Flynn that might be useful later. Pientka wanted to get a close-up look at Flynn, "and also if there was anything specific to Russia, or anything specific to our investigation that was mentioned," he later said. But Flynn wasn't the agent's only area of interest. Pientka also wanted to observe whether the other people in the room, including Trump, made "any kind of admission" or otherwise interesting remark. "Whatever it was," Pientka later told investigators, "I was there to record that."

In preparing for the meeting, FBI officials wanted to make sure their briefing to Trump was identical to the one they would give Clinton and her aides later in the month. The senior FBI officials who approved the Pientka assignment did not tell anyone at ODNI or the Justice Department that they were sending a Crossfire Hurricane investigator to the briefing, and there was no government rule or regulation that the Bureau should consult the Justice Department about using such a briefing for investigative purposes. More than a week after the briefing, Pientka wrote up an account of it. Trump asked two questions, Pientka wrote. Pientka also said Flynn had a number of exchanges with the ODNI briefers but he did not memorialize them because they weren't relevant to the Crossfire Hurricane investigation.

■■■■■■■■■■■■

While Pientka briefed Trump and Flynn, others on the Crossfire Hurricane team were eager to see if they could get surveillance on Carter Page. To do that, they needed to be sure first whether Page had pre-existing relationships with other US agencies like the CIA. The process, called deconfliction, is one of the most basic tasks of intelligence and law enforcement agencies, because it can be maddening, and at times danger-ous, if one agency begins surreptitiously investigating someone who is acting on behalf of a different agency. So the FBI reached out to the CIA to see if Carter Page was one of theirs. In response, a CIA liaison sent the FBI a memo, spelling out that Page had been an operational contact of theirs from 2008 to 2013, a time period that included some of his interac-tions in New York the FBI still considered suspicious.

Carter Page's relationship with the CIA wasn't quite as cloak and dag-ger as it sounded. The agency has a program to try to gather tips from Americans who've recently returned from living overseas. Page had lived in Moscow from 2004 to 2007, so it was not too surprising that the CIA approached him in 2008 to talk. Even though the FBI had a document in hand spelling this out, it would take agents nearly a year to set the record straight even in their own shop. By the time the issue was settled, it would do considerable damage to the FBI's reputation with the courts and Congress.

SATURDAY, AUGUST 20, 2016

Eight days after Stefan Halper had agreed to start reaching out to Trump campaign aides, he sat down with Carter Page at Halper's horse farm in northern Virginia. Going into the meeting, Halper's instructions from the FBI were to bring up the news stories about Russia hacking Clinton's emails, and to ask questions that appeared normal to a discussion involv-ing a campaign's foreign policy adviser. They also wanted him to ask Page if the campaign was planning some kind of October surprise, which had been suggested earlier that month by Roger Stone, the longtime friend and adviser to Donald Trump.

It was a remarkably open-ended idea for the FBI to be exploring, since there is nothing necessarily criminal about an October surprise.

The term "October surprise" is well known to political operatives and candidates, many of whom approach Election Day with a growing dread that their years of planning and hard work may be upended by the sudden revelation of a long-hidden dirty secret, or a false accusation.

Sandy Johnson, who served for years as the Washington bureau chief of the Associated Press before becoming the president of the nonprofit National Press Foundation, would warn her reporters (including me) to be wary of falling for any con games or phony accusations in the waning days of a campaign. "October is dangerous territory in election years, because the stakes are so high, the political strategists are so ruthless, and journalists are so tired," said Johnson. "In this heightened atmosphere at the end of an election, the consultants dig out the meanest, ugliest oppo research and peddle it to sway an election. The worst danger is in those final weeks, because a false narrative or outright lie is hard to disprove or counter."

Stefan Halper gradually worked round to the subject of an October surprise as he chatted with Carter Page. Page claimed to have no ambition for a role in any government job in any future Trump administration, lamented the press linking him to Paul Manafort, and defended his ties to Russia, including his stake in the Russian energy giant Gazprom, which Page said was just a small number of shares. He also bemoaned the fact that others on the campaign joked he was attracting all the media attention and keeping everyone else "off the radar screen."

After Page got that off his chest, Halper asked about an "October Surprise." Somewhat confusingly, Page replied that "there's a different October Surprise . . . although maybe some similarities" to the October surprise of the 1980 presidential campaign. Page was referring to the strange interplay that year between the presidential race and the Iran hostage crisis, in which staff of the US embassy in Tehran were held captive by the Iranian government.

As Election Day neared in 1980, the Republican candidate Ronald Reagan feared the US government would announce a deal to free the hostages that could lift Democratic incumbent Jimmy Carter to a second term. That expectation was heightened by a news column suggesting the

Carter administration planned a military rescue operation. In the end, Carter announced in the closing days of the campaign that the hostages would not be released until after the election, sparking a counter-theory that the Reagan campaign had somehow struck a side deal with Iran to not release them yet. Ultimately, the hostages were released on January 20, 1981, minutes after Reagan's inauguration.

Halper had worked on that Reagan campaign and did not need a history lesson in what had happened. But, following his FBI instructions, he tried to draw more information out of Page about what kind of surprise he meant. He asked if the Trump camp could access any of the information hacked by the Russians, adding suggestively that past campaigns would have used such material "in a heartbeat." Page replied that, because of all the attention on his connections to Russia, he was being "overly cautious" on the subject.

Halper raised the issue a third time, and Page pointed to "the conspiracy theory about . . . the next email dump with 33,000" emails. In conservative circles in 2016, the thirty-three thousand figure had a certain connotation. To many, the thirty-three thousand emails—sometimes rounded down to thirty thousand emails—deleted by Hillary Clinton's lawyers were a kind of holy grail of political ammunition against Clinton, and conservatives inside and outside the Trump campaign spent much of 2016 hoping for the public release, or "dump," of those documents.

The emails Carter Page was referring to were distinct from the ones the Russians had hacked and released via WikiLeaks. At the time Page and Halper had their meeting, the stolen emails being released publicly were primarily from the Democratic National Committee computers. Hillary Clinton's emails, by contrast, were from her State Department days, and were being made public by Freedom of Information Act lawsuits. Although the two separate batches of emails came from two very different places, in the public mind, and apparently even in the minds of some FBI agents, there was some significant blurring of categories.

"We were not on the front lines of this DNC thing," Carter Page told Halper, suggesting the Trump campaign did not have a direct role in the

WikiLeaks email dumps. But Page also asked Halper if he thought the Trump campaign should "egg it along a little bit" while still taking care not to be "seen as the one advancing this in concert with the Russians."

"It needs to be done very delicately and with no fingerprints," Halper answered.

"Okay," said Page, who then asked if it might be worth picking out "a couple trusted journalists" and giving them suggestions for "potential big stories . . . There may be people that kind of work this angle," but he quickly repeated that he was inclined to be "very cautious, you know, right now."

When Halper pushed the key points of possibly conspiring with Russia, an October surprise, or using stolen emails, Page's answers ranged from bland denials to hard-to-follow nonanswers. Halper's handler at the FBI, however, thought Page's answer to the October surprise was particularly interesting. Page's voice "kind of trailed off," the handler told investigators later. "It seemed like that he knew of something, but he wasn't 100% sure and was just kind of alluding to something, but he didn't really give much more information to it. So that kind of piques our interest."

Throughout the conversation, Carter Page came across to agents who later reviewed the transcript as vague in a way that made them both curious and suspicious. The agents debated among themselves whether Page's answers indicated he knew more than he was letting on, a debate that continued as they briefed the higher-ups. To Deputy Director Andy McCabe, Page's answers seemed guarded and evasive. James Baker, the FBI's top lawyer and most senior expert on foreign intelligence surveillance work, said it was interesting to investigators that Halper "couldn't get Carter Page to say anything about the Russians." In the minds of many of the FBI agents, the absence of evidence became evidence of something suspicious.

Halper also asked if Page knew George Papadopoulos, but Page gave every indication they were not close. Halper made one more attempt to draw out Page on the Russia question. He noted that he often arranged fully paid trips for Russians to speak at Cambridge University, and asked if he knew anyone who might be interested in coming to speak in an academic setting. Page demurred, saying he knew a couple of people in London who might be interested, but he wanted to be extra cautious in order "to limit conspiracy theories." Page said he would think it over further before sharing any names.

While the FBI agents briefed their bosses, up to Deputy Director McCabe, about Halper's recorded conversation with Carter Page, no one at the FBI told the Justice Department's National Security Division about it for another ten months. Increasingly, the FBI was not in the habit of telling the Justice Department what it was doing on the most sensitive cases it had. And if they had told the National Security Division lawyers, it's possible Page's denials would have been taken at face value.

THURSDAY, AUGUST 25, 2016

A week later it was Julian Assange's turn to fan the Clinton conspiracy stories. He went on Fox News to promise more document releases and revelations.

"Are we going to see it before the November 8 election?" asked his interviewer, Megyn Kelly.

"Yes of course," said Assange. "People involved in that election have the right to understand who it is they're electing."

When Kelly pressed him to describe the documents, Assange referred to them as thousands of pages that were still being reviewed, but said he didn't want to prematurely spoil his own scoop: "I don't want to give the game away, but it's a variety of different types of documents, from different types of institutions that are associated with the election campaign—some quite unexpected angles that are quite interesting, some even entertaining."

Megyn Kelly noted that Clinton had a five-point lead in the polls and asked if he thought his information, whatever it was, "could be a game-changer in the election."

"I think it's significant. You know, it depends on how it captures fire in the public and in the media," Assange replied.

Kelly turned her attention to an offer made two weeks earlier by WikiLeaks to pay a $20,000 reward "for information leading to conviction for the murder of DNC staffer Seth Rich," a nod to a bubbling conspiracy theory that the young man's unsolved killing in DC in early July was somehow connected to the leaked emails. By all informed accounts, Rich had nothing to do with the hacked emails. And yet Assange hinted darkly that the young man had been murdered to keep him quiet.

"I know you don't want to reveal your source," Kelly said. "But it certainly sounds like you're suggesting a man who leaked information to WikiLeaks was then murdered."

"If there's someone who's potentially connected to our publication, and that person has been murdered in suspicious circumstances, it doesn't necessarily mean that the two are connected. But it is a very serious matter," Assange said. "That type of allegation is very serious, as it's taken very seriously by us."

The Seth Rich conspiracy theory, which has caused great pain to his parents, who have long insisted their son had nothing to do with any hacking, would take many more months to fully develop into a Fox News obsession, but the key elements began swirling a month after his death, as Assange and right-wing pundits concocted other darker and stranger dimensions to the leaked emails saga.

TUESDAY, AUGUST 30, 2016

As conservatives continued to push the notion that someone other than the Russians had hacked Democrats' computers, liberals started demanding the FBI answer their concerns about whether the Trump campaign was in cahoots with the Russians. Four Democratic lawmakers—Elijah Cummings, John Conyers Jr., Eliot L. Engel, and Bennie G. Thompson, the senior members of their committees—wrote a six-page letter to James Comey asking the FBI to investigate the possibility of a conspiracy between the Trump campaign and Russian hackers. The letter was meant to put some congressional heft behind Democratic charges that the Trump campaign appeared willing and even eager to take help from the Russians to win an election.

"We are writing to request that the FBI assess whether connections between Trump campaign officials and Russian interests may have contributed to these attacks in order to interfere with the U.S. presidential election," the lawmakers wrote. At the time of the letter, agents had been pursuing such a case for a month, but it was a closely guarded secret inside the FBI. Still, the letter laid out a number of publicly known facts that closely tracked what the FBI was probing at the time, including the activities and public statements of Trump associates Roger Stone, Carter Page, and the recently departed Trump campaign chairman, Paul Manafort.

The letter cited Stone's declaration earlier in the month that he'd been in communication with Julian Assange, noting that Stone made the statement: "During a Republican campaign event while answering a question about a potential 'October surprise.'" "We do not know," the Democrat lawmakers concluded, "if Donald Trump's public statements or the connections of his campaign officials to Russian interests directly or indirectly led to the cyber attacks against Democratic party organizations, but there is widespread agreement that the United States should take all steps possible to prevent Russia from interfering in our electoral process and prosecute to the full extent of the law anyone involved in such a scheme."

Each side now had an ax to grind with the FBI. But the FBI would respond very differently to the two types of pressure.

THURSDAY, SEPTEMBER 1, 2016

The microphone was working well when Stefan Halper listened as the FBI agent gave final instructions. The professor was about to meet with the national cochairman of the Trump campaign, Sam Clovis. The stakes were getting higher, and the agent wanted to make clear to Halper, and to whomever might listen later to the recording, that the FBI was not sending its informant to work inside the campaign of the Republican nominee for president. Halper's job was to find out what the campaign was up to, but not to join it.

Nonetheless, the FBI was encouraging Halper to climb higher up the food chain of the Trump campaign. Clovis, a conservative radio host from Iowa, oversaw the campaign's often chaotic foreign policy shop. If anyone knew if Carter Page or George Papadopoulos were up to something nefarious, it ought to be Clovis.

After emailing Clovis in late August to introduce himself, Halper used the fact he had met Carter Page earlier that summer to secure a face-to-face with Clovis. Clovis agreed to meet at a hotel café in Crystal City, Virginia, a collection of bland office towers across the Potomac River from Washington, DC. Once they sat down together, Halper got to the question the FBI was still trying to answer. Was the Trump campaign planning some kind of October surprise?

Clovis's reply, if taken at face value, should have squashed the FBI's suspicions of dark international conspiracy. The real issue, Clovis told Halper, was that Trump needed to give voters "a reason to vote for him, not just vote against Hillary."

Halper explicitly brought up the question of Russian interference in the election. "Honestly, I think for the average voter it's a non-starter," Clovis answered. People in New York and Washington thought it was a big deal, Clovis argued, "but I think from the perspective of the average voter, I just don't think that they make the connection."

So far, Halper was zero for two from his teasing pitches. He then asked Clovis about George Papadopoulos, whom Clovis called "very eager" and "a climber." Clovis said he was "always suspicious of people like that." Clovis was more complimentary of Carter Page, calling him "a treasure," though they both agreed that Page could be hard to understand at times.

Halper then tried a more roundabout way of asking about the campaign's view of Russia. Should the Trump team do something to put in better perspective the pro-Russia argument made by Carter Page in his

Moscow speech, he asked. Clovis's answer suggested he thought the issue was a minor one.

"It's not that it's not important," Clovis said, but "I'm not sure it was something that in the grand scheme of things rises to the level of the campaign making an open effort." Better, Clovis argued, just to make clear "we should never have any interference in our electoral process."

The conversation eventually got around to Paul Manafort, who had left the campaign weeks earlier after news stories about his ties to corrupt Ukrainian politicians. Clovis said Trump and Manafort never really clicked, because Manafort "was trying to do a traditional campaign, and Mr. Trump wasn't buying it." Halper and Clovis also discussed a host of internal issues about the campaign, including immigration strategy, outreach to minority voters, and the campaign's strategy for explaining why their candidate would not release his tax returns.

After the two men left the hotel, the FBI felt the discussion had been largely worthless. No one at the FBI transcribed the recording.

⸱   ▬▬▬▬▬▬

Undeterred. Halper and his FBI handlers were back at work the following day, reaching out via email to George Papadopoulos. "Please pardon my sudden intrusion just before the Labor Day weekend," Halper wrote the young campaign staffer. Halper said he was leading a research project into relations between Turkey and the European Union, and offered to pay Papadopoulos $3,000 to write a paper about the oil fields off the coast of Turkey, Israel, and Cyprus, "a topic on which you are a recognized expert." He invited Papadopoulos to come to London in mid-September to discuss the paper, and offered to pay for his travel costs. "I understand that this is rather sudden but thought given your expertise, it might be of interest to you," Halper wrote.

The pitch had been carefully crafted. FBI agents wanted to re-create the circumstances that had led to Papadopoulos's comments in May to the Australian diplomat, when he had said over drinks that the Russians had dirt on Hillary Clinton. The investigators thought Papadopoulos might "feel a little freer to talk outside the confines of the United States," the case agent later explained to internal investigators. The idea, another agent said, was to "have a political discussion over a couple of drinks" and see if Papadopoulos would repeat what he'd said to Ambassador Downer. Or, in the bureaucratic language of the internal FBI paperwork for the meeting, "there will be ample opportunity and various angles to have [him] expound on the initial comments made in May 2016."

The agents were pulling on a thread that led back to a mysterious Maltese professor, Joseph Mifsud. The FBI eventually would determine Mifsud told Papadopoulos in April 2016, well before the Russian hacking of the DNC was known, that the Russians had "dirt" on Hillary Clinton in the form of thousands of emails.

Well after the election, Papadopoulos would plead guilty to lying to the FBI about his interactions with Mifsud, whom the FBI suspected was an operative for Russia. In October 2017, Mifsud told the Italian newspaper *La Republica* that he never got any money from Russia. "I am not a secret agent," he declared before vanishing from public life.

By the FBI's own definition, Halper's offer to Papadopoulos was classic spycraft. The Bureau's counterintelligence agents regularly warn Americans abroad that one of the oldest ways foreign intelligence agencies seek to recruit them as potential sources is to offer to pay, or overpay, young Americans for research of questionable value.

If the person says yes, the recruitment begins, as their new benefactor slowly steers their unwitting target toward more compromising tasks in exchange for bigger payouts. When it came to Papadopoulos, that was not the FBI's ultimate goal, but the method would work well enough for what they wanted, which was to pump him for whatever he seemed to know about Russia. Papadopoulos agreed to Halper's offer to meet in London.

12

Travellers Club

FRIDAY, SEPTEMBER 2, 2016

From Europe, agent Mike Gaeta was getting frustrated at the lack of action in New York. He wanted an investigation started into Steele's information and urged his superiors to get on with it. "Do we have a name yet? The stuff is burning a hole," Gaeta emailed. He had been waiting for guidance from New York before putting Steele's alarming reports in anyone else's hands. While he wanted to be careful, he also felt nervous that nothing seemed to be moving above him.

He got an answer later that day. Joe Pientka, the agent on Crossfire Hurricane, had created a subfile for the Steele reports in the FBI's computer system. Gaeta could put the reports in there. But Pientka didn't send him instructions on how to do it until eleven days later.

THURSDAY, SEPTEMBER 15, 2016

George Papadopoulos met Stefan Halper for lunch at the Travellers Club, a two-hundred-year-old private club on London's Pall Mall Street favored by diplomats. The club bills itself as "a meeting place for gentlemen," replete with the formal furniture and ornate drapery associated with generations of the British upper class. If the FBI agents hoped to crack the case in a setting that looked like it could be a set for a Sherlock Holmes film, they were disappointed.

The professor spoke with him at length about the stated purpose of the trip—Papadopoulos's research on the Arab Spring, Greek energy production, and Cyprus. They also talked about Papadopoulos's studies and his work with the conservative Hudson Institute. There was, Papadopoulos would later recount, a third person at the table: a beautiful young woman who said she was Halper's research assistant, but whom officials would later describe as an investigator on the case for the FBI.

Carter Page "always says nice things about you," Halper told Papadopoulos, who replied that Page was one of the Trump campaign's "Russia people," but had never met Trump or advised him on Russia. It was possible, Papadopoulos conceded, that Page could be indirectly advising the president through a more senior campaign official.

"We have to be wary of the Russians," Papadopoulos said, adding that they'd invited him to a faith conference, but he did not go because it was "just too sensitive," particularly after all the public attention on Manafort's ties to Ukraine.

Halper asked whether there might be more public releases of information harmful to the Clinton campaign. Papadopoulos responded with what was already publicly known: that WikiLeaks' Julian Assange had promised more in October. "Whatever that means, no one knows," Papadopoulos said. Papadopoulos would later describe the conversation with Halper as an annoying, testy back-and-forth over US policy toward Turkey.

After the brunch, the FBI agents who had traveled to London for the operation felt Papadopoulos was behaving deferentially to Halper, and they seemed to be falling into a teacher-student relationship. So the agents decided to set up another meeting for drinks that evening, one where Halper would more directly press him for direct answers on the question of conspiracy between Russia and the campaign.

The two met for drinks at a hotel bar where, Papadopoulos later wrote, Halper pushed his cell phone conspicuously close to him at the table. Halper asked again about WikiLeaks. "No one knows what he's going to release," said Papadopoulos, speculating that the group could release information on Trump in order to undercut the next president, "regardless of who it's going to be." Whatever he'd said in May, Papadopoulos was now squarely in step with the Trump campaign's position that "no one has proven that the Russians actually did the hacking."

The conversation then took an unexpected turn, as Papadopoulos claimed Israelis had tried to hack his cell phone, which shocked him because, he claimed, he'd done "sensitive work for that government," for which he'd been given "quite a high level of access."

Halper worked his way up to asking directly whether WikiLeaks "or some other third party like the Russians, could be incredibly helpful" in winning the election.

"Well, as a campaign, of course, we don't advocate for this type of activity because at the end of the day it's ah, illegal," Papadopoulos said, before launching into a longer explanation that at times got tangled in its own syntax: "First and foremost it compromises the U.S. national security and third it sets a very bad precedence . . . So the campaign does not advocate for this, does not support what is happening. The indirect consequences are out of our hands."

The campaign, he said, was not reaching out to "WikiLeaks or whoever it is to tell them please work with us, collaborate because we don't, no one does that . . . Unless there's something going on that I don't know, which I don't because I don't think anybody would risk their, their life, ah, potentially going to prison over doing something like that. Um . . . because at the end of the day, you know, it's an illegal, it's an illegal activity. Espionage is, ah, treason. This is a form of treason . . . I mean that's why, you know, it became a very big issue when Mr. Trump said, 'Russia, if you're listening . . .' Do you remember? And you know we had to retract it because, of course, he didn't mean for them to actively engage in espionage but the media then took it and ran with it."

By now Halper was no longer gently prodding. He was pushing, repeatedly, for Papadopoulos to talk about how hacking could help Trump.

"Of course it's illegal," Papadopoulos said. "No one's looking to . . . obviously get into trouble like that and, you know, as far as I understand that's, no one's collaborating, there's been no collusion and it's going to remain that way. But the media, of course, wants to take a statement that Trump made, an off-the-cuff statement, about Russia helped find the 30,000 emails and use that as a tool to advance their [story] . . . that Trump is . . . a stooge and if he's elected he'll permit the Russians to have carte blanche throughout Eastern Europe and the Middle East while the Americans sit back and twiddle their thumbs. And that's not correct."

Papadopoulos offered to introduce the professor to more members of the Trump campaign, and to meet again in Washington when Halper was there. Halper demurred, saying he did not want to be in the government again, but did want "to help on China," a topic that had become central to Halper's academic work in recent years.

In a sense, Halper had delivered for the FBI. He had asked the question, and gotten a lengthy answer. Several lengthy answers, in fact. But while the answers were substantive, the FBI agents didn't believe them. An FBI agent emailed Pientka that he felt their target gave "a canned answer, which he was probably prepped to say when asked."

Papadopoulos's demeanor, the agents felt, changed significantly when the conversation turned to the Russia question, from a free-flowing talk over drinks to what seemed like a rehearsed response. "It sounded like a lawyer wrote it," Pientka would later tell internal investigators—a view shared by some of the agents, who questioned whether the campaign staffer had been "coached by a legal team" to deny any involvement. At the same time, Papadopoulos's bragging about his very sensitive work for Israel raised a new potential arena for agents to explore—whether he had violated any federal laws about secretly working for foreign governments.

Although in their secretly recorded meeting with an informant, the FBI had set the table as well as they could—a bar in London, an elder academic able to dominate the conversation with the young man—still, the twenty-nine-year-old had denied the allegation of Russian collusion up, down, and sideways. The Bureau had gotten nothing from him. But the very fact that their target had given them nothing, the agents decided, was suspicious.

MONDAY, SEPTEMBER 19, 2016

In Rome, agent Mike Gaeta emailed six Steele reports directly to Joe Pientka for him to put into the new subfile of Crossfire Hurricane. It had been two and a half months since Steele had given his first report about Trump to Gaeta. No one at the FBI could offer a good explanation as to why it had taken so long to get Steele's reports into the hands of higher-ups at FBI headquarters, particularly since everyone agreed the allegations were serious—a modern-day version of the Cold War–era film *The Manchurian Candidate*. In the months and years that followed, inquisitors from Congress and the Justice Department's Office of the Inspector General would repeatedly press the FBI to explain how it was that something so important could move so slowly up the ladder. Each time, they got, in essence, the same maddening answer: miscommunication and human error. As one longtime agent put it, "At the FBI, bureaucracy is our middle name."

As the FBI failed to engage on his first reports, Steele was peppering the Bureau with new ones, whose rhetoric seemed intended to grab the attention of the so far reluctant Bureau. Steele wanted to be heard, and wanted the FBI to act on his information. "Russia/US Presidential Election: Further Indications of Extensive Conspiracy Between Trump's Campaign Team and the Kremlin," read one, asserting that "a well-developed conspiracy of cooperation" existed between the Trump campaign and the Kremlin, with Carter Page and Paul Manafort acting as intermediaries for the plot. The report attributed much of the information to "Person E," reflecting Steele's alphabetic nomenclature for hiding the identities of his sources. That same report claimed Page and others had agreed to downplay Russian aggression in Ukraine as a campaign issue, in exchange for Russia providing hacked DNC emails to WikiLeaks. Another Steele report, titled "Russia/US Presidential Election: Reaction in Trump Camp to Recent Negative Publicity About Russian Interference and Likely Resulting Tactics Going Forward," claimed the recent release of DNC emails by WikiLeaks was to push Sanders voters toward Trump, and said that effort was Carter Page's idea.

With a crop of new allegations against Carter Page in hand, Pientka and the other agents were more eager than ever to get a warrant from the Foreign Intelligence Surveillance Court to monitor his communications, even though Justice Department officials had pooh-poohed the same suggestion just a month earlier.

FISA

THURSDAY, SEPTEMBER 22, 2016

Sally Moyer, a unit chief for national security lawyers at the FBI, was trying to help agents overcome lingering Justice Department skepticism about getting a Foreign Intelligence Surveillance Act (FISA) warrant to monitor Carter Page. "Since this is essentially a single source FISA, we have to give a fulsome description of the source," the lawyer wrote. The agents worked through several versions until settling on language that called him a former British intelligence officer who "has been an FBI source since in or about October 2013." His information "has been corroborated and used in criminal proceedings," the application said. But that wasn't true. Steele played a key role in helping set the FIFA World Cup case in motion by introducing an FBI agent to another source of information, but he'd never been a court witness or a source for a search warrant in that case. The Crossfire Hurricane team seemed to not understand, or to have not asked, what Steele's actual role had been in the FIFA case. The FBI had paid Steele about $95,000 and "is unaware of any derogatory information" about him, the application would ultimately say.

At the time, FBI officials felt Steele's information dovetailed with what they already knew or suspected of Russian interference efforts. Comey and his advisers were certain the Russians were trying to interfere in the US election, to Clinton's detriment and Trump's gain. Steele's reports seemed to provide the missing link between the benefactor and the beneficiary of all that hacking. The director approved the agents' decision to use Steele as a source.

FRIDAY, SEPTEMBER 23, 2016

The FBI's work was upstaged by a Yahoo! News scoop. "U.S. Intel Officials Probe Ties between Trump Adviser and Kremlin," read the headline on the story by Michael Isikoff, a reporter with a long track record covering investigations into Washington politicians. Citing "a well-placed Western intelligence source," the story said US investigators were trying to determine whether Carter Page had established private communications with Kremlin officials, including about "the possible lifting of economic sanctions" if Trump became president.

Prior to the Yahoo! story, the notion of an investigation into Carter Page was, publicly speaking, hypothetical. But here, Isikoff had confirmed, about six weeks before Election Day, that such an investigation was in fact under way. Isikoff's information grew out of a meeting he'd had with Steele earlier that week, part of a series of sourced, on-background conversations Steele had with reporters from the *Washington Post*, the *New York Times*, the *New Yorker*, and CNN.

Steele would later tell investigators that, because the Isikoff briefing was off the record, meaning the information he relayed was not to be published in any form, he assumed he could not have been a source for Isikoff. The reporter would later say he spoke to a senior law enforcement official about the investigation before he published the story.

Inside the FBI, the Crossfire Hurricane team noticed the story, and worried about what it meant for their work. One of the agents correctly suspected Steele was the "Western intelligence source," and that Steele was "selling his stuff to others."

Joe Pientka was mostly concerned that someone inside the FBI might be leaking. There was a growing paranoia inside the Bureau over leaks. The problem had been exacerbated by the wind-down of the Clinton investigation, the ramping up of the election, and the heightened public scrutiny on the FBI. But Pientka also thought it was at least possible the source could be elsewhere—in some other part of the government or private sector that had gotten wind of Steele's reports. In FBI parlance, an informant who makes problems for the Bureau is called a "control issue," and Pientka thought there might already be control issues with Steele.

Government officials, even ones who deal with the press on a weekly basis, have a spotty record when it comes to guessing the identities of anonymous sources of news stories. Often, officials are such careful students of bureaucratic interests and personal motives that they attribute many things to intent and design that are more the result of chance and confusion.

It is a cardinal rule of source work that reporters do not identify their sources on sensitive matters, even when confronted. A less well known rule is that reporters generally will not rule out sources, because doing so can lead to a guessing game of elimination that ultimately makes identification possible.

In the case of Steele and the FBI, agents were right on their first guess, and in an early draft of their FISA application to secretly surveil Carter Page, they bluntly said so, adding that Steele had been "acting on his/her own volition and has since been admonished by the FBI." Yet when it came time, a month later, to seek a FISA warrant on Carter Page, the final version of that application would state the opposite: "The FBI does not believe that Source #1 [their masking term for Steele] directly provided this information to the Press."

Absolving Steele of the leak was useful to the FBI—it made Steele appear more trustworthy to the court, and it made the FBI look more responsible by not relying on someone who would anonymously publicize such an incendiary allegation. When internal investigators later asked who put those assertions into the different early and final versions of their FISA application, no one at the FBI or the Justice Department could explain either one.

14

Laptop

Special Agent John Robertson did not look much like an FBI agent at first glance. He had long brown hair that he often kept pulled back. Robertson liked to say that the long hair, combined with a frequent work wardrobe of jeans, flannel shirts, and T-shirts, softened his appearance and made him easier to talk to, for the type of crime victims he dealt with. Among colleagues, Robertson was respected as a dedicated agent who had a knack for quickly developing a rapport with witnesses and victims—making personal connections to people that helped uncover critical pieces of evidence. But this empathy also meant that at times he wore his heart on his sleeve, and often became emotionally invested in his cases.

After six years working organized crime and white-collar cases, Robertson had switched over to the FBI New York office's C-20 unit, investigating sex crimes against children. That can be soul-crushing work, requiring mental fortitude to sift through thousands of images of grotesque and often sadistic treatment of children. For that reason, the members of the C-20 squad are essentially volunteers. Under FBI rules, agents working those cases can raise their hands at any time and ask for a new assignment.

"They do say, before you come on this squad, be ready to lose your faith in humanity," Robertson told the television show *Inside the FBI: New York* in 2016. But he added, "There's a sense of satisfaction that I have not had anywhere else."

Working out of his cubicle in an office building in lower Manhattan, Robertson was working in September 2016 on allegations that a former congressman, Anthony Weiner, had sent sexually explicit messages to a teenage girl in another state. The case was another major setback for the young politician who had once seemed to have a stellar career ahead of him. Robertson had handled plenty of sex crimes investigations before, but Weiner was more high profile than most. Part of Weiner's celebrity came from his former job as a lawmaker, an earlier scandal over sexting women, and his troubled marriage to Huma Abedin, a close aide to Hillary Clinton.

Weiner's case itself seemed straightforward enough, however, and in late September Robertson was executing a routine search of Weiner's laptop, looking for any evidence of sexual content shared with minors. Robertson noticed there was a problem with the program processing the data; it kept bogging down. When he looked at a screen of the files it was handling, he immediately noticed what appeared to be a BlackBerry message between Hillary Clinton and Huma Abedin. Then he saw email addresses for Clinton. Shocked, he called over a colleague to look at it, and they both had what would later be described as an "oh shit" moment.

Robertson reported the finding to his boss, who agreed with Robertson that the Weiner search warrant did not authorize them to look at any Hillary Clinton messages. Robertson's boss told him to "stay completely out of" the Clinton messages. Before anyone went any further, they needed to take this up the chain of command.

WEDNESDAY, SEPTEMBER 28, 2016

The House Judiciary Committee summoned Comey to discuss Russian hacking, and he found that as the country moved closer to the election, the political parties had moved further apart, particularly on the issue of the FBI. At the hearing, Democrats tried to get Comey to say as much as possible about the threat posed by Russian hacking of the DNC, and perhaps answer some of the questions raised in their August 30 letter about Manafort, Carter Page, Roger Stone, and Trump. Republicans wanted to talk about the Clinton case, and to berate him for supposed failures in the pursuit of Hillary Clinton.

Rep. John Conyers, the top Democrat on the House Judiciary Committee, went after the Republicans: "In recent weeks, this line of attack has been remarkable only for its lack of substance," Conyers said. "They want to investigate the investigation, Director Comey, and I consider that an unfortunate waste of this committee's time."

For his part, Comey sought against long odds to turn the topic to something other than the election, highlighting the other work of the FBI: "Obviously, as you know, we are doing an awful lot of work through our counterintelligence investigators to understand just what mischief is Russia up to in connection with our election." But he signaled that was as far as he was going to go about that case. He declined to confirm the Yahoo! report by Isikoff that law enforcement officials were investigating Carter Page's contacts with Russia or say whether the FBI had spoken to Roger Stone about his contact with Julian Assange.

Rep. Jerry Nadler, a New York Democrat, pressed Comey to explain why he publicly discussed the Clinton investigation while it was still ongoing, but now would not say whether there was an investigation aimed at Trump.

"Is there a different standard for Secretary Clinton and Donald Trump?" Nadler pressed.

"No," Comey answered. "Our standard is we do not confirm or deny the existence of investigations. There is an exception for that: when there is a need for the public to be reassured; when it is obvious it is apparent, given our activities, public activities, that the investigation is ongoing. But our overwhelming rule is we do not comment except in certain exceptional circumstances."

Nadler seized on the obvious follow-up question—wasn't it exceptional for people close to a major party presidential candidate to be in cahoots, possibly, with a foreign power?

"I don't think so," Comey answered, without elaborating. Nadler moved on to ask about Manafort, before circling back to the matter of Clinton's emails. The litany of criticism of Clinton on July 5, prior to the announcement that she would face no charges, Nadler said, was "highly inappropriate."

Lamar Smith, a Republican congressman from Texas, seized the opportunity provided by Nadler's reintroduction of the subject of the Clinton investigation. He asked Comey a series of questions that would prove both prescient and maddening.

"Would you reopen the Clinton investigation if you discovered new information that was both relevant and substantial?"

Comey replied, "It is hard for me to answer in the abstract. We would certainly look at any new and substantial information."

After going through a number of facts in the investigation that Lamar Smith thought *could* justify reopening the Clinton case, Smith mentioned a number of details about the case that gave him pause and said, "I know you can't tell us whether you have or have not, but I believe that I have given evidence of new information that is relevant and substantial that would justify reopening the investigation."

In that moment, captured on live television, a conservative lawmaker told Comey he was not expected to tell Congress if it had reopened the Clinton case. The Republican signaled, to anyone paying attention, that he at least did not expect the FBI to alert Congress if the email case had been reopened. But he did not press the point, and Comey did not confirm or deny it. Yet it would later become part of conventional wisdom that Congress had forced Comey to commit to notifying them if the case was reopened.

Comey did try, once more, to dispel the idea that Clinton had been treated more leniently than a low-level employee would have been treated in a similar circumstance. "If we were to recommend she be prosecuted, that would be a double standard because Mary and Joe at the FBI or some other place, if they did this, would not be prosecuted," the director said. "They would be disciplined. They'd be in big trouble. In the FBI, if you did this, you would not be prosecuted. That would not be fair."

When Sheila Jackson Lee, a Texas Democrat, asked Comey if he was being criticized unfairly by the right, the director offered a broad defense not just of the FBI, but of a basic principle in government.

"I think questions are fair. I think criticism is healthy and fair. I think reasonable people can disagree about whether I should have announced it and how I should have done it. What is not fair is any implication that the Bureau acted in any way other than independently, competently, and honestly here. That is just not true," said Comey.

With a little more prodding from Jackson Lee, Comey finished his speech with a flourish.

"You can call us wrong, but don't call us weasels. We are not weasels. We are honest people. And . . . whether you disagree or agree with the result, this was done the way you would want it to be done," he insisted.

Since July, Comey had sharpened his answers on the Clinton case. But the political debate around the FBI had, if anything, intensified, and his appeal to the Republicans' sense of trust and respect for the FBI largely fell on deaf ears.

Democrats, though, stayed on his side, even as he refused to give them the answers they sought on any hypothetical investigation into the Trump campaign. "You are a credit to the FBI," Rep. Steve Cohen of Tennessee told Comey.

At the Hoover building, where some of Comey's senior advisers had gathered in his conference room to watch the hearing live, there was a feeling of elation and relief that their practice sessions with the director had correctly guessed, and rehearsed, so many of the questions the director was fielding. "I'm so f*cking proud that we nailed all these Qs in advance of the prep," Peter Strzok texted Lisa Page.

After a tongue-lashing from Republican congressman Trey Gowdy, a former prosecutor from South Carolina, Comey said he thought of the heated political debate around Clinton not as a feature of modern public life, but a kind of temporary insanity.

"I hope someday when this political craziness is over, you will look back again on this," Comey told Gowdy. "Because this is the FBI you know and love. This was done by pros in the right way." To suggest otherwise, Comey said, "is the part I have no patience for. Sorry sir."

The Republicans weren't buying it.

"You blew it," Rep. Doug Collins told Comey, and when the director tried to argue that it was a team effort by career professionals, Collins went further. "They blew it. Anybody else would have been prosecuted under this, in my humble opinion."

"You are just wrong," shot back Comey. "You are just wrong."

The Comey hearing was largely theater; Democrats praised, Republicans criticized, and Comey parried as best he could. Behind the scenes at the FBI, though, the hearing's timing had significant consequences. Because the director was busy on the Hill most of the day answering questions about the now shuttered Clinton investigation, he did not take part in the weekly secure video teleconference, or SVTC, with three dozen of the most senior bosses in the FBI. In his absence, the 3:00 P.M. video meeting was led by Andy McCabe, which in and of itself was not particularly unusual. With plenty of demands on the director's time, there were many occasions when Comey missed such meetings.

But the video call on September 28 was about to introduce a new element into the drama, and Comey crucially would not be there when it was first raised. From this point on, he and the senior execs on the seventh floor of the Hoover building who advised the director were behind the curve. Among the roughly three dozen different FBI executives present on the video meeting was Bill Sweeney, the head of the New York field office. On the call, Sweeney reported that New York FBI agents, while investigating whether former congressman Anthony Weiner had broken federal law while sending sexually explicit messages to a teenager, had found 141,000 emails on Weiner's laptop that might be relevant to the Clinton email investigation.

Paul Abbate, the head of the Washington field office at the time, was also on the video call and later compared Sweeney's update to "dropping a bomb in the middle of the meeting." Everyone understood the potential significance, Abbate said. McCabe told Sweeney they would talk one-on-one after the video call. After he didn't hear from McCabe for a couple of hours, Sweeney called him and told him agents were continuing to look at the laptop and now saw about 347,000 messages on the device.

McCabe summoned Peter Strzok, and told him to figure out what New York had and how important it might be. "Got called up to Andy's earlier," Strzok texted Lisa Page. "hundreds of thousands of emails turned over by Weiner's atty [attorney] to sdny [Southern District of New York], includes a ton of material from spouse." In Bureau-speak, Strzok was telling her about the Weiner laptop, and that a cursory review of the device showed a vast amount of emails belonging to Huma Abedin, Hillary Clinton's close aide. "Sending team up tomorrow to review . . . this will never end," Strzok added presciently.

"Turned over to them why?" Lisa Page asked.

"Apparently one of his recent texting partners may not have been 18 . . . don't have the details yet," Strzok replied.

"Yes, reported 15 in the news," Page confirmed.

Strzok added that he and Bill Priestap had to wait for McCabe at his office door because when they got there Andy was "down with the director." McCabe later told internal investigators he gave Comey a "fly by" heads-up about the laptop, though Comey would say he had only a vague recollection of a brief conversation, and he did not think it particularly important at the time. It didn't stick in his head, Comey said, because he wasn't sure if he even knew the former congressman was married to Huma Abedin.

Sweeney didn't only call McCabe that day. He called three other senior FBI officials at headquarters—Randy Coleman, Mike Steinbach, and Bill Priestap. Asked later if any of those officials mentioned the Weiner laptop to him after the September 28 conversations, Comey told internal investigators: "Unless I'm having a stroke, no. I don't remember any of that."

Peter Strzok knew exactly who Anthony Weiner was but he didn't assume the Weiner laptop was a huge deal, because over the course of the Clinton investigation, random State Department employees would occasionally come forward to provide the FBI with some emails they had found in their own inboxes. The possible new evidence did not immediately alarm him. The Weiner laptop, though, had the potential to become exponentially more important. Among the large cache of Clinton messages might even be the elusive thirty thousand deleted messages—the holy grail to Republican conspiracy theorists. Whatever the emails contained, their discovery was a gold mine or toxic spill, depending on where you stood. Either way, it was a huge deal.

FBI executive Randy Coleman, for his part, reached out separately to McCabe to make sure he understood what had happened. Though their call was short, Coleman said, "There was no doubt in my mind when we finished that conversation that he understood the gravity of what the find was."

Bill Priestap was on the same page. It was "explosive" information, he said, the kind where you didn't schedule an appointment with McCabe, you just go upstairs to make sure the boss knows before he goes home. By the end of the day, McCabe at least, if not Comey, should have been fully aware there was extremely sensitive, politically radioactive information sitting in the FBI field office in New York.

THURSDAY, SEPTEMBER 29, 2016

After notifying his ultimate bosses at the FBI, just after six in the morning the next day, Bill Sweeney sent Priestap an email asking him to call, because he wanted legal guidance on what his agents could or couldn't do with the Weiner laptop.

Lawyers at the FBI and the prosecutor on the Weiner case made clear that agents could not, on their own, go looking at the Abedin emails. The night before, Strzok had contemplated sending the agents from the Midyear Exam investigation—the earlier Clinton probe—from Washington to New York to look at the material. He held off on that after the government lawyers weighed in against it, but in the morning, FBI agents on the Weiner case in New York held a conference call with the Midyear agents in Washington. In that call, the number of emails discussed was the same as the previous day's SVTC call, 141,000, but agents were still processing the data; the 350,000 figure was also mentioned.

Repeatedly in the call, the New York agents emphasized two things. There was a lot of Clinton content on the laptop, and they knew that because they'd seen not just the domain—clintonemail.com—but her private email address. The other thing the New York agents emphasized was that they were not going to go poking around those emails without express approval from the bosses. Both sides of the call seemed to agree they would need a separate search warrant for any clintonemail.com message. The Weiner agents' current warrant was only to look for messages between Anthony Weiner and minors that contained sexual content. Secretary of state emails were far beyond the scope of that court order.

When the call ended, the New York office was sure of what the next step was: they were to await further advice and instruction from headquarters. The ball was in DC, they felt. Strzok and the other Washington agents, however, thought New York would take a closer look at the email addresses and get back to headquarters with a more detailed description, so the bosses could make a call about whether to seek a search warrant. Each team was waiting for the other to make the next move.

Strzok wasn't on the call but was told about it later. Throughout his career, Strzok had a reputation for going all out when he had a "crank lead," something that needed to be run down quickly. But here, Strzok was far more passive, and by his own account he did not have a sense of urgency about the laptop.

Are You Kidding Me?

Andy McCabe called Mary McCord, the acting head of the Justice Department's National Security Division, to let her know about the Weiner laptop, although in his account that day, he mangled significant details, describing the message as the contents of an iCloud account shared by Abedin and her husband. At this early stage, there was confusion at the FBI about how such a large stash of Abedin's emails could have ended up on her husband's computer. McCabe told McCord he was sending one of the Midyear Exam agents up to New York "to look at what it is" and see if there were any new emails they hadn't seen before. They also discussed whether one of them should call US attorney Preet Bharara "to make sure he doesn't charge ahead." Neither seemed to understand that Bharara's office had explicitly instructed the agents not to proceed beyond the sex crimes investigation of Weiner. They briefly discussed whether they might be able to get Weiner and maybe Abedin's consent to look at the messages without a warrant. There was no sense of urgency to the call.

"Hopefully all duplicates," McCord wrote in her notes, and as she later told investigators, she did not call Bharara. She got busy with other things.

The same day in Rome, FBI investigators chasing possible connections between the Kremlin and the Trump campaign had a meeting scheduled with Christopher Steele. The location was convenient to really only one of the attendees, but he was in some respects the most crucial player in the drama: Agent Mike Gaeta, Steele's longtime contact and handler at the FBI, would have to bridge whatever distance might exist between Steele, the man who felt his sourced warnings about a Trump-Russia conspiracy had been ignored for too long by the FBI, and the FBI agents who had decided only very recently that Steele's sources could hold the key to unmasking an unprecedented assault on American democracy.

Steele walked into a secure room and immediately felt a bit out-gunned by the four agents there. Gaeta saw his job as prepping both sides for a tricky conversation. A few days before the meeting, Steele had called Gaeta to give him a heads-up that he had shared his reports with Jonathan Winer at the State Department. The FBI generally wants its informants not to share their information with others, but Steele's move wasn't seen as a deal breaker by the FBI, just another indication that he was not exclusively theirs. Steele also told Gaeta that Winer knew of the upcoming FBI meeting in Rome.

███████████

As the Crossfire Hurricane team prepared to talk to Steele, Mike Gaeta told the agents not to hold back when questioning Steele. Before the meeting, one of the agents asked Gaeta if Steele had said anything about Michael Isikoff's revelatory Yahoo! article describing a counterintelligence investigation into Carter Page, and Gaeta said no. Gaeta himself did not seem to be aware of it.

The Crossfire Hurricane agents hoped Steele could propel the case in a number of ways, including by finding out more about possible connections between Russia and the Trump campaign. Second, they wanted Steele to share as much as he could about his sources. Could the FBI talk to them directly? Could they be tasked with trying to get answers to specific questions? Third, they wanted Steele to make his FBI relationship exclusive. The agents knew Steele had also been talking to the State Department, and they knew Steele was working for Fusion GPS, a client he was unlikely to quit. But it would be better, the agents felt, if the only US government agency Steele dealt with was the FBI.

Over a period of about three hours, the agents gave Steele a broad overview of their investigation into Russian election interference, while generally avoiding the specifics of what they knew and what they suspected. Using a metaphor popular among federal law enforcement, an FBI agent described to Steele the "three buckets" of information they were seeking: any further intel on specific individuals who might be relaying information between Russia and the Trump campaign; any physical evidence, such as emails, photos, or internal documents, of such a Trump-Russia relationship; or any names of sources who could cooperate with the FBI's investigation.

They also offered "significant" compensation for any help Steele could provide. He would be paid $15,000 for the Rome meeting alone, the agents said, and more could follow, particularly after the election, when, presumably, Steele would no longer be doing such work for Fusion, but could keep going for the Bureau.

The FBI's pitch did not go well. Steele sat with his arms folded through much of the discussion, and when the "three buckets" were mentioned, Steele sarcastically suggested that maybe he would go back to the Russian hotel "and get the manager for you to meet to talk about the prostitutes being there." The more Steele spoke, the more the agents realized he was going to be difficult to manage.

When the topic of Carter Page came up, Steele said his information about him grew out of research he had done for a lawsuit Russian oligarch Oleg Deripaska had filed against Paul Manafort. The Englishman explained that it was too dangerous to say much about his sources and complained leaks and news stories about these issues were causing his network to dry up. The FBI agents started to feel Steele was holding out on them.

A general air of distrust and paranoia about leaks hung over the exchange, but the FBI agents did not press Steele too forcefully, in part because they were trying to get him to "play ball," as one participant put it. Come fully over to our side, they were telling Steele, and give us, and only us, everything you have.

An FBI "electronic communication," the bureaucratic term for an internal memo that is different from a formal 302 write-up of an FBI interview with a witness, would later note that Steele "was admonished" that if he and the FBI "were going to have a reporting relationship regarding the specific terms of interest to the CROSSFIRE HURRICANE team," then he must have "an exclusive reporting relationship with the FBI, rather than providing that information to the clients" that hired him.

Gaeta said the understanding reached with Steele that day was that he would not speak to anyone else in the US government except the FBI. In other words, no more dalliances with the State Department. Some agents thought they had gotten a tacit commitment from Steele to provide any additional information exclusively to the FBI and not to Fusion GPS, but that was not how Steele viewed it. Steele came away from the meeting thinking he had made it clear that he was not going to stop working for Fusion or shut them out of what he called "the election project."

As he'd been with Gaeta when they met in July, Steele was guarded about the identity of the ultimate client for his Trump research. He was doing it for Fusion GPS, obviously, and said Fusion had been hired by "people seeking to prevent Trump becoming president." Clinton's name wasn't spoken, but it probably didn't need to be, either.

Steele wanted to be helpful, but only up to a point. He wanted the FBI to investigate what he'd found, and he wanted the press to investigate it as well, and he wanted those things to happen quickly, before the election. But he also didn't want to be exposed as a source of the allegations, and he didn't want his sources exposed either.

From Steele's point of view, there was one intriguing and optimistic moment in the discussion, when the agents asked him what he knew about someone named George Papadopoulos.

One agent's notes, which referred to Steele as "CHS" for confidential human source, showed that the agents were willing to show a little leg about what they were chasing. "The CHS was then given a general overview of the FBI's CROSSFIRE HURRICANE investigation and told that it was a small cell that was exploring a small piece of the overall problem of Russian interference in the U.S. Electoral process. CHS was advised that the CH team was made aware of [Papadopoulos'] May 2016 comments in the U.K. in late July by a friendly foreign service," the agent wrote in a summary. The Papadopoulos tip "had predicated a small analytical effort that eventually expanded" to include Paul Manafort, Mike Flynn, and Carter Page.

Steele didn't know anything about Papadopoulos, but the question meant a great deal to him, and later to Fusion GPS when Steele recounted the conversation. If the FBI was asking about another member of the Trump campaign, one whose name meant nothing to Steele, then they must have some evidence of their own, Steele reasoned. There must be other suspicious behavior the FBI had found and was now hunting, independently of his own reports. To Steele, it validated what he'd done so far. Amazingly, Steele had no information on Papadopoulos; the FBI had very little on him, and yet both were quickly convinced of his involvement.

Mike Gaeta had felt it was a risky move to mention Papadopoulos in front of Steele. In any interview, agents have to make calculations about how much to say. Questions can reveal to a witness what the FBI knows, and what it doesn't know. Telling Steele about Papadopoulos was a hint—one liable to be misinterpreted.

Overall, the meeting had not gone well. To the FBI agents, Steele had not provided any meaningful new information, and seemed noncommittal about working with them exclusively. "We need to be realistic about that," one agent wrote at the time. "Whether that happens or not remains to be seen."

Before the month was over, the agents would come to believe Steele had not even been honest with them and had cynically blamed the FBI for leaks that were his own handiwork. "Clearly he wasn't truthful with us," one agent later told internal investigators. Steele has denied ever lying to the FBI.

That night, back in Washington, FBI executive Dave Bowdich sent an email to McCabe, Comey, and Comey's chief of staff, Jim Rybicki, saying he'd asked Randy Coleman "to stay behind tomorrow to quickly brief you on the Weiner matter which is growing more complicated, but it can wait until then." Comey's calendar entry for the following day shows a briefing with Coleman. However, when asked about it later, both men told investigators they could not remember such a conversation.

TUESDAY, OCTOBER 4, 2016

Special Agent John Robertson, the case agent investigating Anthony Weiner's sexting, had needed the help of an FBI computer specialist to unpack the tremendous volume of emails on the ex-congressman's laptop. A week later, the work was finally done. As is standard Bureau practice, the computer expert mirrored the data—made a copy of it—and worked off the copy. That part was easy, but it was days before the entire contents of the laptop were sorted and catalogued.

That work finally done, the computer expert looked at the contents. The first file he clicked on was a document marked "Sensitive but Unclassified" with the handwritten initials "HRC." When Robertson came by to look, he told the tech: "We can't be looking at this."

At headquarters, Randy Coleman, who had scheduled a meeting with Comey to talk about the Weiner laptop, scribbled down notes: "Initial analysis of laptop—thousands emails. Hillary Clinton & Foundation . . . Crime Against Children." The cryptic notes could be interpreted any number of ways, from benign to conspiratorial.

Coleman's notes marked the last moment anyone at FBI headquarters would write down anything about the laptop issue until weeks later, when the FBI was facing tough public questions about its handling of

Clinton cases. When investigators with the inspector general's office later tried to piece together what had happened, they found the written record stopped cold on October 4. Coleman told investigators he wasn't even sure what his notes meant—whether they were a discussion at a staff meeting, or a discussion with Comey. By that Tuesday, the Weiner laptop issue had been described to a host of senior leaders, principally Andy McCabe, but also Mike Steinbach, Bill Priestap, and Randy Coleman. Yet after Coleman's scribbles, the documentary trail dries up. Like many investigations in the digital age, those conducted by inspectors general rely primarily on the written record. Michael Horowitz, the Justice Department's inspector general who would spend more than a year probing the FBI's handling of the Clinton case, was generally reluctant to extrapolate too much beyond emails, memos, and officials' handwritten notes. Horowitz's investigators spent months trying to determine what exactly Comey knew about the laptop and when he knew it, but ultimately could not reach a firm conclusion. Comey told them he had only a very vague memory of being told something about it but did not understand the significance. Within the inspector general's office, there was some skepticism about Comey's answers on that point, including his claim that he wasn't aware Weiner and Abedin were married, but lacking a better paper trail, investigators would keep those doubts to themselves.

WEDNESDAY, OCTOBER 5, 2016

For weeks, the Obama administration, nearing the end of their term in office, had been kicking around the notion of whether to speak out forcefully about Russian interference efforts in the election. Comey proposed that he write a newspaper op-ed warning of the danger. That struck National Security Adviser Susan Rice and others as bizarre—election interference by a foreign power was a far bigger issue than one man's throat-clearing exercise in a newspaper. The op-ed idea was nixed, but

Comey and the FBI began working with the White House on a joint statement warning of the problem.

Then, without warning at a meeting of the National Security Council, Comey announced he would not be signing any statement about election interference. It was too close to the election, he had decided. Rice was floored and gave Comey a look across the table that said, "Are you kidding me?" according to people who were there. For a guy who'd once been so gung-ho on the issue he wanted to write a solo op-ed warning America, his sudden unexpected reversal felt strangely flakey.

Despite Comey's concerns, the CIA and Director of National Intelligence (DNI) would go ahead with a statement, but the FBI would stay out of it, Comey decided, fearful of being accused of playing politics.

"I think the window has closed on the opportunity for an official statement," Comey wrote to CIA director John Brennan in an email that day, laying out his rationale. "I think the marginal incremental disruption/ inoculation impact of the statement would be hugely outweighed by the damage to the [Intelligence Community's] reputation for independence," Comey wrote. The director was arguing that in order to protect the reputation of the country's intelligence agencies, they had to hold themselves scrupulously separate from the politics of the moment. "I could be wrong (and frequently am) but Americans already 'know' the Russians are monkeying around on behalf of one candidate. Our 'confirming' it (1) adds little to the public mix (2) begs difficult questions about both how we know that and what we are going to do about it and (3) exposes us to serious accusations of launching our own 'October surprise.' That last bit is utterly untrue, but a reality in our poisonous atmosphere."

Without citing it explicitly, Comey was drawing on a longstanding Justice Department practice to avoid making moves, before an election, that could be taking sides. Comey had precisely articulated the potential danger of an October surprise by government decree, and yet within weeks he would fire off his own, far more consequential announcement, over the objections of his bosses. But by that point, Comey would be more focused on the politics of the bureaucracy than the politics of the election.

FRIDAY, OCTOBER 7, 2016

According to the traditional rhythms of government and press, Friday afternoons are for "news dumps"—releases of embarrassing information that, officials hope, might get lost or just plain forgotten in the rush of Americans trying to get out of the office and enjoy their weekend. The strategy often works, but this was not going to be one of those Fridays.

At 3:30 P.M., the DNI-CIA joint statement publicly accusing Russia of election interference was released. "The U.S. Intelligence Community is confident that the Russian government directed the recent compromises of e-mails from U.S. persons and institutions, including from U.S. political organizations," the statement said, warning that some states had noticed scanning and probing of their systems "which in most cases originated from servers operated by a Russian company. However, we are not now in a position to attribute this activity to the Russian government." The statement also tried to reassure Americans they should not fear the worst, because "it would be extremely difficult for someone, including a nation-state actor, to alter actual ballot counts or election results by cyber-attack or intrusion."

The statement didn't say it, but the reason the US voting system was hard to hack was because it was so fragmented, decentralized, and in many cases, too old and creaky to be manipulated by hackers. The best defense of America's votes wasn't the NSA or cyber experts; it was little old ladies in public school gymnasiums poring over printouts.

Shortly after the statement's release, I asked a senior FBI official why Comey wasn't on it. "It's too political," the official said. "We don't want to be a part of that."

White House officials assumed they had just pulled the pin on the biggest news of the day, but barely a half hour later, at 4:03 P.M., the *Washington Post* reported, with accompanying audio, that Donald Trump had made shockingly offensive comments about groping women in a conversation with Billy Bush of the television show *Access Hollywood*. The audio, with the now infamous "grab 'em by the pussy" line, became the talk of every news show across the country. While the election interference statement was news, the *Access Hollywood* tape was a political earthquake. Republicans privately huddled to consider the unthinkable—whether Trump should drop out of the race.

The Friday afternoon news dump wasn't even over. About thirty minutes after the *Access Hollywood* tape was released, WikiLeaks released emails from Hillary Clinton's campaign chairman, John Podesta. It was the first of what would become a daily drip of leaks of his emails. Both campaigns were reeling, reacting to events beyond their control, and staring at potential disaster. In their desperation, each was prepared to lash out at the other.

"Jesus," Peter Strzok texted Lisa Page after seeing a story about a former National Security Agency contractor suspected of removing reams of secret documents from his workplace. "And I made the mistake of reading some stupid *NY Post* article about how agents are ready to revolt" because of the Clinton case. "Now I'm really angry . . . There are a bunch of really ignorant people out there blinded by their politics."

Page tried to calm him down. "You can't really read that sh*t. And honestly, let them. The bu [Bureau] would be better off without them."

"I can't help it. It's click bait. I emailed it to you," he answered.

"I don't want it!" she replied.

Like a lot of people in Washington that week, the conversation between Page and Strzok circled back to discussing whether Trump's candidacy could survive the revelations about his *Access Hollywood* recording.

"Currently reading about Trump," Strzok wrote. "Wondering if he stepped down if Pence could actually get elected."

"That's probably more likely than Trump getting elected," Page replied.

SUNDAY, OCTOBER 9, 2016

The FBI's relationship with the Clinton campaign had not improved; if anything it was getting worse. The glaring absence of the FBI on the official statement about Russian interference grated on those at Clinton's campaign headquarters in Brooklyn. Earlier in the campaign, the Clinton team had declined the Bureau's offer of a classified briefing about Russian hacking. The Clinton team had asked for an unclassified version instead, but the FBI refused. Neither side trusted the other. The FBI agents wanted to keep the campaign from blabbing whatever they were told about the investigation. The campaign staffers, including John Podesta, felt like a classified briefing was a trap; if any of the information leaked later, congressional Republicans or maybe even the FBI would accuse them of being the leakers, and they'd be right back in the same kind of mess as the email investigation.

That weekend, Podesta traveled to St. Louis, Missouri, to prepare for the upcoming presidential debate there. An FBI agent called and left a message for him. "You may not know this," the agent said, "but you've been the subject of a hack."

"I'm very well aware of this," said the exasperated Podesta, given the seemingly endless headlines about his hacked emails. The agent didn't offer anything in the way of new information; he seemed to mostly be trying to open a line of communication. That night Peter Strzok tuned in to the presidential debate. He saw Donald Trump trying to turn the story back to the Clinton emails.

"Trump saying agents at FBI are furious at the MYE [Midyear Exam] outcome and he's getting a special prosecutor," Strzok texted Page. She immediately replied, "I'm not watching." "I am. Just getting aggravated," Strzok answered.

TUESDAY, OCTOBER 11, 2016

The Clinton campaign thought talking about emails, any emails, was a losing issue for them. Many voters didn't seem to distinguish between different batches of emails, or their contents, or whether or not they said anything positive or negative about Hillary Clinton. The campaign's internal polling suggested that any stories about emails tended to have negative consequences for Clinton. But Podesta wanted to punch back over his own hacked messages, and remind voters about Roger Stone's suspicious text from August, the one in which he had claimed it would soon be Podesta's "time in the barrel."

"Stone pointed his finger at me, and said that I could expect some treatment that would expose me and ultimately sent out a tweet that said it would be my time in the barrel," Podesta told reporters on the campaign trail. "So I think it's a reasonable assumption to—or at least a reasonable conclusion—that Mr. Stone had advance warning and the Trump campaign had advance warning about what Assange was going to do . . . I think there's at least a reasonable belief that Mr. Assange may have passed this information on to Mr. Stone."

WEDNESDAY, OCTOBER 12, 2016

The following day, Roger Stone all but confirmed Podesta's suggestion when he sat for a television interview with the CBS local news affiliate in Miami, which ran a breaking news banner for the story: "CBS 4 Confirms Connection between Trump Ally and WikiLeaks."

"I do have a back-channel communication with Assange, because we have a good mutual friend," Stone told the station. "That friend travels back and forth from the United States to London and we talk. I had dinner with him last Monday." Stone denied any direct contact with Assange, saying he had not spoken to or met with the man who had been holed up for years in the Ecuadorian embassy in London.

Not surprisingly, the local interview quickly became national and international news. Here was an informal adviser to the Trump campaign—though not an actual member of that campaign—publicly declaring to have a line to WikiLeaks as it released emails stolen from Democrats. Stone appeared to be admitting, if not to a crime, then to being in regular contact with people in possession of hacked, unreleased emails. In the coming months and years, as those boasts became legally problematic for Stone, he denied having contact with Assange, or knowing beforehand that Podesta's stolen emails would be released.

Podesta seized on the report as further evidence the Trump campaign was in cahoots with the Russians. The FBI was also alarmed that Stone appeared to be bragging about his supposed relationship with Assange.

"The Roger Stone comments are scary as sh*t," Lisa Page texted Strzok. "Roger Stone is horrible," he replied.

THURSDAY, OCTOBER 13, 2016

In response to Stone's claims, WikiLeaks publicly denied any connection to Stone, tweeting: "WikiLeaks has never communicated with Roger Stone as we have previously, repeatedly stated."

The denial angered Stone, who sent the group a private message over Twitter. "Since I was all over national TV, cable and print defending wikileaks and Assange against the claim that you are Russian agents and debunking the false charges of sexual assault as trumped up bs, you may want to rexamine [sic] the strategy of attacking me- cordially R."

WikiLeaks replied: "We appreciate that. However, the false claims of association are being used by the democrats to undermine the impact of our publications. Don't go there if you don't want us to correct you."

"Ha!" answered the ever combative consultant. "The more you 'correct' me the more people think you're lying. Your operation leaks like a sieve. You need to figure out who your friends are."

MONDAY, OCTOBER 17, 2016

The FBI was continuing to keep tabs on Carter Page, and agents found out he'd made plans to go abroad. Wanting to know who he was meeting and why, the agents had Stefan Halper set up another secretly recorded meeting.

By that point, Carter Page had left the Trump campaign over the public questions about his ties to Russia. In this meeting with Halper, Page sketched out an ambitious plan to become a kind of high-profile foreign policy intellectual, a latter-day George Kennan. Page said he wanted to create an institute like Kennan had, "to be a rare voice that talks against this consensus" of Russian containment, which he called "too hawkish and aggressive in a lot of ways against the Russians."

"I don't want to say there'd be an open checkbook, but the Russians would definitely . . ." Page said, trailing off without finishing the sentence. He laughed. When Halper tried to finish the thought, saying, "They would fund it, yeah, you could do alright there," Page replied, "Yeah, but that has its pros and cons, right?"

Page then returned to one of his regular themes in public and private conversation—that the United States was being unnecessarily antagonistic toward Russia, and that approach was self-defeating. He, on the other hand, "had a longstanding constructive relationship with the Russians going back" years. "I could talk for the next five hours about all these sneaky little approaches that the [US] has been taking against Russia" in the last two decades, Page said. If that practice continues, Page predicted, the two countries will end up "on the brink of war."

Halper asked Page about connections between the Russians and WikiLeaks. "I know nothing about that," Page answered. "On a personal level, you know, no one's ever said one word to me. But it's interesting, you know, off the record between us, if the only source of transparency and truth is an external source, you know, c'est la vie, right?" Page was arguing, in essence, that it didn't matter where the emails came from, as long as they became public.

Page continued, adding that this next piece of information was "very deep off the record"—the Clinton camp had "hired investigators to come after me, including some in London." Page said his own very good sources told him the names of the investigators. It wasn't clear from the conversation if Page was talking about Christopher Steele, Fusion GPS, or some other people he imagined were investigating him, but by that point, after numerous stories had been written about him, it would not be surprising if he surmised simply from the news coverage that private actors were digging into his background.

Halper also steered Page to talk about another one of the accusations that had been floating around about him—that he had pressed for a change in the Republican National Committee platform language about Ukraine, to make it more to Russia's liking. Page told Halper he had steered clear of that, but acknowledged "there was a lot of conspiracy theories that I was one of them." He added "totally off the record" that members of the Trump team were working on that. "In retrospect, it's way better off that I . . . remained at arm's length."

When Halper brought up Russia, the "core lie," Carter Page told Halper, was that he "met with these sanctioned Russian officials, several of which I've never even met in my entire life." This was a key point for Halper and his FBI handlers, and he pressed further. Page sounded exasperated talking about it. He'd never met Sechin, the head of Rosneft. "And there's another guy I had never even heard of, you know, he's like in the inner circle." Asked by Halper who he meant, Page said he couldn't even remember the man's name. "It's just so outrageous."

Page also said his lawyer had advised him there was no law against meeting with officials under US sanctions "as long as you don't take gifts or have any sort of business dealings." The lawyer had told him, "'Don't even take a pen,'" Page said.

Halper asked Page if he could introduce him to Russians who might be interested in speaking at Cambridge, to which Page laughed and said his lawyer would probably not want him to do that. Halper pressed his luck and asked again, but Page said doing anything like that "would be setting off such big alarm bells," and besides, he said, he didn't have their contact information anyway.

To the agents listening, this secretly recorded conversation had been more successful than the earlier one in August. Page had thrown out the idea that he could publicly defend Russia, and Russian money might bankroll such an effort. To the FBI, this sounded suspiciously like Page was interested in setting up a propaganda machine for Putin.

However, the agents chose to overlook other key statements that were, if anything, more important. Page had denied knowing about any WikiLeaks connection to Russia. He'd denied having any involvement with changing the RNC position on aid to Ukraine. He'd denied having any meetings with sanctioned Russian officials, or even knowing who one of them was. The FBI quickly disregarded those exculpatory statements. In fact, the agents didn't bother to transcribe whole sections of the Halper-Page conversation, deciding they were not relevant or interesting. The agents thought they were days away from getting court approval to secretly monitor Page's communications.

16

A Letter to Himself

WEDNESDAY, OCTOBER 19, 2016

The pressure had been building on Special Agent John Robertson for weeks, and the case agent tasked with investigating Anthony Weiner's electronic correspondence with a fifteen-year-old girl felt the weight of the world on his shoulders.

The Weiner case wasn't the problem. Or at least, it wasn't the biggest problem. The real issue was the hundreds of thousands of Huma Abedin's emails, including many that were to or from Hillary Clinton. After flagging the emails to his supervisors at the end of September, he had heard nothing.

"The crickets I was hearing was really making me uncomfortable because something was going to come down," Robertson later told investigators. "Why isn't anybody here? Like, if I'm the supervisor of any CI squad in Seattle and I hear about this, I'm getting on with headquarters and saying hey, some agent working child porn here may have [Hillary Clinton] emails. Get your ass on the phone, call [the case agent], and get a copy of that drive, because that's how it should be. And that nobody reached out to me within, like, that night, I still to this day I don't understand what the hell went wrong."

Robertson was hoping to get some real answers, or at least some as-surance that the issue was not being swept under the rug. He wondered if the prosecutors on the Weiner case, Amanda Kramer and Stephanie Lake, could get the attention of the US attorney in Manhattan, Preet Bharara. Robertson thought Bharara might "kick some of these lazy FBI folks in the butt and get them moving."

When he got to Kramer's office, she asked him, "What's up?" Sitting in a chair, Robertson exhaled deeply and began talking, his knee pump-ing much of the time. He'd told his bosses about the Clinton emails weeks ago. Nothing had happened. Or rather, the only thing that had happened was his boss's boss had instructed Robertson to erase his computer work station. Ostensibly, that was in order to ensure there was no classified material on it. But it also meant there was no record of what he'd done, and hadn't done, with the laptop information. He was starting to feel like he was going to be made a scapegoat, and he was freaking out. He had already talked to a lawyer. The prosecutors tried to both calm him down and warn him that going outside regular channels could destroy his career.

"I'm a little scared here," Robertson told Kramer and Lake. "I don't care who wins this election, but this is going to make us look really, re-ally horrible." Chief among his concerns was that Comey's testimony to Congress about the number of emails was outdated and now incorrect.

A big admirer of Comey, Robertson worried the FBI director had not been told what was going on, and that ignorance would come back to bite not just him, but the entire FBI. And Robertson feared that when that happened, he, the lowly case agent, would be blamed. Robertson couldn't help but think that someday angry members of Congress would come after him. The prosecutors, Kramer and Lake, thought Robertson was get-ting paranoid. They also gave him a blunt warning: if Robertson decided to tell Congress or the press about the emails, he could be prosecuted. The legal rationale behind such a scenario is faulty at best—the fact of the emails' existence on the laptop was not classified. If Robertson had de-cided to tell a lawmaker or a reporter about them, that could be a fireable offense, but probably not a criminal one. Rather than having his doubts and suspicions quelled, Robertson left the meeting even more alarmed.

━━━━━━

In Washington, the FBI was upping the pressure on Justice Department officials to move forward with seeking a FISA warrant on Carter Page. At Justice, national security lawyer Stu Evans had pried some answers out of the FBI, but was still worried that FISA surveillance might be too aggressive, given the politics of it all. McCabe felt pretty strongly that it was time to stop debating it and just get the surveillance up and running.

McCabe told Evans in a pull-aside conversation after a meeting between senior FBI and Justice officials that they shouldn't pull any punches; they should get the FISA and let the chips fall where they may. To McCabe, the danger was not in getting too deep into politics; it was in being too fearful of politics to investigate it.

With prodding from McCabe, Evans agreed to go ahead, and the nearly final version of the Carter Page FISA application was sent back to the FBI agents on the case to approve the edits Justice had made. That evening, Peter Strzok let Evans know they were comfortable with the accuracy of the latest version. Sally Yates, the deputy attorney general, also read it and gave it her green light.

Once the FISA seemed to finally be moving, Strzok was upbeat. He wasn't that worried about the outcome of the election, and envisioned a happy hour, "HH," somewhere with colleagues. "Came up with election night plan—we should all hit HH somewhere," he texted Lisa Page. "Figure this damn thing better be called early."

THURSDAY, OCTOBER 20, 2016

At SDNY, the two prosecutors on the Weiner case were worried about their case agent, and thought he might act out in some way. So the day after their meeting with Robertson, they went to see their bosses, and let them know of the laptop issue and Robertson's concerns. Joon Kim, the second in command at the US Attorney's Office, decided to bring the issue to Preet Bharara. They wanted to take some action that would satisfy Robertson, but they also didn't want to meddle in the FBI's internal chain of command. Kim thought it wasn't really SDNY's business.

Bharara was generally on the same page as Kim. If the agent was so agitated, they should do something, but Bharara was wary of getting out of his lane on a high-profile case like the Clinton matter. Bharara's office did not have a role in the Clinton email investigation; he couldn't just go butting into it without potentially angering a whole slew of senior officials at both the Justice Department and the FBI. Better to reach out to Deputy Attorney General Sally Yates's office just to be safe, Bharara decided.

Robertson, however, continued to privately boil at the, as it seemed to him, inaction all around him. That lunch hour, he sat down at a computer and wrote an email, with the subject "Letter to Self." In the coming years and months, FBI and Justice Department officials far higher up than Robertson would write similar memos, seeking to document sensitive conversations in real time and protect their personal reputations as they dealt with investigations of political figures. Robertson's email was the first in that pattern, revealing a crisis of conscience that would repeat and reverberate throughout the FBI, the Justice Department, and the country in ways no one could have predicted.

"I had a conversation yesterday w/ AUSA Amanda Kramer and AUSA Stephanie Lake," the email began, using the government acronym for their formal titles, "Assistant US Attorney." "I have very deep misgivings about the institutional response of the FBI to the congressional investigation into the Hillary Clinton email matter. However, I am not an institutional representative of the FBI. I do not have the authority (or competence, I suppose) to make determinations of this nature," he wrote.

Robertson had also talked to his lawyer, who had told him to tell his boss, a supervisory special agent, and leave any further action with his superiors. "Put simply: I don't believe the handling of the material I have by the FBI is ethically or morally right. But my lawyer's advice—that I simply put my SSA on notice should cover me—is that I have completed CYA. And I have done so," the agent wrote, using the acronym for "cover your ass."

"Further, I was told by AUSA Kramer that should I 'whistleblow,' I will be prosecuted, and she wished to 'talk me out of it' should I want to whistleblow. I was informed that this material"—Robertson meant the Clinton emails on Weiner's laptop—"was obtained after the subpoena was served, and that the subpoena is only for materials possessed at the time of service." He meant the congressional subpoena that applied only to the original tranche of roughly thirty thousand Clinton emails. Robertson wrote:

> I consider that lawyerly bullshit. I possess—the FBI possesses—20 times more emails that Comey testified to (approx. 30,000 I believe. I have 600,000+). While Comey did not know at the time about what I have, people in the FBI do now, and as far as I know, we are being silent. Further, while I have no authority in my warrant to look into the emails (and I have stuck to my limited search authority), the mere existence of these emails is sufficient to give me pause when I see that we (FBI) have been served with a subpoena for all materials related to HC.
>
> I am not going to whistleblow.
>
> If I say or do nothing more, I am falling short ethically and morally. And later, I may be accused of being a Hillary Clinton hack because of the timing of all this. Nothing could be further from the truth. I am apolitical.
>
> But if I say something (ie, whistleblow), I will lose my reputation, my career, and risk prosecution. I will also be accused of being a Donald Trump hack. Again, nothing could be further from the truth.
>
> If this were for a cause greater than a politicized congressional investigation that will have no bearing on the outcome of a pathetic presidential race, I would consider speaking up against legal advice. But I suppose I shall lose sleep over this, and not my career and reputation.

At 12:44 P.M., Robertson clicked Send on the email to himself. He had put it all down in writing, should someone come looking. He was certain someone would.

At the Hoover building, another FBI agent, Joe Pientka, was going through the final steps of preparing the FISA application on Carter Page, checking the document against what intelligence agents call the "Woods file." Woods files arose out of a problem years earlier in the FISA process, when the court came to doubt the honesty of at least one of the agents who had submitted sworn statements to the court. As a result, the FBI had to keep a separate file, dubbed "Woods," that documented each assertion made in the FISA application. It was not a foolproof system, because in some ways it was an exercise in repetition. But it was a way to force agents involved in FISA applications to double-check their work. But the very nature of the double-check procedure suggested the potential problem. The Woods file system still too often relied on an agent to spot their own errors, and second-guess their own judgment.

Director Comey signed a lot of FISAs, but he did not read them all. There were simply too many, and he had too many other responsibilities. He did read the Carter Page FISA, knowing it was a particularly sensitive case. James Baker, Comey's general counsel and point man on all matters in intelligence law, read it as well, and spoke to Comey about it. Part of Comey's comfort in signing the Page FISA derived from Baker's confidence. Baker had spent decades of his life working on intelligence law issues in both the Justice Department and the FBI, and he'd developed a reputation within the FBI and Justice as a stickler, even a persnickety reviewer of such applications. He was, most colleagues thought, a cautious man who pressed those around him to be more careful.

█████████

Christopher Steele didn't know that the FBI director had approved a surveillance application in large part on his say-so. On the same day the FISA was formally approved, Steele sent a new bit of information to Gaeta, the FBI agent in Rome. Steele had gotten a report, from State

Department official Jonathan Winer, that claimed Russian intelligence operations toward Trump were an "open secret" in the Kremlin, that sex videos of Trump existed, and that the FSB, the Russian security agency, had funneled money to Trump through an Azerbaijani family.

———

There was another presidential debate that night, and Peter Strzok wanted Lisa Page to watch it with him. "I'm not watching. I honestly don't want to know," she texted in reply. "It is not worth the stress to me." Strzok couldn't let it go. "I cannot believe what I am hearing. I am riled up. Trump is a fucking idiot, is unable to provide a coherent answer," he added. "Please. I honestly don't want to know," she replied. "It's not worth your stress either."

But the election was less than a month away, and, completely absorbed, Strzok was getting all-caps angry. "I CAN'T PULL AWAY. WHAT THE FUCK HAPPENED TO OUR COUNTRY, LIS?!??!?!" he tweeted. "I don't know. But we'll get it back," she texted back. "We're America. We rock."

When the debate touched on Russia, Strzok began texting blow by blow. "Hillary: Russia and WikiLeaks and highest levels of Russian Government and Putin!!! Drink!!!!!" Strzok typed. "Oh hot damn. HRC is throwing down saying Trump in bed with Russia." After Page simply stopped responding, Strzok texted again: "Sigh. I'm sorry. Just don't turn on this goddamn debate." "There's no chance," Page replied. "What is watching going to accomplish? . . . You can read about it in the morning. Even watch clips if you must."

Strzok couldn't let it go. "She could do SO MUCH BETTER. But she's just not getting traction." Page again tried to talk him down. "You DO have control over this anger and frustration." "Maybe," he answered. "I have to watch this. And I'm so damn mad Lisa. And disgusted. And disappointed. Trump just said what the fbi did is disgraceful."

Republicans had been pounding the FBI with criticism for months, but now the criticism was starting to bubble up from inside the organization. The July announcement of no charges had surprised or alarmed agents of all stripes. Some of the agents involved in politically sensitive investigations were starting to have doubts about the Bureau's leadership. Comey's actions, inspired in part by his time with Ray Dalio, seemed like a wild departure from the FBI's past practice, and among the relatively small number of agents who knew of the political donations Virginia governor Terry McAuliffe had steered to McCabe's wife in 2015, there were deep suspicions of McCabe's involvement in Clinton cases—particularly when, it seemed to them, he had sought to curtail some of those efforts.

Around this time, I began to hear of those concerns. As a reporter for the *Wall Street Journal* covering the Justice Department and the FBI, I had been tracking the Clinton email case for more than a year, and been part of the reporting efforts surrounding Trump's possible connections to Russia. To the criminal agents who had long doubted the real-world savvy of McCabe and other national-security-focused FBI executives, McCabe's role in the Clinton cases was highly suspect, and only looked worse when they learned agents on the Clinton Foundation case had been told in August to "stand down" and "knock it off."

I was skeptical. When I was told of a stand-down instruction inside the FBI, I suspected someone had watched too many movies. But as I dug into the McCabe issue, it was clear his wife had taken hundreds of thousands of dollars in campaign donations from someone closely tied to Clinton. That was a matter of public record, and that alone seemed worth a story. And as I asked around about the stand-down instruction, others said they were told the same thing. To me, the story was always about ethics in the FBI, and whether the Bureau had made the wrong decision in letting McCabe play a role in the Clinton investigations.

There was another reason it struck me as important. Earlier that year, Comey had short-circuited the regular Justice Department process when, in essence, he made the announcement closing the Clinton email case as if the FBI, and not the Justice Department, were the prosecutors. Comey had taken control of the entire decision-making process. For that reason, how he and his people reached that decision seemed even more important than it would be otherwise. And perhaps most importantly, the reporting suggested Comey, McCabe, and others were losing the confidence of some of their own people inside the FBI. That was unquestionably newsworthy. The very act of investigating the Clintons was acting like a kind of kryptonite inside the FBI, corroding the trust and unity of the typically tight-lipped organization. In October 2016, more and more people inside the FBI were starting to harbor serious doubts about decisions made above them, and they were starting to talk.

So I kept pulling on the thread, and was continually surprised by what I learned. Readers sometimes assume that because I worked at the *Wall Street Journal*, a conservative newspaper, I am assigned to cover things with a political slant or starting point. That's not how it works. I do, on occasion, get asked by bosses to try to find out answers to questions—I do work for them, after all. And I do, at times, disagree with an editor or three about how to describe things in the fairest way possible. Reporting is often a messy process. But all of the reporting I did in October 2016 was entirely at my own instigation. I wasn't looking to advance any agenda or please anyone; in fact, early on I was pretty certain that if anything, my reporting would just make a lot of folks mad. And far from pushing me in any particular direction, my bosses by and large had no idea what my reporting was turning up until I filed the story, as later events will show.

FRIDAY, OCTOBER 21, 2016

The Foreign Intelligence Surveillance Court approved the Carter Page FISA. The meat of the application consisted of the Steele allegations, the tip about George Papadopoulos, Page's past association with Russian intelligence officers, and some mentions of his secretly recorded meeting with Halper.

In a footnote, the FBI noted, without naming Fusion GPS, that the entity that had hired Steele "was likely looking for information that could be used to discredit" the Trump campaign. It also said the FBI did not believe Steele was a direct source for the Isikoff story on Yahoo! News on

September 23, though, of course, he was. There were bigger factual problems with the application, too. Though the FBI had been sent a memo from the CIA stating Page had been an operational contact of the agency from 2008 to 2013—covering some of the time period in question—that was not reflected anywhere in the FISA application.

The agents also didn't tell Justice Department lawyers about the denials Carter Page had made to Halper that undercut many of Steele's claims, including that when Halper had asked Carter Page about Manafort, Page said he had "literally never met" him or exchanged a single word with him. Nor did they tell the Justice Department about Papadopoulos's secretly recorded statements to Halper that no one in the Trump campaign was collaborating with the Russians.

The FISA application did relay a number of Steele's allegations, which came from a person described in documents as his "Primary Sub-source." First of these was that the Kremlin had been gathering compromising information about Hillary Clinton for years, and was feeding that information to the Trump campaign. Second, that during Carter Page's July 2016 trip to Moscow, he attended a secret meeting with a Russian oligarch close to Putin, Igor Sechin, the chairman of Rosneft, as well as a second meeting with another high-level Russian official. Third, that Page was a go-between for Russia and Manafort, as part of a "well-developed conspiracy." Fourth, that Page had come up with the idea of Russia releasing stolen DNC emails to WikiLeaks, which would then publish them to sway American voters. None of those claims would stand up to scrutiny. The application was signed by the chief judge of the FISC, Rosemary Collyer.

███████████

Joon Kim, the deputy US attorney in New York, called Sally Yates's office, which Justice Department officials call "ODAG," short for the Office of the Deputy Attorney General.

Kim was calling with some troubling news about an FBI agent who was upset that his bosses seemed to be sitting on a politically explosive development. Kim was quickly redirected to George Toscas, the senior

National Security Division lawyer who played a key role in the Justice Department's most critical cases involving classified information.

Kim described the situation to Toscas: Anthony Weiner's computer contained hundreds of thousands of Huma Abedin emails, and many appeared to be communications with Hillary Clinton. The description was more detailed than Toscas remembered receiving earlier, and it seemed in Kim's telling that the emails in question were likely to be relevant to the now shuttered Clinton probe.

Toscas later told investigators the talk with Kim went far beyond what Deputy Director McCabe had told him in early October about the laptop. It was, Toscas said, "The first time that I actually got information like something you could actually think through and analyze." Toscas immediately instructed his deputy to call Peter Strzok, and Justice Department lawyer David Laufman.

That afternoon, around four o'clock, Kim emailed Kramer and Lake, the two New York prosecutors who'd had the heart-to-heart with Special Agent Robertson two days earlier, to let them know he had spoken to Toscas about the laptop.

One of the prosecutors then called Robertson to share the news that the issue had been raised with Main Justice. "Thanks for the call," Robertson wrote in an email. "I feel much better about it. Not to sound sappy, but I appreciate you guys understanding how uneasy I felt about the situation."

Robertson also emailed his boss, letting him know the federal prosecutors had taken the issue up their own chain of command:

Just got a call from SDNY. [The AUSAs] understood my concerns yesterday about the nature of the stuff I have on Weiner computer (ie, that I will be scapegoated if it comes out that the FBI had this stuff). They appreciated that I was in a tight spot and spoke to their chain of command who agreed.

So they called down to DoJ, who will apparently now make a decision on what to do. This is a good thing according to SDNY because it means we (FBI C20) went above and beyond to make known that the material was of potential concern. It is out of my hands now so now I know I did the right thing by speaking up. . . . I feel much better about this now.

By this point, Robertson and his lawyer weren't the only ones thinking about the bureaucratic imperative of covering their asses. Bharara decided to take another step to protect SDNY. He instructed his chief counsel to write up a memo describing his office's involvement with the Weiner laptop and Hillary Clinton emails. Like Robertson a day earlier, Bharara felt that someday, someone would come asking what, exactly, he and his staff had done, and why.

Asked later by investigators why he took this step, Bharara answered that "things seemed unusual," and he expected to face questions. The leadership at SDNY, Kim recalled, "concluded at this point that we should have something in the document, either email or memo, that laid out the chronology as, to make sure that if people did ask that, you know, we had it, we had it down on paper."

The memorandum recounted recent events in the driest, cleanest possible terms. The warrant

did not provide authority to search for evidence of any other crimes (beyond Weiner's sexual interactions with a minor). We advised the agents of the proper scope of the search warrant and they understood the scope . . . [The] search of emails stored on the computer apparently recovered in excess of 700,000 emails. In order to stay within the scope authorized by the warrant, [Robertson] sorted the emails recovered by sender. In performing that sort, we understand that header information for all of the emails was visible, and he noticed a very large number of emails that appear to be between Huma Abedin and Hillary Clinton. [Robertson] believes that, although Weiner's counsel provided the computer to us, the computer was used by both Anthony Weiner and Huma Abedin.

We understand that the FBI agents in our case will not be reviewing the contents of the Abedin-Clinton emails because it would not be appropriate to do so under the search warrant issued in support of our child exploitation investigation. The agents, however, have reported the existence of the emails up their chain of command at FBI to enable other agents to take any action that is appropriate for their cases.

Because we understand that another component of DoJ may be conducting an investigation related to Hillary Clinton's emails, we have advised [the office of the Deputy Attorney General] and George Toscas at [the Justice Department's National Security Division], who we're told is the most senior career prosecutor involved in investigations of Hillary Clinton and the Clinton Foundation, of the existence of the emails so that they can take any steps that may be appropriate in their investigation, including, if proper, making an application for the content of potentially hundreds of thousands of emails that are outside the scope of the warrant in our case, which authorized a search only for evidence of child exploitation crimes.

Though records indicate the SDNY memo writing began Friday, it would not be finalized until the following week, by which point public questions were flying around Washington and the campaign trail about how the Justice Department and the FBI had handled another Clinton investigation.

Also that Friday, FBI deputy director Andrew McCabe emailed others in the office about a series of questions I had been asking about the donations McAuliffe and the Virginia Democrats had made in 2015 to his wife's campaign. By then, I had been asking those questions of senior FBI officials for days, but the reporting was now far enough along that I let them know I was getting close to publishing.

"In the more bad news category," McCabe emailed Comey, Rybicki, and Bowdich, "Devlin Barrett of the *Wall Street Journal* is putting together an article claiming I had a conflict of interest on midyear as a result of Jill's campaign. Connections to Governor McAuliffe. I'll work with Mike to provide some basic facts to push back." Comey replied, mixing sarcasm with moral support: "Outstanding. Don't sweat it."

The email exchange between Comey and McCabe is noteworthy in two respects. First, it underscores how much the FBI leadership at that point considered the questions about his wife's political donations to be a headache, but not a crisis. In my conversations with FBI officials that week, they made clear they believed the story was rooted in Republican opposition research. The donations were a matter of public record, and it didn't take more than a cursory search of Virginia election records to find them. So the donation story seemed to FBI leadership a shot fired by political actors, not an indication of internal FBI dissent. For my part, I was content to let them believe that, since I was still reporting on internal workings at the Justice Department and the FBI; if FBI executives had understood right away it was their own personnel talking, they would have tried to clamp down, and it would have made my job harder.

That evening, Peter Strzok texted Lisa Page: "Toscas now aware NY has hrc-huma emails via weiner invest[igation]." The Justice Department, in the form of Toscas, was officially looking over the FBI's shoulder when it came to the Weiner laptop. Page replied, "I'm sure Andy is aware, but whatever."

17

Roller Coaster

SUNDAY, OCTOBER 23, 2016

The bosses at the *Wall Street Journal* had looked at a draft of my story about the McCabe donations and wanted to publish it that day, catching me a bit by surprise, since I'd taken my family to an amusement park. I'd already written most of the McCabe story with the goal of publishing it Monday, but by lunchtime the *Journal*'s editors were adamant that we publish by the end of the day.

So I called Jill McCabe's cell phone, and asked her for comment. I didn't know it at the time, but I had reached her in her car. She was driving with her husband. Jill and I had a perfectly amiable conversation, despite my having to shout at her over the roar of a roller coaster.

Andrew McCabe gave Comey a fresh heads-up on that story, telling the director that McCabe and the FBI's top spokesman, Mike Kortan, "spent a good part of the day trying to shape the *Wall Street Journal* story on my alleged conflict. That can only be background information. Looks like they may try to release it online tonight."

Jill McCabe sent me a statement, underscoring the FBI assertion that her husband had "no formal role" in her campaign "other than to be a supportive husband to me and our children." I then got an official comment from the FBI's press shop, and sent all that in to the editors at the paper. In a scene that many reporters can identify with, I wrote the final version of the story on my phone with my thumbs.

The pushback from McCabe and the FBI consisted of a few basic points. First, McCabe had cleared everything with the Bureau's ethics officials. That seemed fair enough, and a definite mark in his favor, whether the ethics decision had been a wise one or not. Second, McCabe did not take on any meaningful oversight of the Clinton email investigation until after his wife lost her race. By the measure of the FBI's top ethics official, Patrick Kelley, any ethical question about his wife's candidacy ended when she was no longer a candidate or an office holder. In other words, once the race was over, the ethics issue was also over.

This rationale didn't sit with me as easily. As I worked on the story, I remembered that, when I was a kid, my mother had run for the state legislature in New York. I was nine years old at the time, and paid little attention to my mother's political aspirations. But I also remembered, years later when I was in high school, riding in her rusty Subaru sedan one day, she noticed a local businessman strolling down the sidewalk of our hometown. My mother sighed and reminisced about how the businessman had donated to her long-ago campaign. She not only remembered the donation, which was for no more than a few hundred dollars, but she still felt somewhat guilty about it, like she'd let him down.

So when FBI officials argued strenuously to me that the ethical issues raised by Jill McCabe's donations from McAuliffe ended the day she lost her race, it didn't jibe with my experience, including five years I had spent covering Congress. More importantly, I knew it didn't square with the concerns of a number of people inside the FBI.

I had another nagging concern as I listened to senior FBI officials defend McCabe. Many of them didn't defend the facts—they conceded that more than $600,000 in political donations to the wife of a senior FBI official looked bad. "But it's Andy," I was told again and again. "Andy is a good guy." Knowing someone is a "good guy" and arguing it mattered more than the facts didn't feel to me like much of an ethics policy.

There was one more reason I felt like the FBI answers did not quite add up. It was one thing to argue McCabe's role as the number two official in the Bureau was not critical to the outcome of the Clinton case. But that argument was weakened by Comey's move in July to assume publicly the role of prosecutor. If the Justice Department had decided whether or not to charge Clinton, that was one thing. But the decision had been made preemptively by the FBI, and it was clear no one at the FBI had revisited McCabe's history when Comey made his July announcement. Again, this reflected the FBI posture that, as an ethical matter, the day Jill McCabe lost her race, it was as if the hundreds of thousands of dollars in donations had never happened. That struck me as odd.

The story about the donations posted online that evening. Because it was the weekend, many folks at the FBI were out of the office and could not see the story behind the *Journal*'s strict paywall, FBI officials asked me to send it to them.

When he finally read it, McCabe's reaction was blunt: "Sucks pretty much," he wrote in an email. "Buckle in. It's going to get rough." The immediate reaction to the story inside the senior leadership of the FBI was anger.

For Lisa Page and Peter Strzok, the *Journal* story sparked a heated text exchange over whether or not Strzok should give the investigators on the Clinton email case a heads-up about it. Page was incensed at the idea he would spread a bad story about McCabe inside the Bureau.

"Give me a break," Strzok typed. "Go look at EVERY article I've sent the team. Count them. Then count every Godd*mn heads up I get from [FBI's top spokesman Mike] Kortan. . . . But NOT this one. Then tell me I should sit on THIS one and let them hear from someone else. You're not being fair about this. I really cannot believe you're taking this position and it angers me. I'm going to hope your anger about Andy and Jill getting dragged into this is clouding things."

"I AM being fair about this," wrote Page. "I asked you not to. I don't care that [the FBI press shop] sucks. 1) This is about trust, and 2) WHAT THE F DIFFERENCE DOES IT MAKE TO ANYONE ON THE TEAM? Is there some investigative step to take? Some mitigation measure?"

"The fact that everyone is treating this so hush hush differently is part of the problem," Strzok said.

The intense secrecy surrounding the case had created pressure—and suspicion—even inside the Bureau, where some people were indeed losing faith in each other. The criminal agents were losing trust in the national security branch, and vice versa. The seventh floor at the Hoover building was losing the trust of other parts of the building. And Lisa Page and Peter Strzok were losing trust in each other. The argument also revealed the degree to which Page, in many ways Andy McCabe's closest confidante in the building, was worried about how FBI agents would react to the story.

MONDAY, OCTOBER 24, 2016

The next morning, Strzok and Page were no longer fighting, but they were still going back and forth over the *Journal* story. "And it's above the fold," Strzok texted, referring to the prominent placement it got on the Monday-morning front page. "Jerks. I wonder how Devlin got a hold of the story. I have theories. And Devlin is saying, not implying there's a connection here, but look at the timing—server, then meeting, then case, then funding. The point we need to highlight isn't the March date of discovery of the server, because to us, who cares?—it's the date anyone realized there was classified on there."

"A) He did. And he's right B) I agree we can't just drop it where it is—I just hate that this case is so all-consuming and I'm so tired of it," he added.

As Republicans began in earnest to talk up the story, the FBI shifted into damage control mode. To Page, the story had set off "an enormous fire storm . . . It's not only all over the news, but there's just a lot of swirl and churn associated with that fact coming out."

That day, I called Mike Kortan, the head of FBI press. "You ready for Round 2?" I said, trying to keep it light. I explained that I was told McCabe had given instructions for FBI agents working the Clinton Foundation case to stand down from the investigation.

Kortan gave a long sigh and asked me to put my questions in writing, so I sent him an email later that day. The key point of the email was that I had been told McCabe relayed an instruction down the chain of command to agents that "given that it was the height of election season and the FBI did not want to make a lot of overt moves that could be seen as going after her or drawing attention to the probe." Kortan said he would work on it.

That morning, McCabe attended a regularly scheduled 9:00 A.M. briefing for the attorney general, Loretta Lynch, and her staff. Toward the end of the meeting, George Toscas, the senior career national security official, asked McCabe about the Weiner laptop. Though Toscas would later describe the conversation as "just a passing comment at the end of our briefing," the question posed by a senior Justice Department official in front of other senior officials was an unmistakable message to the FBI to figure out if they had a major problem on their hands. McCabe said he would find out.

With McCabe's name on the front page and on cable news, and a host of new questions buffeting the FBI, the Bureau suddenly kicked into high gear on the Weiner laptop. Robertson, the FBI agent in New York, had spent weeks agonizing over the silence from the top. Now, the high command was fully engaged. After Toscas's question, McCabe reached out to two people: Mary McCord at the Justice Department and FBI intelligence executive Bill Priestap. Priestap, in turn, told Peter Strzok the bosses needed answers.

That afternoon, Jill McCabe sent her husband an email. It was a story she wanted him to see, on a little-known website called True Pundit, which piggybacked off of the *Journal* story, but made a number of startling additional claims. The story claimed McCabe "lobbied" internally for no charges to be filed against Clinton in the email case, adding darkly: "According to one FBI insider, the McAuliffe-generated campaign funds may have ultimately bought Clinton some strategic breathing room," going far beyond the ethical questions raised by my original story. The story then went on an odd tangent describing a recently retired FBI executive, John Giacalone, as a "true heavyweight agent" inside the Bureau, who had overseen the email investigation in its early days, but chose to retire when it went "sideways," according to the story. "He felt it was simpler to quietly step aside, walk away instead of fight to keep the investigation on its proper track," the story asserted.

The True Pundit piece was less than a blip in the public consciousness, but it sparked a curious reaction inside the FBI. The sourced assertions in the piece were a grab bag of rank speculation, yet senior FBI officials took it somewhat seriously. John Giacalone hadn't been angry about the Clinton email investigation. He had left the FBI because, after a stellar career, he had kids to put through college, and that was going to be difficult if not impossible on his FBI salary.

But for Comey, the McCabes, and others, the True Pundit piece was something to consider as they worried about what their employees thought of them. Throughout the Clinton email case, Comey, McCabe, and others had worried about how the FBI workforce would view their handling of the Clinton investigation, and Comey's July press conference had been written, in part, to convince his own agents he'd handled the case the right way. Now, suddenly, the workforce knew that while McCabe's wife had campaigned for office, she had received hundreds of thousands of dollars from one of Clinton's closest allies. Senior FBI officials were worried how their agents in the field might react to that.

McCabe forwarded his wife's email to Comey and his chief of staff, Jim Rybicki, with a terse, sarcastic "FYI. Heavyweight source." Comey replied with skepticism a couple of hours later: "This still reads to me like someone not involved in the investigation at all. There is no way John would say he left because of the investigation," wrote Comey. "This strikes me as lower level folks who admire John (which is fine, because I do) telling yarns."

The exchange highlighted one of the difficulties law enforcement faced in the summer and fall of 2016. There was a powerful desire on the seventh floor of the Hoover building to find out immediately who exactly was saying bad things about McCabe or the Bureau.

At the same time, it seemed like the public was often drowning in disinformation and misinformation, much of it coming from all manner of websites, and much of it proclaiming alleged corruption or malfeasance by law enforcement officials when it came to the Clintons. No one—not even FBI directors or their senior advisers, with access to reams of the most sensitive classified information—was completely immune to the innuendo and suspicions raised by a steady barrage of conspiracy theories, false accusations, and shaky assertions floated online. The post about Giacalone was a lesson in the effectiveness of propaganda that has still not been fully absorbed by government officials, the press, or the public, who even in 2020 seem to still too readily consider rank BS as holding at least a kernel of truth.

Within the FBI, some officials immediately credited True Pundit with being on to something. Some had come to see the site as irresponsible and often wrong, but also felt True Pundit did, in fact, have someone inside the federal government talking to them. Their hunch was "they must know something," said one law enforcement official at the time.

Far more clear-cut within the FBI was that the bureaucracy had been roused to push back forcefully against any doubters or leakers. That evening, officials in the Hoover building were trying to keep their own employees from losing faith in the seventh floor. The FBI press shop issued a memo to every special agent in charge and higher, telling the leaders of every field office around the country that my *Journal* story was misleading and unfair.

"Overview of Deputy Director McCabe's Recusal Related to Dr. McCabe's Campaign for Political Office," the memo was titled. The two-page document said the timeline presented in the story "makes invalid associations between the events."

The memo repeated the statement the FBI had issued to the *Journal*, emphasizing McCabe consulted with FBI ethics officials, followed their advice, and had nothing to do with his wife's campaign: "During the campaign, he played no role, attended no events, and did not participate in fundraising or support of any kind." He did not take on a role in the Clinton email investigation until months after his wife's race ended.

The memo proceeded to offer a series of FAQs, noting McCabe had no role in the Clinton investigation while his wife was running for office.

It also said he stayed out of cases involving Virginia politics while his wife was running for office. The memo also sought to draw a bright line separating the Clinton email case and the McCabe candidacy.

"Is it relevant that the existence of Secretary Clinton's email server was reported in the same month that Dr. McCabe announced her candidacy for state senate?" asked another of the FAQs.

"No," the FBI memo replied. "The FBI was not conducting an investigation regarding Secretary Clinton in March 2015. Four months later in July 2015 the State Department Inspector General made a referral to the FBI for investigation. The allegation centered on the possibility Clinton had classified e-mail on her personal system. At the time of the referral Mr. McCabe was serving as ADIC at WFO and was not supervising the Clinton investigation."

For its last question, the memo asked: "While at WFO did Mr. McCabe provide assistance to the Clinton investigation?"

"After the referral was made, FBI Headquarters asked the Washington Field Office for personnel to conduct a special investigation. McCabe was serving as ADIC and provided personnel resources. However, he was not told what the investigation was about. In February 2016 McCabe became Deputy Director and began overseeing the Clinton investigation."

As suspicions seeped further inside the FBI building, and spread to the field offices as well, the FBI's leadership had staked their credibility with the rank-and-file on a technical and precise reading of the timeline. Key to the FBI's defense of McCabe was the assertion he played no role in investigating Clinton during the Jill McCabe candidacy. But for that explanation to fly internally, they also had to convince employees that as the head of the Washington field office, McCabe had no idea he was providing staff support to the Clinton probe—an assertion that struck many veteran FBI agents as implausible at best.

"You get asked to provide people to support a special case run out of headquarters, and you see what kind of people are being tasked, you will know what it's for, even if someone doesn't say the name 'Clinton,'" said one FBI veteran. "And I cannot imagine no one said the word."

To others at the Bureau, the very existence of that all-SAC memo seemed alarming, because it suggested a high degree of concern about the story among FBI leadership. "I have never seen a memo like that, ever," said one longtime employee. The FBI is a large place with a wide variety of opinions on all sorts of topics, and for many agents, McCabe was a divisive figure well before the events of 2016. But this controversy amplified those divisions, raising new questions about how decisions were made on the seventh floor.

Minutes after the memo was sent, Bill Sweeney, the head of the FBI in New York, called an FBI official at headquarters on his cell phone. As it happened, the official was getting a ride home from McCabe, and the executive put the phone on speaker mode so the three could speak. Sweeney told McCabe that federal prosecutors in New York had already spoken to officials at Main Justice about the Weiner laptop. After weeks of silence, it seemed federal officials in New York and Washington suddenly couldn't stop talking about it.

McCabe still had plenty of defenders inside the FBI. Steve Richardson, the Criminal Division executive who had previously told agents to "stand down" on the Clinton Foundation probe, was particularly livid at a staff meeting that Monday. "It's one thing to take a shot at us, but to go after a guy's wife is just awful," Richardson said. In the room, his anger was palpable.

That evening, Lisa Page texted Peter Strzok: "I hate this case . . . Just all of it."

18

Leak Hunting

Donald Trump had begun to escalate his attacks on the FBI, weaving and warping the McCabe donation story into his growing list of grievances against the entire political system and the person he painted as the main beneficiary of that system, Hillary Clinton.

At a campaign appearance in Sanford, Florida, Trump whipped the crowd into a frenzy of "Lock her up!" chants.

"We have just learned," Trump declared, "that one of the closest people to Hillary Clinton, with longstanding ties to her and her husband, the closest—the closest person I can tell you that, gave more—listen to this, just happened yesterday—gave more than $675,000 to the campaign of the wife of a top FBI official who oversaw the investigation into Mrs. Clinton's illegal e-mail server. In other words, the man who was in charge of the investigation of Hillary Clinton accepted essentially from Hillary Clinton $675,000 that went to his wife."

The crowd booed lustily. As would happen so many times in the 2016 race, it didn't matter that Trump was drawing a straight line from Hillary Clinton to Andy McCabe, when the reality was far more nuanced. Donald Trump had declared the FBI was crooked, and out to protect Clinton.

In many other years, that kind of accusation would have been political poison to whomever uttered it. In 2016, it found an audience willing to believe it.

At the Hoover building, McCabe was acutely aware of the criticism directed at him and the FBI, but was trying to focus on the most immediate investigative concern, the Weiner laptop. He called Mary McCord at Justice to talk about it. As McCabe told it, he had assumed the Strzok and the Clinton email investigation team had gotten in touch with the agents in New York and begun working on how to handle the Weiner laptop question. But that was not what had happened. New York agents had flagged the issue, made clear they would not proceed to look at the emails without explicit instructions, given the legal issues between the two very separate cases, and never heard back. And now their inaction was becoming evident at the peak of election season, enabling the Republican candidate for president to publicly accuse senior FBI officials of corruption. Senior Justice Department officials were demanding answers about what exactly was going on.

As McCord pressed McCabe for the details, the deputy director confirmed that prosecutors in New York had asked the FBI to hold off on reviewing the Clinton emails on the Weiner laptop while the SDNY prosecutors studied the legal issues involved.

That afternoon, FBI executives held a quarterly strategy review conference call. In a bureaucracy as large as the FBI, such calls are a regular part of running FBI field offices, but when the two-hour call finished at 4:30, Comey, McCabe, and Bill Sweeney, the head of the New York office, remained on the call to talk about the Clinton Foundation investigation—the subject of my inquiries the day before.

Sweeney's notes from that call show they discussed the Clinton Foundation case, the Weiner investigation, and what legal steps needed to be taken to get a search warrant for the Clinton emails on the Weiner laptop. Here in one combustible swirl were all the issues that suddenly seemed dangerous to the FBI's reputation. Sweeney wrote that McCabe said they needed to move forward and take action consistent with the Justice Department's policy of not taking overt investigative steps that could suggest a preference in an upcoming election. The deputy director was arguing, in essence, that whatever the FBI did next, they should do it quietly, in a way that the public did not find out, because it would make the Bureau look like it was trying to sway the election.

Asked later about this conversation, McCabe and Comey told investigators they did not remember it. For Comey in particular, the distinction is key because he has long insisted he was not made aware of the laptop issue until he was formally briefed later that week. By reputation, Comey did not have a great memory. By reputation, McCabe did. Yet it is remarkable that here, in a moment in which the personal and professional reputations of both men were on the line, and critical decisions needed to be made that would have a huge impact on those reputations, neither of them remembers the discussion. Sweeney's notes indicate not only that they discussed the Clinton Foundation case, but also that Sweeney followed up that evening by calling senior FBI officials in New York, as well as the head of the FBI's Criminal Investigative Division, Comey's chief of staff, and then McCabe. In his personal notes for each of those calls, Sweeney wrote that they discussed the Clinton Foundation investigation. Yet McCabe, Sweeney, and Comey all said later they had no recollection of discussing the topic, and Comey said he did not even remember discussing the Weiner laptop.

Meanwhile, the questions from the top were filtering down to the Clinton email agents at FBI headquarters, who were finally starting to ask questions about the Weiner laptop. Peter Strzok would later admit to investigators that the effort by FBI headquarters to find out the status of the laptop investigation would likely not have happened on October 25 without the prompting from senior officials at the Justice Department.

WEDNESDAY, OCTOBER 26, 2016

The distrust between the Justice Department and the FBI boiled over the next day behind closed doors. Loretta Lynch, the attorney general, usually so calm and soft spoken was now neither: she was ripping into the FBI officials, blaming them for what she viewed as a damaging leak about a high-profile civil rights case.

It had nothing to do with Clinton, or emails, but it was enough to shred the few strands of trust between the two departments, especially because it looked to Lynch like there were damaging leaks coming out of the New York FBI office. A day earlier, the front page of the *New York Times* revealed that Justice Department officials had replaced the FBI agents and prosecutors investigating the 2014 death of a Staten Island man, Eric Garner, after NYPD officers grabbed him and pulled him down to the sidewalk. As he struggled with the officers, Garner uttered what would be his last words: "I can't breathe." The arrest was videotaped, and when the video was released, an outraged public demanded justice for Garner. The death was part of a string of lethal police interactions with unarmed black men recorded by passers-by, spawning the Black Lives Matter movement.

In some ways, the Garner case was incredibly simple. A video of less than two minutes showed what happened, but processing those events through the lens of federal civil rights law would take far longer. By October 2016, the Justice Department had spent more than two years investigating Garner's final moments, and had yet to reach a conclusion. The FBI agents and federal prosecutors originally assigned to the case were based in New York, and they came to believe no charges should be filed against the police officer who wrapped his arm around Garner's neck. In Washington, lawyers in the Justice Department's Civil Rights Division disagreed with that view, and convinced higher-ups to assign new agents and prosecutors to the case.

The *Times* story revealed the internal dispute, and noted there was a plentiful paper trail of the disagreement, making it more difficult to pursue a theoretical prosecution of the police officer, even if the new prosecutors and agents decided to file charges. Hence, the usually serene Lynch was furious, and ordered a conference call with senior FBI officials in New York and Washington, as well as prosecutors in the Civil Rights Division at Justice Department headquarters. Bill Sweeney, the head of the New York FBI office, was one of the people on the call who got "ripped by the AG on leaks," as he later put it.

Lynch got to the point—she felt she knew the leaks had come from the New York FBI office. She also felt she knew all too well the squeamishness some law enforcement officers can have over prosecuting others who carry badges.

"You don't like prosecuting cops—get over it," she told the officials on the call, and railed against how leaks like this one would harm any case, and all the people involved. "You have a family who watched his father die. You have an officer's life which will never be the same . . . I do not want to hear or see any more of these leaks. We all know who it is. I know who it is. I want it to stop." She then called out each section by name.

"Civil rights, am I clear?"

"Yes, ma'am," came back the answer.

"New York field office, am I clear?"

"Yes ma'am."

It was easy to assume the Garner leaks came from the FBI's New York office, given that was where the original agents had come to the conclusion they could not prove the officer violated Garner's civil rights. But that didn't explain why Lynch had faced a similar problem with leaks during the prosecution of Dylann Roof, the racist gunman who opened fire inside a historically black church in Charleston, South Carolina. And it didn't explain why the first two reporters on the *Times* story were based in Washington. And it didn't explain why, when I'd heard about the issues in the Garner case earlier, it hadn't been from anyone in New York. Despite the certainty of Lynch and other officials, there was, ultimately, very good reason to believe the information had not come from New York agents.

━━━━━━

By 2016, it had become common practice in federal law enforcement for officials in Washington to blame their New York counterparts for leaks, and vice versa, even blaming the other for their own disclosures. The practice stretched back more than a decade, and was part of a tradition of bureaucratic finger-pointing that went on inside the government every time there was a news story that displeased senior officials.

The ritual was so formalized that officials would occasionally ask a DC journalist, before a story was published, to make sure that a New York reporter's name was on the byline of particular stories involving the FBI, in order to make it easier for them to blame New York if they had to. That request could cut the other way, too. In 2016, the New York versus Washington blame game would metastasize into a more virulent, nasty public allegation that would hang over the FBI for years.

███████████

By midafternoon, Clinton email agents and prosecutors in Washington were on a conference call with FBI agents and prosecutors in New York working the Weiner case; it was the first time Robertson, the Weiner case agent, spoke to anyone on the email team.

"They were asking questions that I had already repeatedly answered in other calls," Robertson later told the inspector general. The Midyear Exam prosecutors wanted to know what domains he had seen, how many emails, and who the senders and recipients of the emails were on the laptop. At one point, he was asked to speculate on what he'd seen so far. "Based on the number of emails," he replied, "we could have every email that Huma and Hillary ever sent each other. It's possible, given the pure volume. It's possible."

For Robertson, the exchange was both a relief and a source of further frustration, because most of what the Clinton email investigators wanted to know, he had already provided to his bosses weeks earlier. Strzok, who was also on the call, described the conversation as a "triggering event" for the Clinton agents, because it crystallized to him what was on the laptop.

For the agents in Washington, the key distinction was the sheer volume of emails—some 675,000 by Robertson's estimate. The other point of Robertson's presentation that stuck out to them was that they might be looking at Huma Abedin's entire email history from recent years, including BlackBerry emails from a critical three-month period at the start of Clinton's term as secretary of state, which the FBI had not been able to find.

Abedin was key because, as Strzok later explained. ""Huma was frequently used, my recollection, as kind of a proxy for the, for Secretary Clinton. So if people wanted to get something to Clinton, they'd email it to Huma and say please print for the Secretary. And she would; she was a gatekeeper in that way." Lisa Page, in her notes from the call, was blunt: "Good news, in a bad news way." She couldn't quite believe they were considering reopening the Clinton case that had caused so much grief. The presidential election was less than two weeks away.

After the call, it was clear to the FBI and Justice officials that they had to get a search warrant to review the emails. Toscas, who was on the call, was "on board" with getting a warrant; he felt like the information he'd gotten from McCabe in early October was wrong in significant respects, in terms of the sheer scope of potential new evidence, and how it might be able to fill in some of the blanks the Midyear Exam agents couldn't before. He attributed the earlier misunderstanding to "a garble," or miscommunication.

In a conference call later that evening, McCabe said they would need to reopen the case. It was an incredible moment for the Bureau. Having stood still for weeks on potentially critical information, the Bureau was now racing forward to revive the most controversial case they'd had in years. The election was only a couple of weeks away, and the Republican candidate for president had publicly accused the FBI of being in the tank for Hillary Clinton.

That night, as he often did in 2016, Rudy Giuliani—the former mayor of New York, the former US attorney in Manhattan, and now media surrogate for the Trump campaign—appeared on Fox News to talk about the presidential race; specifically, how polls seemed to still show his candidate trailing Clinton. Speaking to Martha MacCallum, Giuliani said he didn't trust polls that showed Clinton with a comfortable lead.

To make his point, Giuliani reminisced about Election Night 2004, when, he said, television executives confidently predicted John Kerry would be the next president, though in Giuliani's telling, he misstated the year, claiming it was 2008. Still, Giuliani had a point. That year, early exit polls had indicated a strong lead for Kerry, which never materialized as the votes were counted.

When MacCallum sounded a note of skepticism that Trump was really in a position to win the election, Giuliani teased, "I think he's got a surprise or two that you're going to hear about in the next few days. I mean, I'm talking about some pretty big surprise."

MacCallum asked what he meant. Giuliani laughingly replied, "You'll see," and went on to insist the Trump campaign was not going to roll over in the final stretch of the election, whatever the polls said. "We're not going to go down, we're certainly not going to stop fighting, we've got a couple things up our sleeve that should turn this around—in a way that even liberal pollsters will get to see," he said.

His remarks went largely unnoticed at the time. Lisa Page and Peter Strzok were busy talking about the plan for the following morning. "Hey guess what," she texted Strzok a bit after eight that night. "We're going to have a mye [Midyear Exam] meeting tomorrow," referring to the acronym for the Clinton investigation. "Like old times . . . The whole band! We're back on tour!"

Amid the intense pressure of the Clinton email case—the case that wouldn't die, not just because congressional Republicans wouldn't let it go, but also because a disgraced ex-congressman had apparently inadvertently downloaded his wife's entire email inbox—the two FBI officials joked to try to release some of the pressure.

"I feel (hopefully don't look as old) like Keith Richards," Strzok replied. "Andy joining via call? There's nothing classified . . ."

"Yes, he is," she answered.

"It's a Banner Day," wrote Strzok. "What special occasion outfit should I wear?"

"No idea. But I did just realize that we all should have dressed up as classified emails for Halloween," she answered.

After the tension and anger, Strzok was enjoying the jokes, replying, "or blackberries. Or B1 redactions. Or sketchy big brown shaddy shit."

For weeks, the lack of instruction from McCabe about how to handle the Weiner laptop had worried some FBI agents. Now that he was moving rapidly to getting a search warrant, senior FBI officials began to doubt if he should be involved at all.

The World of Really Bad

THURSDAY, OCTOBER 27, 2016, 5:20 A.M.

"Boss, The MYR team has come across some additional actions they believe they need to take," McCabe emailed Comey before the sun was up. Inside the FBI, MYR or MYE were both used as acronyms for Midyear Exam, the formal name of the Clinton email investigation. "I think we should probably gather today to discuss implications if you have any space on your calendar. I am happy to join by phone."

At 6:49 A.M., before Comey had responded to McCabe's email, Lisa Page sent an email putting the key players on the Clinton email team on notice that they would be needed: senior executive Dave Bowdich, Comey chief of staff James Rybicki, FBI general counsel James Baker, FBI national security lawyer Trisha Anderson, agent Peter Strzok, analyst Jonathan Moffa, executive Bill Priestap, and McCabe.

"Team, The Deputy has asked that we convene to inform the Director about what we know regarding the laptop in NY. Time is TBD, but I just wanted to alert you all now," Page wrote. Five minutes later, Strzok asked two members of the team to get him specifics on when New York agents first got the Weiner laptop, and when they initially talked to headquarters about possibly getting a warrant for the Clinton emails. A little after seven o'clock, Comey responded to McCabe's email in the clipped shorthand of cops: "Copy."

Comey would later tell internal investigators this was the first time he heard about the issue surrounding the Weiner laptop, though both McCabe's and Sweeney's recollection is that they told him days, if not weeks, earlier.

At 10:00 A.M., Comey walked into a conference room with a grin on his face and he quickly made a joke about getting "the band" back together. The others at the meeting were grim. As they began talking, Baker, the chief legal counsel in the meeting, interrupted.

"Hold on, can we pause for a second?" Baker asked, turning to Comey. "We haven't quite decided the recusal issue and whether Andy should re-cuse himself or not," Baker said. "Should he just out of an abundance of caution not be on the call right now?"

"Yeah, I think that's right," Comey agreed.

McCabe had been traveling, and was joining the meeting by speaker phone. Comey asked, "Andy, you're okay with that?"

"I guess," McCabe replied. He didn't have much of a choice, since the director was putting it to him, but it was clear McCabe was not happy about being removed from the discussion. He had spent days pushing hard against the mere suggestion of recusal only for his boss to push him out.

"I don't need you on this call," Comey said, finally.

The FBI kept the decision tightly under wraps. Publicly, the FBI press office was still forcefully defending the deputy director from questions about his possible ethical conflict. Privately, they cut him out.

After McCabe hung up, Lisa Page asked if she should also leave, since she worked directly for McCabe. "Yeah," said Baker. "While we're work-ing on this, why don't you step out."

McCabe and Page were livid, feeling that he was being unfairly locked out of the FBI's most pressing issue. Page, never one to hide her displea-sure or impatience with colleagues, inevitably texted Strzok. "I obviously don't need to tell you how completely INFURIATED I am with Jim right now," referring to Baker, who was the FBI's top lawyer and, on paper at least, Page's boss.

That same day, Baker had a separate conversation with Patrick Kelley, the FBI ethics officer who had okayed the arrangement in 2015 for the FBI to screen political cases while Jill McCabe was running for Congress. Now, after the *Journal* article, Kelley told Baker he thought it was "desirable" for McCabe to recuse himself from the Clinton cases, not because of any law or regulation, but because of the appearance of a potential conflict. Kelley based that view on what officials informally called the "*Washington Post* test"—if you didn't want to see something on the front page of the paper, don't do it.

Once the Clinton email meeting resumed without the deputy director or his top aide, the investigative team began describing to Comey the huge volume of emails on the Weiner laptop, and how the metadata showed some of those emails appeared to be from the early months of Clinton's time as secretary of state, the critical missing piece in the FBI's understanding of how the private server had come to be used.

The team said they wanted to get a search warrant for the emails, to see if they would reveal any further information about how and why Clinton had decided to use private email while running the State Department. Bill Priestap explained there could be information they hadn't seen before, and that not looking at the Weiner emails would amount to dereliction of duty. "We have to do it," Priestap said.

In Priestap's mind, there was little chance the emails would reveal anything they didn't already know. But that wasn't the point. The FBI had an obligation to be thorough and careful and make sure. They had to investigate it thoroughly, in order to be able to say for certain there was nothing of consequence.

Bill Priestap was also consumed by the burgeoning investigation into Russian election interference. By late October, the FBI was certain Putin was behind a brazen information war against Clinton, and the integrity of the election increasingly appeared to be at risk. Priestap, the assistant director of the FBI's Counterintelligence Division, was overseeing not just the Russia probe, which now had secret wiretap surveillance on former Trump adviser Carter Page, but also protecting the United States' diffuse and in many places outdated election systems. The Bureau had largely succeeded in keeping the details of that investigation out of the public eye. The reasons for the secrecy were not just that any stories could make it look like the FBI was trying to influence the outcome of an election; the Russia investigation was also, by FBI standards, very young. There was still so much the FBI didn't know about Carter Page, George Papadopoulos, Michael Flynn, Paul Manafort, and a whole host of characters who moved around them. And now Priestap and his crew were whipsawing back into the Clinton case.

Comey agreed quickly with the decision to seek a search warrant. There could, in theory, be some kind of "golden emails" that would fill in some of the gaps in the Clinton case. No matter how skeptical Priestap and others were, it was worth finding out for sure.

The conversation then moved to whether Congress should be told. "I couldn't see a door labeled, 'No Action Here.' I can only see two doors, and both were actions. One is speak, the other is conceal," Comey said later. "Let's see what's behind the speak door. It's really bad. We're 11 days from a presidential election. Given the norm I've long operated under, that's really bad. That will bring such a storm. Okay, close that one, really bad. Open the second one. Catastrophic. And again this is something reasonable people can disagree about, but my view was to conceal at that point given all I had said would be catastrophic. Not just to the Bureau, but beyond the Bureau and that as between catastrophic and really bad, that's actually not that hard a choice. I'll take really bad over catastrophic any day. And so I said to the team, welcome to the world of really bad."

When Justice Department officials learned of Comey's thinking, they were infuriated, and many today still speak with undisguised contempt for Comey's rationale, particularly the decision to notify Congress. It flew in the face of the department's long-standing practice not to make overt moves on political cases before an election. Rather than proceed quietly to figure out what secrets the laptop held or didn't, Comey set on a course to loudly reopen the Clinton email investigation, knowing very little about where it would lead.

Some of Comey's critics say his next moves were the unavoidable re-sult of his earlier decision to speak at length about the Clinton case when he announced its closure on July 5, 2016. Once he had opened the door to a public discussion of the evidence and his thought process, which in turn led to further elaboration in his congressional testimony, it was inevitable that if new evidence was discovered, he would have to tell law-makers.

Comey, though, has insisted his July 5 statement was not a factor in his decision to notify Congress about reopening the Clinton case. The driving factor, he has maintained, was that he had an ethical obligation to update Congress. Completely forgotten was his public exchange with a Republican lawmaker in which the assumption was that he would not tell Congress if the case was reopened.

As the meeting went on, Comey asked the members of the team if they thought he should tell Congress. Most of the team thought he should. When it came time for Jonathan Moffa, the lead analyst on the Clinton case, to weigh in, he said, "Sir, every instinct in my body tells me we shouldn't do it, but I understand your argument that you have to make a factual representation, a factual correction to Congress to amend essentially what you told them."

James Baker, the person in the room most free to disagree with his boss, also felt Comey should tell Congress. As Baker saw it, whether the director had given a press conference or not, he would have ended up talking to Congress about the case. And after talking to them about it, he would have an obligation to tell them he was reopening it.

Overwhelming in the minds of the people gathered around the con-ference table was the idea that if they didn't say something, the FBI would be accused of covering up a major development in order to help get Hil-lary Clinton elected. They spent almost no time discussing a different possibility—that it could tip the scales in favor of Trump and hand him the White House. At the end of the meeting, it seemed clear to many in the room that the FBI would do two things: seek a search warrant for the Weiner laptop, and tell Congress they were reopening the Clinton case.

Getting the Justice Department to go along with the decision was another matter. That afternoon, Peter Strzok and two other FBI officials held a conference call with the main players at the Justice Department, to let them know about Comey's plan. The Justice Department lawyers were universally shocked and upset by what was described to them. "This is bullshit," George Toscas told Strzok. "We don't talk about our stuff publicly. We don't announce things. We do things quietly." David Laufman thought the impact of the announcement would be "disproportionate" to the actual importance of the investigative step the FBI was about to take.

For one thing, it was not uncommon for additional evidence to emerge after an investigation had ended. Typically, the FBI would quietly take a look at such evidence without any announcement or fanfare. If the new evidence changed their understanding of the facts, then a decision could be made about whether to say something publicly. But mostly, it seemed to the Justice Department that announcing the reopening of the case would unavoidably have political repercussions for the presidential race. "It particularly struck us as exceptionally inappropriate to make a statement that unmistakably would be construed as the Bureau's having reopened this investigation in that close a proximity to the day of the election," Laufman said.

Part of Laufman's disagreement stemmed from his own understanding of what they already knew about Clinton, Abedin, and the emails— the evidence gathered at that point indicated that as important as Abedin was to Clinton's work and personal life, she was just not immersed in the policy discussions or management issues like Clinton's other aides. Abedin "wasn't as substantively engaged in, in some matters that would have occasioned access to classified information or dealing with classified issues," Laufman said later.

The protestations of the Justice Department lawyers seemed to have no effect. One recalled that Peter Strzok seemed to be pretending to hear them out, without actually offering taking any feedback or reconsidering. "Nothing we said mattered on that call," one of the prosecutors ruefully recalled.

Similar conversations were going on elsewhere. Comey had instructed his chief of staff, Jim Rybicki, to notify senior DoJ leaders, by which he meant, call Matt Axelrod. "Tell DoJ that I think I need to inform Congress of this step. And please tell the [Deputy Attorney General Sally Yates] and the AG that I'm happy to speak to them, but that's what I'm thinking."

In contrast to his decision in July to announce on his own that no charges would be filed against Clinton, Comey decided in October to tell the Justice Department ahead of time what he planned to do. Comey said he thought the approach left an opening for Lynch or Yates to engage him directly and try to talk him out of it. One of the stranger elements of this episode—and Comey's decisions throughout this process—was his decision, time and again at critical moments, to not speak directly to either of his bosses, the attorney general, or deputy attorney general. And it's all the stranger because, even when his bosses knew what he planned to do, they didn't speak directly to him, either.

Instead, Comey's chief of staff, Rybicki, spoke to Yates's deputy, Axelrod. When it came to the Clinton case, the FBI and Justice Department were engaged in a kind of bureaucratic duel, but a particularly passive-aggressive one. The leadership of two buildings that sat across Pennsylvania Avenue from each other preferred to let their seconds do the talking.

From the first of what ended up being several tense phone calls that day, Axelrod was angry. "No, we just don't do that," he told Rybicki. "It's contrary to how we do business."

Rybicki made a number of points to Axelrod, who dutifully relayed them to Lynch and Yates. Comey believed he had a personal obligation to correct a misimpression Congress currently had that the Midyear investigation was over. If they didn't notify Congress, it would leak anyway, Rybicki relayed. "If he doesn't," Rybicki added, "it's not survivable for him."

While Lynch and Yates were angry and upset over Comey's rationale, the "survivable" comment raised new red flags to them. Was Comey going public to preserve his own job, at the expense of the FBI and the

Justice Department? Comey had said to Baker and others at the FBI that he thought he should probably be fired if he didn't come clean quickly about the laptop. He had "raised the issue of, you know, potentially he could get impeached for this if he doesn't tell them," Baker said later.

Lynch, Yates, and Axelrod were apoplectic, but they also felt powerless to stop Comey. Ironically, part of their fear was the closeness to Election Day—the very same concern that made them certain Comey should not say anything public made them afraid that, if they ordered Comey to stop and the order leaked out, they would have created a similar but different problem. Then, Republicans would presumably denounce the department for trying to bottle up damaging information to preserve the viability of their political candidate, Clinton.

The other issue was Comey's reputation as the guy with the ethics and the guts to stand up to the powerful, up to and including his bosses. It would be easy enough, Yates reasoned, for Comey to again present himself as the honorable public servant fighting his political bosses, as he had done in the confrontation at the bedside of John Ashcroft more than a decade earlier.

"We weren't at all convinced he would follow such an order not to do it," said Yates. "We couldn't figure out a scenario that was not going to, again, take a bad situation and make it even worse when we ordered him to do it when it had been framed as his personal ethical obligation." Lynch put it more bluntly in her private conversations with aides. Whatever they told Comey, she thought, he was going to do what he wanted.

In the meantime, there were other fires to put out. Shortly after noon, Lisa Page went to Kortan's office in order to have a conference call with me on the story I was writing about McCabe, the Clinton Foundation, and the instruction given to agents that the deputy director wanted them to "stand down" on the case until the election was over. In an era of endless leak hunting, the Page-Kortan conversations with me would have major repercussions for the Bureau long after the election.

McCabe later told investigators he viewed the account being provided to me about keeping the foundation case on ice to be "incredibly damaging," and decided that in order to beat back the accusation, he would authorize Lisa Page to relay some details of the phone conversation with Axelrod.

At the same time Page and McCabe were deciding what to do about my pending story, they were also picking up signals about what Comey planned to do regarding the Weiner laptop. Page in particular had deep misgivings about the director's decision. She was also still furious about Comey and Baker squeezing McCabe, and consequently her, out of the room.

Strzok tried to keep her up to date on what was being discussed in the Clinton team meetings from which she and her boss, McCabe, were now excluded. Strzok told her Comey "is going to call Andy, we should talk before then." "He already did," Lisa answered.

Strzok tried to make clear he was still on her side, and McCabe's. "JB told me there was no requirement to recuse you, that it was optics, we went round and round playing that out," he texted. "Please, let's figure out what it is we HAVE first," Page texted Strzok. "What if we can't make out PC?" she asked, referring to the probable cause standard necessary to getting a judge to sign a warrant to look at the emails on the Weiner laptop. "Agreed," Strzok replied.

There wasn't much time to debate the point. Within an hour, she and Kortan would be back on the phone with me to talk about McCabe and the Clinton Foundation case.

Toward the end of the day, Lisa Page decided to confront Baker about the forced, semi but not official recusal. "I'm not recused, but I'm not sitting in on this meeting," Page said, trying to point out what she felt was the deeply unfair decision to freeze her and her boss out of the ongoing Clinton discussions. "Just go chill out," Baker told her. Strzok considered it good advice.

McCabe was also pressing Baker and Comey further on the recusal issue, but try as he might, the most they would commit to was not making a decision while McCabe was out of town. "I spoke to both," McCabe texted Page. "Both understand that no decision on recusal will be made until I return and weigh in."

Around ten o'clock that night, McCabe texted Page, saying that Baker's follow-up discussions with Comey were "mostly about the notification and statement which the boss wants to send tomorrow. I do not agree with the timing but he is insistent." Page again voiced misgivings. "Fwiw, I also wildly disagree that we need to notify [Congress] before we even know what the plan is. If we can't get in, then no investigative step has been taken. Whatever. I hope you can get some rest tonight."

By that point, McCabe had been cut out of the decision about reopening the investigation or notifying Congress, but he and Page were both still engaged in conversations about it with some of the key players. Page was frustrated that such momentous decisions were being made without them, and anxious to, as best she could, relay her concerns to those still in the room where decisions would be made. McCabe was simply angry, and in no mood to back down.

"The Death of Me"

FRIDAY, OCTOBER 28, 2016

Something was eating at Trisha Anderson, the senior national security lawyer at the FBI who had stewarded so much of the Bureau's work on the Clinton email case. The discussion about notifying Congress that Comey and his aides had held the day before had centered largely around what it would look like to Republicans when they found out the FBI had known about the Weiner laptop emails and not told anyone until after the election. The team had debated it largely in terms of the harm that could do to a new Clinton administration, or to the FBI's reputation.

That Friday morning, Anderson went to see her boss, Baker. "I have serious reservations about going down this road," Anderson said. In Baker's recollection, she added: "We're going to inject ourselves into the election in a way that potentially or almost certainly will change the outcome. And I'm concerned about us being responsible for getting Donald Trump elected." Would the FBI notifying Congress be fair to Clinton? Anderson wondered. And if it wasn't fair to Clinton, was it fair for the FBI to prioritize its own interests above that of the election?

Anderson later insisted she did not put it so bluntly—that she raised concerns about the FBI having an impact on the election, without naming a specific candidate or outcome. To Anderson, telling the public of the reopening of the investigation before knowing what the emails were seemed fundamentally unfair to Clinton, a violation of the spirit of the rules that govern investigations of public figures.

Her alarm only grew that morning when Comey told a group of senior officials he planned to reopen the Clinton case. Anderson had thought there would be another meeting that morning among the MYE team to consider the issue one more time. But now, the director had already told a wider group of executives the case was being reopened; he was committing to it. The whole thing seemed to her to be flying ahead.

When the small group of senior FBI officials on the email case met later that day, Comey immediately started discussing the wording of his letter to Congress. Baker interrupted to allow Anderson to raise her concerns to the director. In Comey's description of what followed, Anderson asked him, "How do you think about the fact that you might be helping elect Donald Trump?" Comey's answer was emphatic. "I cannot consider that at all," he told her. "We can't think that way."

Anderson would later recall the conversation much differently when she described it to the Justice Department inspector general. In her telling, she again raised questions of fairness and evidence, and whether they were unfairly punishing one candidate.

Comey would make the argument, and repeat it for months and years to come, that it would have been fatal to the FBI's reputation for him to even consider the impact on the outcome of a presidential election. He would later tell internal investigators that when Anderson raised her concerns, he replied, "Down that path lies the death of the FBI, because if I ever start thinking about whose political ox will be gored by this or that, who will be hurt or helped, then we are done as an independent force in American life and so I appreciate you raising it, [but] I cannot consider it."

"The director often talks in parables, and he thinks in parables," said one person involved in the discussion that day, "and sometimes, he remembers things in parables. That doesn't mean that's an accurate description of what happened."

In Comey's telling, he quickly dismissed Anderson's concerns and the hypothetical scenario that ended up being closest to what actually happened. He discarded it because in his mind it would be improper to consider the electoral consequences of what the FBI was about to do. Yet Comey and his aides were very comfortable discussing at length scenarios in which Clinton was elected president, and how the FBI's reputation might be affected. A Clinton victory was almost a given; a Trump victory, they reasoned, was too hypothetical.

Comey's inner circle was also comfortable discussing the polling that showed Clinton ahead, and how that should factor into their decision making. "There was some discussion about if she, if we do this and she wins, then nobody can allege that it was a rigged system and things had been hidden to try to benefit her," James Baker later said. "Somebody may have said in that context, well, she's ahead in the polls anyway and that's probably what's going to happen, and so on . . . But it was more like, you know, if we do this and she gets elected, then she should be thanking us."

The senior FBI leaders assembled that morning expressed confidence in the polling predicting the outcome of an election less than two weeks away—most pollsters generally put Clinton ahead by about six points. It was a good lead, but as pollsters like to remind people, potentially much closer given a margin of error, which on many polls is about three points. Also, national polls can mask the true nature of a presidential contest, where the winner is determined not by who wins the most votes, but who wins 270 or more Electoral College voters. As it turned out, the polls were fairly close to the actual votes tallied.

But on October 28, in Comey's mind, the polls were clear, and he viewed as unbroachable the possibility of a Trump victory. By his own telling, he seemed to feel the FBI's reputation was more important than public trust in the outcome of the US election, which probably wasn't in doubt anyway. Speaking later to skeptical investigators with the Justice Department's Office of Inspector General, Comey conceded: "I am sure I was influenced by the tacit assumption that Hillary Clinton was sure to be the next president."

███████████

Comey's letter to Congress would have taken only a single sheet of paper, if not for all the political names and titles it had to mention. Formally addressed to the eight Republican chairmen of House and Senate committees, and cc'ing the eight senior Democrats on those committees, known in political circles as the ranking members, the letter was three paragraphs long. The missile he had dramatically defused at a July press conference was suddenly rearmed and sailing through the air.

When it came to the wording of Comey's letter to the Hill, Comey's team went back and forth about exactly what it should say. Comey wanted to leave the wording as vague as possible, given the many unknowns regarding the investigative work that still needed to be done. But a vaguely worded letter would likely cast the issue in the darkest possible light, allowing people to read into it the worst-case scenario for Clinton. "That thing was edited within an inch of its life, maybe even edited to death," said one senior FBI official involved in the discussions. "Every word of it was debated and re-debated."

"Dear Messrs Chairmen," it began.

> In previous congressional testimony, I referred to the fact that the Federal Bureau of Investigation (FBI) had completed its investigation of former Secretary Clinton's personal email server. Due to recent developments, I am writing to supplement my previous testimony.
>
> In connection with an unrelated case, the FBI has learned of the existence of emails that appear to be pertinent to the investigation. I am writing to inform you that the investigative team briefed me on this yesterday, and I agreed that the FBI should take appropriate investigative steps designed to allow investigators to review these emails to determine whether they contain classified information, as well as to assess their importance to our investigation.
>
> Although the FBI cannot yet assess whether or not this material may be significant, and I cannot predict how long it will take us

to complete this additional work, I believe it is important to update your Committees about our efforts in light of my previous testimony.

Sincerely yours,

James B. Comey

Director

■■■■■■■■■■■

It took just minutes for the shock wave to ricochet around Washington. Within moments of Comey's letter reaching the Hill, Rep. Jason Chaffetz tweeted: "FBI Dir just informed me, 'The FBI has learned of the existence of emails that appear to be pertinent to the investigation.' Case reopened." At the same moment inside the FBI, Kortan and Page were talking to me on a conference call about my story on the Clinton Foundation, while Strzok texted Page what he was seeing on television.

"Still on with Devlin," Page texted Strzok. "Mike's phone is ON FIRE."

"You may wanna tell Devlin he should turn on CNN, there's news going on," Strzok replied, adding a wink emoji.

"He knows. He just got handed a note," Page replied.

"Ha. He asking about it now?" asked Strzok.

"Yeah. It was pretty funny."

In one tweet, the race for president was upended. About twenty minutes earlier, the Clinton campaign had notified reporters she would be campaigning in Arizona, a traditionally Republican state. The decision to go to Arizona was a show of confidence that in the final two weeks of the campaign, Clinton was running from a position of strength, and might look to pick up additional, tougher states in the Electoral College. Her team was confident that she held a comfortable lead.

Within hours, Trump seized on the gift he'd been given by the director of the FBI. Speaking at a campaign appearance in New Hampshire, the Republican candidate summoned all the hyperbole he could muster. "They are reopening the case into her criminal and illegal conduct that threatens the security of the United States of America," Trump said.

"Hillary Clinton's corruption is on a scale we have never seen before. We must not let her take her criminal scheme into the Oval Office."

Later that afternoon, the *New York Daily News* reported that mysterious new evidence had been found in a laptop from the Weiner case.

"Christ," Lisa Page texted Strzok that evening, marveling that the story was the lead item on NPR's *Marketplace*, a segment devoted to business reporting. "Our statement affected the stock market."

Even as the senior leadership of the FBI marveled at just how big a crater they had put into the news cycle, they were still fighting internally over the question of McCabe's recusal. Comey's chief of staff, Rybicki, called Page to discuss it. "He very clearly 100% believes that Andy should be recused because of the 'perception,'" Page texted Strzok. "God," Strzok replied.

As news of the reopened investigation engulfed cable news, Special Agent John Robertson in New York wrote himself another email. The fear and anger of the past month had given way to satisfaction and relief. "Someone in the chain of command had the sense to inform the director and I am elated to have learned that he did the right thing," Robertson wrote at 4:30 that day. "I suppose I should have had greater faith in the FB, but this is a different matter."

For Clinton and Democrats, the devastating consequences of Comey's letter were immediately apparent. In July, when he'd held his press conference closing the case but criticizing her, the general consensus among Clinton's team was that they should try to put the entire email controversy behind them.

There was no chance of that now. There was only one choice left, to fight back, not just against Trump, and the Russians, but the FBI. At Clinton's campaign headquarters in Brooklyn, aides set up a conference room as a round-the-clock response team for the email issue. With very little time left, they were ready to throw whatever they could at the FBI.

Democrats, including former Justice Department officials who had held their tongues after Comey's July press conference, now started taking public swings at him.

"This is great, but where the hell were you back in July when it might have mattered?" thought Matthew Miller, the former Justice Department spokesman who had waged a lonely war against Comey in the summer. "If Democrats on the Hill or high-profile former Justice Department officials had criticized him for violating the rules in July, he might never have sent the letter in October."

To Clinton's campaign chairman John Podesta, who had been hacked by the Russians, and seen his boss skewered by the FBI twice, the letter seemed like a knife in the heart of the campaign.

Hillary herself found out about the letter when her campaign plane landed in Cedar Rapids, Iowa. As aides scrambled to figure out what was going on, each piece of news seemed more infuriating than the last. Huma Abedin, who was traveling with Clinton, burst into tears when she learned her estranged husband's laptop was at the heart of the latest, gravest threat to her boss becoming president.

"This man is going to be the death of me," she sobbed. Clinton hugged her before going to speak to reporters.

"We are 11 days out from perhaps the most important national election in our lifetimes," Clinton said. "So the American people deserve to get the full and complete facts immediately."

In fact, the American people would have to wait years as the political campaigns, politicized media, and rumor mills of every stripe went into overdrive. The truth was buried in the shouting. The smoke and noise of October 2016 hung thick in the air for years, and in some ways has never lifted. A campaign marked by ill-defined accusations of crimes by the two candidates has evolved into a national politics where conspiracy theories spread quickly and elected officials are regularly, casually accused of committing crimes, or casually accuse each other of crimes. Onlookers, pundits, voters were lost in the fog.

Hours after the Comey letter landed on the Hill, a senior FBI official called me with a question. "Where's your story?"

"The one about McCabe?" I asked. "Well, I'm not running that today. You guys made too much news. I will do it soon."

"Oh, okay then," the official replied, sounding disappointed.

SATURDAY, OCTOBER 29, 2016

The secret of the Weiner laptop was out, which caused a seismic shift inside the FBI and Justice Department. People were talking. One person in particular wanted me to know a lot more about what had been happening with McCabe. All that week, senior FBI officials had been refusing to provide answers or explanations to certain parts of the story, leaving me to get those answers elsewhere, or not. Now someone new was filling in many of the blanks, airing out a number of incidents I had heard about, but hadn't understood completely. What became apparent, as the conversations wore on, was that this person was sticking up for McCabe forcefully because they felt the Bureau was not defending him enough.

In my previous conversations with FBI personnel about the Clinton cases, there had been essentially two camps. The first was FBI's senior leadership, the decision makers on the seventh floor and those who worked closely with them. The second camp consisted of people who were largely outside that decision-making group. They were unquestionably less informed than Comey and his tight circle of trusted advisers, but they also had enough interactions with the decision makers to become, in some instances, deeply distrustful of how the cases were being handled.

There is a moment, rare but recognizable to experienced reporters, when even senior federal law enforcement officials decide the public heat of a crisis is too much for them to bear in silence. One such moment was during the US attorney firing scandal in 2007 when Alberto Gonzales was the attorney general. As those firings led to tough questions from reporters and lawmakers for senior Justice Department officials about possible political motives for removing senior law enforcement officials from their jobs, some officials broke ranks (though usually not on the record), deciding they would not silently accept whatever reputational damage the controversy might inflict on them.

In the FBI's frantic days of late October 2016, a similar dynamic consumed the Justice Department and FBI. Suddenly, a number of people who would not regularly speak to reporters about sensitive internal discussions felt compelled to defend their own honor as agents, lawyers, and civil servants. The result was a significant number of new behind-the-scenes details about the Clinton investigations, in which turf rivalries, differing interpretations of the law, and competing views about the best course of action all got a public airing.

In the wake of Comey's decision to reopen the Clinton email investigation, these conversations revealed a new dynamic, one in which there was disagreement even within the seventh floor about how to handle political investigations. The implication was as obvious as it was jarring—the deputy director of the FBI was no longer lined up with his boss, or other members of the senior leadership. It wasn't every man and woman for themselves, but the cracks inside the crumbling brown concrete of the J. Edgar Hoover Building were growing.

SUNDAY, OCTOBER 30, 2016

The Sunday morning political shows were consumed with the reopening of the Clinton investigation, and how it might affect the outcome of the election.

"October surprise," declared NBC's Chuck Todd as he opened *Meet the Press* that morning. Democrats, having spent July thanking Comey for his wise judgment and moral compass for not recommending charges against Clinton, were now castigating him as a wrecking ball in the election aimed only at one side.

"Your actions in recent months have demonstrated a disturbing double standard for the treatment of sensitive information, with what appears to be clear intent to aid one political party over another," Senate minority leader Harry Reid wrote to the FBI director. Reid even went so far as to suggest Comey might have violated the Hatch Act. Then Reid sought to move the story away from his grievously wounded candidate and back onto the possible sins and omissions of her opponent.

"In my communications with you and other top officials in the national security community, it has become clear that you possess explosive information about close ties and coordination between Donald Trump, his top advisors, and the Russian government—a foreign interest openly hostile to the United States, which Trump praises at every opportunity," Reid wrote. "The public has a right to know this information . . . And yet, you continue to resist calls to inform the public."

While the political class debated the impact and propriety of Comey's move, at the Justice Department and FBI the infighting and finger-pointing was spreading.

"Justice Officials Warned FBI That Comey's Decision to Update Congress Was Not Consistent with Department Policy," read the headline on the *Washington Post* story Peter Strzok forwarded to Lisa Page that morning.

Strzok guessed the information had come from Matt Axelrod, the senior Justice Department official who had spent hours on the phone trying to convey his bosses' desire that Comey not notify Congress about the reopening of the Clinton email investigation. To the FBI, the story showed that Justice Department leaders were not willing to shoulder the blame coming Comey's way.

"Yeah, I saw it," Page replied to Strzok. "Makes me feel WAY less bad about throwing him under the bus in the forthcoming CF article," she added, referring to the Clinton Foundation story I was set to publish later that day. "Yep, the whole tone is anti Bu," Strzok said.

The weekend had been a rush of work for them both—trying to manage the public fallout from Comey's decision, working with the Justice Department to draft a new search warrant application for the Weiner laptop, all while dealing with the distrust inside the FBI and anger emanating from the Justice Department.

I had gone into the office to work on the Clinton Foundation story. Things were moving so fast now—calls seemingly every two minutes—that I told the editors only that I was working on something big and interesting about the FBI, DoJ, and Clinton, but needed a couple hours to write it all up.

They tried to leave me alone, but other news organizations, from the *New York Times* to the *Washington Post* to Fox News, kept trumpeting breaking news, making my bosses anxious to get something out as quickly as possible. At one point, I got a call out of the blue from someone at Fox News. "I hear you have a big story coming on the FBI," said the reporter. "I have a big one too. Can we compare notes?"

This was bizarre. I didn't know this person, had never spoken to them before, and I wasn't about to trust a reporter outside my own news organization—a competitor—with anything I was doing. Readers and viewers sometimes assume that because the *Wall Street Journal* and Fox News are both companies in Rupert Murdoch's empire, there is some kind of connection between the reporting at the two places, but the truth is, I'd never received a call like that before or since.

"Look, I'm not trying to be a dick, but I can't talk about anything I'm working on," I said, and quickly got off the phone. Soon after the discussion, Fox's Bret Baier reported that the FBI was preparing for likely indictments in the Clinton investigation. Big, if true. But it wasn't.

My editors were understandably excited and upset, not knowing the specifics of my story and concerned I might have let a big scoop slip away. Our story would, by describing the dormant nature of the Clinton Foundation investigation, show just how wrong the Fox News report was. "Just give me another thirty minutes," I pleaded, "and you'll see that what they are saying cannot possibly be true."

About three thirty that afternoon, the *Journal* posted my story with the headline "FBI, Justice Feud in Clinton Probe." It described Weiner's laptop as having roughly 650,000 emails on it, a giant cache of data for the FBI to process. It recounted the angry phone call about the case back on August 12, though it did not name Axelrod, calling him instead a senior Justice Department official. And it detailed how suspicions had festered inside the Bureau over months about the handling of the Clinton cases, and much of that suspicion had come to be directed at McCabe. But it also had people close to McCabe defending him, arguing that he had pushed back against unseemly demands from the Justice Department.

Right around the time the *Journal* story posted, Page texted Strzok, saying, "Sorry, utterly terrible day. I'm not sure I can identify one single redeeming thing about it." "Stupid f*cking election," Strzok replied. "The bureau honestly doesn't deserve us," Page vented. "God, I'm so incredibly furious. I would just walk out if I had anywhere to go."

Soon, Page and Strzok wouldn't have a choice. Around five o'clock that afternoon, McCabe called Bill Sweeney in New York to yell at him about leaks. Sweeney pushed back against the accusation the leaks came from his shop, arguing that a lot of the information in the story was stuff his people in New York didn't even know. It was particularly frustrating to Sweeney because, as far as he knew, McCabe was now off the Clinton Foundation case, so they really shouldn't be talking about it at all. Mc-Cabe had a similar phone call with Paul Abbate, the head of the Washington field office. When questioned by investigators, McCabe would later say he didn't remember calling either of them.

Halloween

MONDAY, OCTOBER 31, 2016

After several days traveling—days in which his entire reputation as an FBI agent and the second in command of the organization had been publicly attacked and privately doubted—McCabe was back in the office and eager to talk to his boss.

At a meeting with his staff that morning, Comey complained about the leaks from within the FBI, and he told them they needed to figure out a way "to get our folks to understand why leaks hurt our organization." McCabe, the consummate briefer, liked to have difficult, sensitive conversations after meetings, not during. So after the meeting, he pulled Comey aside.

Comey would later tell the inspector general that he walked away from the conversation believing McCabe was not involved in talking to the *Journal*, though he still thought it possible Lisa Page had done so in an effort to defend her boss. McCabe would give a drastically different version of this conversation with Comey, saying that not only the director but a number of senior FBI officials knew that McCabe had authorized both Lisa Page and Mike Kortan to have conversations with me.

McCabe's most pressing concern, though, was getting himself back on the Clinton cases. Comey tried to dodge the issue, telling his deputy to connect with Jim Baker, the FBI's general counsel. "You guys should talk about that," Comey said. "Talk to Baker and see what you think." Comey wanted McCabe off the case, but wasn't comfortable saying so directly. Besides, he had a bigger face-to-face confrontation on his plate that morning.

Loretta Lynch was in the Hoover building again for a meeting. When it was over, she asked Comey to come to her office. After not speaking to each other about critical decisions, the two would have something of an airing out. However, in keeping with their dysfunctional relationship, two very different versions of what was said would emerge.

In Comey's version, the first thing Lynch did when he appeared in her office was to come out from behind her desk and hug him, a moment made all the more awkward given the huge height disparity between the attorney general and the FBI director. Lynch "pressed her head, her face against my solar plexus and wrapped her arms around me and hugged me, saying, 'I just wanted to give you a hug,'" Comey later said.

Lynch asked how he was doing, and Comey said, "Okay. . . . Look, this is really bad, but the alternative is worse." "Yeah, would they feel better if it had leaked on November 6th?" two days before the election, Lynch asked, in Comey's telling. "Exactly," Comey responded, though he would continue to insist the worry about leaks had not played a role in his decision. Lynch then said, "I hope you're holding up."

The brief discussion over, Lynch then walked Comey over to her office door, telling him, "Try to look beat up," the implication being that Lynch wanted to create the appearance she had been tough on him, when she hadn't.

Comey described the meeting as a kind of setup by Lynch and her staff. When he emerged from her office, her staffers were in the hallway waiting. "And then somebody puts it out within moments that the attorney general had taken me aside to give me a woodshedding or something; it was in the media, I think, that morning," Comey recalled later.

Lynch, however, had a remarkably different version of the same meeting. In her account she indicated to Comey that they had to talk about the "aftermath" of his letter to Congress, and that he knew she had not wanted him to send it. And she said the letter had been widely reported and perceived by the public as the FBI reopening the Clinton investigation, and it was her understanding Comey had not meant to convey that message.

"You ought to think about sending another letter, a clarifying letter," Lynch said. "You've already done this now, you have created a misimpression as to what is going on." Comey asked how he would phrase such a letter, and Lynch said it shouldn't come from her; it should come from him because he had sent the first letter. "I'll think about that," Comey said, according to Lynch.

"I really think you need to clarify this," Lynch pressed again. "I hear you," Comey replied, though he added he was concerned a second letter would do more harm than good at this point. "Look, I've known you for a long time," Lynch went on. "You and I have been in the department a long time. My view is you would never have done something like this if you didn't feel tremendous pressure to do it. I don't understand that pressure, but it was conveyed to me that you were very concerned about leaks, specifically. I can only assume that you were thinking of leaks that would have been of this information in a much, much worse way."

It was at this point, according to Lynch, when Comey said, "Exactly." She then pressed him: "Do you think that this was the right way to deal with the issue, the concern about leaks?" Comey didn't really answer the question, Lynch thought, but she kept going. "We've got to talk about the New York office," Lynch said, keeping the discussion on leaks. Comey replied: "It's clear to me that there is a cadre of senior people in New York who have a deep and visceral hatred of Secretary Clinton," adding, "it is deep," and admitting he had underestimated the extent of the anti-Clinton sentiment among FBI agents in New York.

That struck a chord with Lynch. In the early 1990s, as a young prosecutor, Lynch had handled intake for new arrests and arraignments in federal court, a position in which she interacted constantly with FBI agents.

Even then, she recalled, agents would make passing comments sharply critical of Hillary Clinton. Many of the agents were conservatives, and they loathed Clinton, even that early in her time on the national stage, Lynch remembered.

The conversation turned back to the question of a clarifying letter from Comey, who said he feared it would just throw more fuel on the political fire. "Well, let me know what you decide about whether to do something else or not, particularly as we go through the process of finding things out," Lynch replied.

Lynch and Comey would share their accounts of the conversation months later with the Justice Department inspector general, the office investigating the handling of the Clinton case. The two versions agree, more or less, on how the conversation started and ended. But the gulf between the two accounts is cavernous. Comey describes a meeting lacking substance—a fake tongue-lashing aimed at getting a story favorable to Lynch in the press quickly. Lynch describes something completely different—a long discussion in which she pressures him to take an action to walk back his prior letter, his demurral, followed by her asking him to think about it.

And the back-and-forth about leaks and the New York FBI's supposedly blind hatred of Hillary Clinton simply doesn't exist in Comey's telling. For years to come, Comey would insist that concerns about leaks played no role in his decision to send the letter, yet virtually everyone he spoke to about the decision in that time frame said they discussed their concerns about leaks. The two versions of the Lynch-Comey conversation are so starkly different, so fundamentally contradictory in meaning, specifics, and import, that it is hard to read them as descriptions of the same conversation.

Some of Lynch's subordinates recalled that later that day she described her Comey meeting in the same terms she would later give to the inspector general. Mary McCord, the acting head of the Justice Department's National Security Division, later turned over notes she took later that day at a meeting with Lynch. According to the notes, Lynch said she had spoken to Comey about issuing another letter, and "he wanted to think about it." The notes also said Lynch felt there was a "need to correct misimpressions out there" and that any such letter should "come from Comey."

No one has offered a similar corroboration of Comey's account. The differing versions of the Comey-Lynch meeting are perhaps the starkest example of a disturbing feature of what was by then a broken relationship between the FBI and the Justice Department—at key moments involving the Clinton or Russia cases, Comey's version of events is starkly at odds with accounts provided by Justice Department officials. "It's not that there's an outright lie in it, but the meaning gets all mangled," opined one former senior Justice Department official. By mid-2016, Justice Department officials had come to suspect Comey viewed himself as the most moral, ethical actor in any room he was in. Much later, several of them came to believe his sense of moral superiority was driven in part by viewing even straightforward conversations with his superiors in a sinister light.

Later the same day, David Corn of the magazine *Mother Jones* posted a story online with an explosive headline: "A Veteran Spy Has Given the FBI Information Alleging a Russian Operation to Cultivate Donald Trump."

The story infuriated FBI officials, because it seemed clear that Christopher Steele had broken a basic rule the FBI applies to its informants—telling others what they have told the FBI. The Yahoo! story had alarmed the FBI, but they had been willing to ignore the signs pointing to Steele. The *Mother Jones* story went much further, and agents felt it could only have come from one person. Steele was so angry, he didn't care. The former British spy had trusted the FBI to pursue his leads, find out the truth, and keep a potential Manchurian candidate out of the White House. Instead, from Steele's perspective, the FBI seemed to be trying to ensure Clinton's defeat.

The Corn story was important, and greatly alarmed the Russia investigators inside the FBI, but it did not generate the same kind of public heat the reopened FBI investigation into Clinton had, in part because of another story that was about to land. That night, as many Washington families were out on the streets trick-or-treating, the *New York Times* website trumpeted a story with the headline "Investigating Donald Trump, FBI Sees No Clear Link to Russia."

The *Times*'s verdict was unquestionably a blow to those like Steele and Fusion GPS who'd been pursuing and promoting the Trump-Russia connections, but it was a curious piece in some ways. The first three words of the headline declared the FBI was investigating Donald Trump—an amazing development in a presidential race that had already seen one candidate under investigation more than once—yet Washington's main takeaway from the piece was that there wasn't evidence to support the idea of a conspiracy between Trump and Russia.

A month earlier when testifying to Congress, Comey had studiously avoided answering Democrats' questions about whether the FBI was investigating the Trump campaign. Yet here it was in print for all the world to see. The FBI's announcement days earlier that agents had reopened an old probe into Clinton was the political equivalent of an earthquake. By contrast, the *Times* story declaring a newer investigation into her opponent generated a short flurry of attention before most politicos went back to discussing the Clinton probe.

Steele, whose fury over the reopening of the Clinton investigation had not cooled, was even angrier after reading the *Times* story. To his mind, the FBI already had a lot of information pointing to some kind of Trump-Russia conspiracy. For one thing, there were his reports. For another, his meeting with agents in Rome indicated the Bureau was pursuing some kind of separate investigative thread involving George Papadopoulos. Yet the *New York Times* was all but declaring the issue irrelevant.

Comey relied on Jim Baker. Baker had a key job—the top lawyer of the nation's top investigative agency. In that role, he oversaw a large office of FBI lawyers, but the skill he brought to the job was not management expertise. Baker was one of the government's foremost experts on intelligence law, surveillance, and the often complex relationship between criminal investigations and intelligence gathering. It was an important task in the FBI, but if anything it was Baker's second most important attribute, after his unique relationship with Comey. Among the FBI's senior executives, Baker was one of the few who were willing to regularly disagree with Comey, and push the director to change his mind. Any FBI director wields an incredible amount of unspoken influence among his senior staff; with Comey that influence was, if anything, stronger because he was so openly solicitous of not just their thoughts, but their feelings. Comey's open-faced empathy inspired a kind of loyalty that was different and in some ways stronger than his predecessor, Robert S. Mueller III, enjoyed.

But loyalty inside the upper echelon of the Bureau had exposed it to an unexpected problem. In 2015, Comey had given his blessing to McCabe's wife running for office. But he hadn't known about the amount of money Jill McCabe received from Terry McAuliffe. Now that reporters and Republicans were asking questions about the McCabes, McAuliffe, and the FBI, Comey wanted McCabe to stay out of whatever remained of the Clinton case. But he didn't want to tell McCabe himself. So he sent Baker to do it.

On Monday, Baker went to see McCabe for what he knew would be a difficult conversation. McCabe, back at the office, was adamant that he would not be letting go of the Clinton case. Baker made the case, painfully at times, considering McCabe was his own boss, that it would be better for him and the Bureau for McCabe to recuse from the Clinton case. It was a question of appearances, Baker argued. They could do the job more credibly without him, and it would be politically messy for McCabe to stay on it.

McCabe vehemently disagreed. It would undermine him with the workforce, McCabe argued. It would undermine all the work the FBI had already done on the Clinton case to recuse the deputy director now, at the very end of the process. It would call into question the integrity of the entire enterprise, and make it look like the criticism of McCabe and the Bureau was justified to some extent, he told Baker.

Baker said McCabe was probably right that, legally, there was no obligation to recuse. Baker thought the situation might be different if Jill McCabe was a career politician, or had won her race; then the argument for her husband's recusal would be stronger. But now that the stories about the donations and McCabe's involvement in the Clinton Foundation case were public, he should step away from it, for the good of the Bureau and his boss.

But McCabe would not budge. The FBI, Comey liked to say, was an organization that put tremendous value on "face," in the sense that the higher up FBI agents moved in the organization, the more important it was to them to save face, not be embarrassed, or lose respect in front of their bosses or subordinates. Comey thought that at the FBI, that degree of anxiety could be crippling and counterproductive, and he tried, usually in small groups, to encourage those around him to speak more and worry less. It was part of what he brought with him from Ray Dalio's Bridgewater, and one of the things he most hoped to change in his remaining seven years at the Bureau. But it was a tough sell to many at the FBI, and a nearly impossible one to McCabe in that moment. To the deputy director, it seemed as if his authority to be the chief operations officer of the FBI would be crippled, perhaps permanently, if he was made to step aside.

TUESDAY, NOVEMBER 1, 2016

Mike Gaeta, the FBI agent in Rome who handled Steele, got an email from Joe Pientka, the agent in Washington on the Crossfire Hurricane case, telling him about the *Mother Jones* article describing the FBI investigation of possible Trump-Russia connections. Inside the FBI, everyone seemed to be mad and getting madder. Gaeta called Steele and asked him if he'd been a source for the story, and Steele confirmed he had. Gaeta told him he should stop gathering information for the FBI, and he should not expect the FBI to continue working with him.

One of Pientka's bosses, Assistant Director Bill Priestap, decided they had to cut off Steele as a source. If Steele was going to reveal a major investigation on the cusp of a presidential election, he was a colossal control problem. As angry as the agents were, they did nothing to reassess their other assumptions about the credibility of the former British intelligence officer. They did not revise their view of Isikoff's Yahoo! story from September about Carter Page and blame Steele for that. The agents still felt he was a truthful person supplying valuable intelligence. But they had to take him off the books. Gaeta halted payment of $15,000 that had been on its way to Steele; as a result, the former intelligence agent would end up receiving no money from the FBI for his work on US election interference.

Inside the Hoover building, the bureaucracy somehow found new, creative ways to make things worse. One office within the FBI handled requests for documents under the Freedom of Information Act. On a typical day, the office would release old, often heavily redacted records involving a celebrity or former politician who had died (it is far easier for the public to get records on the dead than the living). On this Tuesday, exactly one week before the election, the FBI's automatic document release system provided a new offering. "William J. Clinton Foundation: This initial release consists of material from the FBI files related to the William J. Clinton Foundation," the FBI Records Vault declared on Twitter.

No one running the Bureau's FOIA work had bothered to check if any releases might be poorly timed just before the election, let alone the same day the *Journal*'s front page carried a story about divisions inside the Bureau over a current investigation of the foundation.

The files themselves were dull—a number of documents regarding a fifteen-year-old FBI investigation into pardons Bill Clinton had granted in his final days in office, and whether any of those pardons had been granted in exchange for donations to the foundation. But that wasn't the point. The Bureau appeared to be going out of its way to make Clinton look bad. They had poured gasoline on the still-burning fires of the previous day's decision.

"Utter complete disaster," Lisa Page texted Strzok, who replied, "I mean, wtf?!?!? We're getting crucified in the news. We should have waited." "It was automatic," Page replied.

On the seventh floor, McCabe was still angry he was frozen out of the Clinton case, and was only getting angrier debating the issue with Baker. They spoke again Tuesday morning, and Baker, who had until then tried to simply convince McCabe that recusal was the right thing to do, decided he had to be blunt. It wasn't just Baker who thought McCabe should step aside from Clinton. It was Comey.

"He wants you to recuse," Baker told McCabe. "He's not going to tell you that, but that's what he wants." "Well, I need to hear it from him," McCabe insisted.

Later that day, the deputy director walked into Comey's office, and sat down on the couch to make his case—a case Comey did not want to hear, did not want to touch, but that was now unavoidably his problem to solve. McCabe made many of the same arguments he'd made to Baker. Comey told McCabe he thought McCabe's legal analysis was probably right, but there was too much "tension" created by the stories about the donations, and about his role in the Clinton Foundation case.

"I just think in light of that it's better that you recuse," Comey told him. With that, McCabe had run out of options. At the insistence of his boss, he recused. "As of today I am voluntarily recusing myself," McCabe wrote in an email to fellow FBI executives. But he still seethed.

In the minds of FBI leadership, the McCabe recusal came about largely because of the *Wall Street Journal* story and concerns about the appearance of a conflict. However, Comey and his advisers also decided they would tell no one about the recusal. They were especially concerned about a public relations nightmare in which McCabe was seen to recuse himself after the FBI had staunchly defended him and argued the reporter was wrong.

After the *Journal* story, Senator Charles Grassley (R-Iowa) wrote a long letter full of questions to the FBI, including what steps the Bureau was taking "to mitigate the appearance of a conflict of interest in the Clinton email investigation and to reassure Congress and the American people that the investigation was not subject to political bias?"

When the FBI finally responded to Grassley's letter in mid-December, it made no mention of the McCabe recusal, and instead continued to argue it was unnecessary. "Based on these facts, it did not appear that there was a conflict of interest—actual or apparent—that required recusal or waiver." FBI officials justified this obfuscation by arguing it was a narrow answer to the question. In one early draft of the letter, the FBI planned to tell Congress of the recusal. "No way," replied Lisa Page, and the sentence was cut.

The logic of the FBI's handling of McCabe's ethics issue was, at best, hard to follow. During his wife's campaign, they considered it a question of local politics, and tried to keep him out of cases involving elected officials in Virginia. As he ascended up the ranks and took a more critical role in the Clinton case, no one revisited the issue, even after the FBI in July 2016 announced, in essence, a prosecutorial decision on the case without telling the Justice Department. Then, when the facts of the donations came to light, the FBI insisted there was no ethics issue. But as more details of McCabe's interactions around the Clinton case emerged, the FBI reversed course and secretly recused him, arguing it was a question of appearances. Yet ethics recusals over the appearance of a potential ethics conflict are premised on the notion that the public will know of the recusal. In McCabe's case, the FBI refused to tell even Congress the truth.

22

Margin of Error

Inside the Clinton campaign, the polling numbers had turned ugly. Before the Comey letter to Congress, Clinton had been in good, but not great shape. In part that was because in the months of September and October, polls showed many Republican-leaning voters had "come home," deciding to support the GOP nominee.

Clinton still held a good lead on the morning of October 8. Her campaign's internal polling on October 27 showed she was up by nine points in Michigan, up by six in Pennsylvania and Wisconsin. Those states were part of what some Democrats called their "blue wall"—traditional midwestern blue-collar clumps of voters who would back the Democratic nominee.

Then came the Comey letter. Good polls take days to conduct, and the impact of news takes days to show up. The key results came to the Clinton campaign on November 2, and they were as bad as had been feared. Clinton had lost six points off her lead in Michigan, and was barely three points ahead. In Pennsylvania and Wisconsin, Clinton's internal polling put her six points ahead before Comey's letter. After, she led in those two states by just three.

To pollsters, a three-point lead is not really a lead, because it is typically within the margin of error. "We had developed a lead outside the margin of error, in the battleground states" John Podesta later said. "Comey upended that. The structure of the race changed."

The danger for Clinton wasn't just that she was losing support; it was where she was losing support. Michigan, Pennsylvania, and Wisconsin are states with comparatively little early voting. Pennsylvania did not allow early voting in 2016. Neither did Michigan, although in that state hundreds of thousands sent in absentee ballots before Election Day. Wisconsin did allow early voting, and hundreds of thousands voted early, but in that state turnout still trailed well behind previous years.

So Clinton had not been able to bank votes the way she could in other places. This meant that, whatever drag effect Comey had on those likely to vote for her, it was likely more pronounced in places where votes couldn't be cast early—before his letter. In Pennsylvania, 95 percent of votes were cast on Election Day, while in Michigan the figure was 73 percent, and in Wisconsin 72 percent.

Other data gathered by the Clinton campaign pointed to voters breaking away from Clinton in the final days. In Iowa, for instance, the campaign had calculated she would receive about 55.1 percent of the early and absentee vote. As it happened, that estimate was right on the nose. When the campaign estimated the Election Day result in the same state, however, they were way off—estimating 42.7 percent of the vote, when they actually got 37.8 percent. She would lose Iowa. It was more proof, in the minds of the Clinton campaign, that Comey had delivered a lethal blow.

It wasn't only the Clinton campaign that saw it that way. Nate Silver, the poll expert who runs the website FiveThirtyEight, would analyze the data and also see a 3 percent chunk taken out of Clinton's lead. In a piece published in 2017, Silver noted the possibility of other explanations— maybe voters just decided to abandon Clinton at the end of the race, for reasons unrelated to the FBI. Maybe she was already declining and Comey's letter, in essence, masked that decline.

But, Silver noted, a three-point drop in a single week is not what erosion of support looks like; it's what news-driven change looks like. "So while one can debate the magnitude of the effect, there's a reasonably clear consensus of the evidence that the Comey letter mattered—probably by enough to swing the election," Silver wrote.

In any election, there are a host of factors that, taken together, determine a winner and loser. In the 2016 race, there were other factors that unquestionably played a role—the candidates themselves, a fountain of online propaganda from Russia, and the social, economic, and political forces of the moment. During the months leading up to the election, millions of Americans saw propaganda from Internet Research Agency, the online troll farm based in St. Petersburg, Russia, but it is exceedingly difficult to measure how that disinformation may have swayed voters.

Comey's letter, though, is unique. First, it was a distinct event in time whose effect could be measured. Second, it came less than two weeks before Election Day, meaning it simply mattered more than other events, such as the *Access Hollywood* tape, and the July 5 press conference by Comey, because it occurred much closer to the actual voting. And third, its impact was larger than those moments, according to pollsters. All of those conditions mean the Comey letter had the single largest measurable impact on the outcome of the race.

THURSDAY, NOVEMBER 3, 2016

Lisa Page was increasingly worried that Clinton's victory was no longer a sure thing. "The nyt probability numbers are dropping every day. I'm scared for our organization," she texted Peter Strzok in the morning.

By that point, the FBI's review of the emails was going faster than agents had initially predicted, thanks to deduping software that let them sift through the hundreds of thousands of documents and be able to quickly toss out messages they had already seen.

But Page felt a growing sense that the outcome of the election might depend on what the FBI did next. The election, she texted Strzok that evening, "and thus, the state of the world, actually hangs in the balance."

That morning, the *Wall Street Journal* ran another story of mine, this time about secret recordings of a campaign finance suspect talking about the Clinton Foundation, which some FBI agents thought could be important evidence, but federal prosecutors viewed as largely worthless hearsay. The Clinton Foundation case was always weak, but there were disagreements inside the FBI and Justice Department about why that was. To some agents, Justice had hamstrung them for a long time. To the Justice Department, the agents were chasing gossip, conjecture, and conspiracy theories.

The story also highlighted the odd role Robert Capers, the US attorney in Brooklyn, had played in the fractious debates over the foundation case. Both the FBI and the Justice Department came to view him as exacerbating the friction by telling each side what they wanted to hear, rather than picking a consistent position.

That evening, McCabe emailed the story to Sweeney, the head of the FBI's New York office, and told him to call him in the morning.

FRIDAY, NOVEMBER 4, 2016

By 7:00 A.M., McCabe was already furious. As promised, he was letting Sweeney have it over the latest *Journal* story about the Clinton Foundation investigation. McCabe vowed to "get to the bottom" of who was talking to the press, once the election was over. The leaks were harming the FBI and needed to stop, he told Sweeney. Once the election was over, he and others would conduct a serious search for leakers, the deputy director said, and there would be "consequences."

While those in the FBI continued to point fingers at each other behind closed doors, in public the leak hunting had already begun in earnest. The questions about what Rudy Giuliani knew and when he knew it had been building for days. Since Comey's announcement on October 28, reporters had zeroed in on Giuliani's reference earlier in the week to Trump preparing to drop "a big surprise." As McCabe was yelling at

Sweeney, Giuliani was sitting on a couch on the set of one of Trump's favorite shows, *Fox & Friends*.

Cohost Steve Doocy brought up the issue of FBI leaks and asked him: "What did you know?" As Giuliani started to answer, cohost Brian Kilmeade chimed in asking if Giuliani "was a part of that?"

"I'm not a part of it at all," Giuliani replied. "All I heard were former FBI agents telling me that there's a revolution going on inside the FBI and it's now at a boiling point, and— "

"So you had a general idea that something was coming?" Kilmeade interjected.

"I had expected this . . . to tell you the truth, I thought it was going to be about three or four weeks ago, because back, way back in July this started. They kept getting stymied looking for subpoenas," Giuliani said, referring to agents on the email case supposedly unhappy they had been told they could not subpoena Clinton's health records.

"They weren't allowed to get the medical records," he continued. "You do that to an honest FBI agent, I mean just an honest guy doing his job, he gets angry. This has been boiling up within the FBI. I did nothing to get it out, I had no role in it. Did I hear about it? You're darn right I heard about it, and I can't even repeat the language that I heard."

Political reporters' ears perked up at Giuliani's "You're darn right I heard about it" remark, many taking it to mean he knew about the emails on Weiner's laptop from disgruntled FBI agents. "You're darn right I heard about it" became the clip of the moment. "Rudy Giuliani Cracks, Confesses after Merciless Interrogation by Steve Doocy" announced the mocking headline on *New York* magazine's website.

That night, Giuliani returned to Fox, and tried to explain that the suspicions about him were wrong, even though the sole fuel for those suspicions had been his characteristically know-it-all moment on live television. The Clinton campaign and Democrats on the Hill called for an investigation of what Giuliani knew, and the former mayor was asked about the accusation he had been fed information from angry FBI agents trying to damage Clinton's chances.

"Oh my god! This is the 'vast right-wing conspiracy' garbage all over again!" said Giuliani, referring to the phrase made famous by Hillary Clinton in the 1990s when she said the investigations of her then president husband were the result of a sprawling Republican effort to gin up phony scandals at the Clinton White House.

"You can investigate me," the former mayor went on. "I've had no communications with them. I haven't destroyed any of my emails. I haven't hammered my cell phone. All of my communications were with former FBI agents. The information I got from former FBI agents who were friends of mine who put the mafia in jail, the Colombian drug dealers in jail."

Building steam, Giuliani plowed ahead, saying the FBI, "from the time of the Comey investigation until the day Jim came forward with what he said, were in revolt about an investigation they believe was being sabotaged. I actually didn't know the dimensions to which the Justice Department sabotaged this investigation until it actually came out."

Giuliani was asked what he'd meant when he'd teased a "surprise" earlier on Fox.

"You know what I was talking about?" Giuliani answered. "I was talking about his [Trump's] advertising this weekend. Because we were having a debate about whether he should give a big speech or do a bunch of advertising. That is what I was talking about. That he was going to go on television and talk directly to the American people."

Giuliani continued to insist he was, in fact, ignorant of what the FBI was working on or wrestling with behind closed doors. "I had no idea that Jim Comey was going to do what he did. Not the slightest idea. What I did know, absolutely truthful with you, what I did know is, from three or four former FBI agents that the people within the FBI, they were telling me this, were outraged at Jim Comey's decision in July, they believe it was a prosecutable case."

On the seventh floor of the FBI, Giuliani's apparent claims of advance knowledge further fueled the growing fears among the Bureau's leadership that more of their G-men were venturing dangerously far off the reservation when it came to FBI policy on talking to the press. Just as important, the world outside the FBI increasingly suspected Giuliani knew something, because many of them looked at the ten-second sound bites on Twitter, rather than watching the entirety of the exchanges. Those suspicions also overlooked an essential element of Giuliani's behavior in 2016—that he frequently went on Fox to make a wide variety of suspect claims, including many that were demonstrably false.

More than a month earlier, on September 1, he had claimed in a Fox interview that he and his firm, Giuliani Partners, had eradicated the drug cartels in Mexico. "Mexico is a very different country than it was 10 or 15 years ago. It's a rejuvenated country because they got control of it. They got rid of the cartels," Giuliani said. In the same interview, he said of Hillary Clinton, "She helped create ISIS. I mean, Hillary Clinton could be considered a founding member of ISIS."

Throughout 2016, Giuliani appeared often on Fox News, sometimes more than once a day, serving as a bombastic cheerleader for Trump, and frequently invoking his hefty law enforcement résumé to bash Clinton. In a February appearance with Sean Hannity, Giuliani laid out what he said his FBI sources had told him would happen if Clinton wasn't indicted.

"I know the FBI really well, as you know," Giuliani told Hannity, who then asked if he had heard anything about agents who believed Clinton should be charged with crimes. "I know there are FBI agents on the case who feel very, very strongly about it," said the ex-mayor. "I have been told, I don't know how true it is, that if there isn't [an indictment] they may very well resign."

Hannity followed up by asking, "But you heard what I heard, that a criminal referral will be made to the Justice Department?"

"Yes," Giuliani replied. "They will recommend indictment on several counts."

Giuliani's claims were not that far afield from what a number of high-profile personalities in the conservative media ecosystem were saying at the time, but as "America's Mayor" and the prosecutor who had paraded Wall Street defendants before cameras back in the 1980s, he brought a degree of legitimacy to such claims that Hannity could not. Those claims, however, were simply wrong. A criminal referral was not made to the Justice Department. The cartels in Mexico are anything but eradicated. Hillary Clinton did not help create ISIS.

But in 2016, reporters generally did not spend their time fact-checking, or even tracking, Giuliani's frequent television appearances. If some poor soul had committed themselves to the task, they would have found Giuliani often tossed out wild accusations and assertions that did not hold up to any serious scrutiny.

In the days, weeks, and months leading up to Election Day 2016, Giuliani made a host of spurious claims on Fox News, including that the Clintons stole from the foundation to pay for their daughter Chelsea's wedding, something everyone involved in the ceremony has denied. He also claimed there had been "hundreds of millions of dollars of fraud" involving the Clinton Foundation and the State Department. No such charges have ever been filed, and the foundation has long denied any wrongdoing. Giuliani also claimed Clinton was hiding a secret illness, urging viewers to "go online" and search for videos with the term "Hillary Clinton illness."

Giuliani spent much of 2016 leveling outrageous accusations on right-wing programs. When one of his vaguer claims later seemed prophetic, first Democrats then reporters were quick to invest it with a sinister meaning, ignoring the former mayor's long track record for hyperbole and falsehoods. Investigators with the Justice Department inspector general's office and the FBI would spend years examining phone records and interviewing witnesses to see if anyone inside the FBI told or relayed sensitive information to the former mayor, and found nothing of value. While many of the investigators came to the conclusion that Giuliani had been spinning out of thin air, as of late 2019, senior officials still claimed the leak investigation into Giuliani was an open case.

SATURDAY, NOVEMBER 5, 2016

After taking a public beating for more than a week, Comey and his crew were increasingly confident the Weiner laptop did not upend their theory of what Clinton and her team had done with their emails. The laptop contained some new emails they hadn't seen before, but no smoking guns, no confessions of criminal intent, none of the far-fetched scenarios that would constitute a Republican dream and a Democratic nightmare for an election just three days away.

Nevertheless, Lisa Page had come to doubt the wisdom of updating Congress yet again, this time with the news that the Weiner laptop emails had led nowhere. The seventh floor of the FBI had been scarred by the reaction to the first letter and the stories that followed about strife inside federal law enforcement.

"I don't want to make a statement anymore," Page texted Strzok that night. "Yeah I don't either. We're kind of out of the news cycle, let's leave it that way," Strzok answered.

Strzok and others worked past midnight Saturday to apply deduping software to the mirrored hard drive of the laptop and then eyeball the new, unique messages. The software radically reduced the workload for the FBI agents, but Strzok and his superiors still wanted investigators to read the messages to make sure they didn't miss anything.

Late that night, Strzok texted Page. "Leaving finally now. . . . no new classified." Once she was up, Page replied, "I still don't know that we should make this statement." "I don't either," he said.

SUNDAY, NOVEMBER 6, 2016

It was time to tell the world what a handful of people in the FBI knew. The Weiner laptop had changed nothing for the FBI. There was no evidence to justify Comey's October surprise.

Comey's second letter to Congress was succinct. "Based on our review, we have not changed our conclusions that we expressed in July with respect to Secretary Clinton," he wrote. "I am very grateful to the professionals at the FBI for doing an extraordinary amount of high-quality work in a short period of time."

It was another remarkable moment in the election, a "never mind" for the ages. On the surface, it seemed a kind of second exoneration of

Clinton. But to many in the FBI, the Justice Department, and elsewhere, a worry persisted that the second letter, merely by raising the issue again in the public's mind of *her emails,* did more harm to the Democratic candidate for president.

MONDAY, NOVEMBER 7, 2016

"OMG THIS IS F*CKING TERRIFYING," Peter Strzok texted Lisa Page the night before the election. The uppercase outburst was fueled by a *New York Times* story that compared Clinton's chance of losing the election to "the probability that an N.F.L. kicker misses a 38-yard field goal." "Yeah, that's not good," Page replied.

Strzok had had a frustrating day dealing with what felt like a pointless debate over what the FBI should do about leaks and critics. Of particular concern was James Kallstrom, who had run the FBI's New York field office in the 1990s—the same job Bill Sweeney held. Long retired, Kallstrom had become a common sight on Fox News, berating the current Bureau leadership as inept or incompetent, and Clinton as corrupt.

Kallstrom drove Page, Strzok, and others crazy. He was probably the most senior former FBI official who had become an outspoken critic of the current FBI. In 1996, Kallstrom had led the investigation into TWA 800, a giant passenger jet that exploded shortly after takeoff from JFK Airport, killing all 230 people on board. Kallstrom quickly became the face of the investigation, but the investigation was slow to come up with meaningful answers as to what had happened. Kallstrom and his FBI team were initially very suspicious of the circumstances. 747s didn't simply fall from the sky, so there was plenty of reason to suspect terrorism or some other form of foul play. The lack of quick answers combined with questionable eyewitness accounts of a flash of light before the crash led to a small cottage industry for conspiracy theorists. One of the theories that gained the most traction was that the plane was taken down by an accidental missile launched by the US Navy, and that the FBI helped cover up the mistake. As the years wore on, Kallstrom spent more and more time beating back various conspiracy theories. Those conspiracy theories drove him batty at times, but he felt he owed it to the victims' families to speak up publicly when hogwash was in the air.

By 2016, Kallstrom was, in the eyes of some of the Bureau leadership, the kind of crackpot he used to denounce. Strzok, Page, and others in Comey's small circle were fairly certain he did not, in fact, have any sources inside the FBI telling him about the Clinton investigations, but he was treated, at least by Fox, as something of a Bureau whisperer, and Strzok was tired of hearing people argue that the FBI should investigate Kallstrom for making claims not based on facts or access to the FBI, a notion he called "wildly infuriating."

In earlier times, the FBI "formers" tended to be a powerful chorus publicly defending and championing the FBI. But the Clinton case had exposed a large rift between the Bureau's current staff and the old guard of retirees. Some of the old guys, many of whom hated Clinton, were not just willing but eager to publicly accuse the FBI of going soft on her.

"Maybe we should go to war with them, if they're spouting bile like Kallstrom," Strzok mused to Page. "He's really out of bounds. That is a valid debate. Talking—telling—me how we should have done it is what's infuriating. There's not a crime. So you publicly shame or disavow him. And you find out who's talking to him and go after them with opr," he said, referring to the Office of Professional Responsibility, an internal watchdog that sometimes chases leak issues. "It's a legitimate criticism that we might have looked sooner at all these people running their mouths to the press."

TUESDAY, NOVEMBER 8, 2016, ELECTION DAY

Finally, the voters were going to the polls.

Before Comey's October 28 letter to Congress, some in the Clinton campaign had thought the outer edge of their success might mean winning Florida. After the letter, their internal polls seemed to indicate that was out of reach, but the Clinton team was still hopeful the "blue wall" in the Midwest would propel her to victory. There was a sense of nervousness, though, since the Clinton campaign's polling had shown Comey's October 28 letter shaving three percentage points or more off her leads in those key states.

In Michigan, Donald Trump edged out Clinton by fewer than 11,000 votes, or a margin of 0.3 percent of the more than 4.5 million votes cast. Green Party candidate Jill Stein garnered 51,000 votes, while Libertarian candidate Gary Jonson collected 172,136. By any measure, Trump's margin in Michigan was razor thin.

In Pennsylvania, another state Clinton had been favored to win (Obama won there in 2012 by 5.4 percentage points), Trump beat her with a margin of about 44,000 votes, or 0.7 percent of the more than 6 million cast.

In Wisconsin, Trump beat Clinton by about 23,000 votes, which, like Pennsylvania, was a margin of 0.7 percent. In 2012, Obama had won Wisconsin by nearly 7 percent. Some of the returns suggested Wisconsin voters had not embraced Trump as much as they had gone cold on Clinton. Republican incumbent Senator Ron Johnson won his race by nearly 3 percent.

Those three states, with their close margins of Republican victory, put Trump over the top to win the presidency. Trump also won Ohio, Florida, and North Carolina more convincingly, giving him 304 votes in the Electoral College, well above the 270 needed to win.

Nationally, the final vote counts indicated the polls were accurate in the aggregate. Clinton got 65.8 million votes, 2.8 million more than Trump. But she didn't get enough of those votes in enough battleground states. So she lost.

PART 3
INTEGRITY

Hangover

The FBI team on the Clinton email investigation was in varying states of shock the day after the election. Trisha Anderson, who'd argued against sending a letter announcing the reopening of the case, was horrified. Among themselves, they debated whether the FBI had made Trump the next president of the United States.

Kevin Clinesmith, a young FBI lawyer who had worked on the Hillary Clinton investigation and was now handling legal issues in the Crossfire Hurricane probe of Trump campaign aides, unburdened himself to a co-worker over an internal FBI messaging system.

"I am so stressed about what I could have done differently," he wrote.

"Don't stress," the coworker wrote back. "None of that mattered."

"I don't know. We broke the momentum," Clinesmith replied. "The crazies won finally. This is the tea party on steroids. And the GOP is going to be lost, they have to deal with an incumbent in 4 years. We have to fight this again. And Pence is stupid . . . And it's just hard not to feel like the FBI caused some of this. It was razor thin in some states."

He then added ruefully: "Plus, my goddamn name is all over the legal documents investigating his staff." Clinesmith was right to think it would come back to haunt him.

Inside the FBI, and inside the Midyear Exam team, Clinesmith was far from alone in thinking the FBI had altered the trajectory of the presidential contest. Senior FBI officials tried to lessen the anger and self-doubt among their subordinates. "A number of people were upset, and felt the FBI was responsible for what happened," said one former official.

The bosses, many of whom had been part of the skinny group discussions in which Comey decided to send the letter to Congress, were now in a position of trying to persuade their subordinates it wasn't their fault, that the director's letter had not been a decisive factor. In those conversations, FBI supervisors sounded at times like they were trying to convince themselves as much as anyone else. "We tried to assure people that no single person was responsible," said the former official.

Sounding almost like a defense lawyer, one former official called Comey's letter "deeply unfair," but argued it's ultimately unprovable if the FBI gave Trump the presidency. "It's fair to say we did, but I have no way of knowing. If it did, it put into motion a series of events that left our country in a very bad place." If Comey had not announced the reopening of the Clinton case on October 28, "perhaps we'd be in a terrible place anyway . . . but I think we are worse off now."

While some FBI officials wrestled with their guilt, others channeled their frustration into leak investigations. After the election, Peter Strzok was quite busy running the Russia investigation, but still got a special assignment from Deputy Director McCabe: to scan all the phones and emails of FBI employees, looking for contacts with reporters. The frustration over leaks about the Clinton Foundation, the email case, and the Weiner laptop was still fresh in the minds of senior officials, particularly McCabe, whose integrity had been publicly called into question by unnamed people inside the Bureau.

When it came to FBI agents' and analysts' work-issued phones, Strzok oversaw what he and McCabe called a "media data pull." To do the search, they got the reporters' numbers and emails from the FBI press shop. Old-school investigators call those kind of phone call record searches "slugs and lugs." In past leak investigations, it would be commonplace to pull the slugs and lugs of a select number of government employees who knew a piece of sensitive information before it leaked, to see if anyone had been in touch with reporters. In the digital age, however, the FBI had the capacity to pull the slugs and lugs of huge numbers of FBI work phones, to search for a needle-in-a-haystack phone call. So they searched.

The examination of FBI employees' phone records was such a closely held secret that some of Strzok's bosses didn't learn about it until much later. The record scan found evidence of leaks in the New York field office and elsewhere on unrelated cases, but did not find evidence showing anyone in New York leaked about the Clinton Foundation case, according to people familiar with the matter. McCabe and Strzok told almost no one about the data search.

███████████

Out of the debris and distrust of the 2016 election, the one thing the FBI was more sure of than ever was the need for leak investigations. It no longer mattered if there was classified information involved, or even grand jury material, the two basic standards that had guided leak investigations in the past. What mattered was finding out who inside the FBI had talked, and punishing them.

In talking the issue over with Andy McCabe, Comey conceded there was no classified information at stake, and none of the type of material that would normally justify a leak investigation. "I told him I don't care," Comey recalled later. "I want to find who is making disclosures and nail them to the wall and so see if we can do it internally."

As the pressure on Comey and McCabe had escalated, they both increasingly looked to the FBI's New York field office as the source of many of their problems. It was an attractive notion for FBI leadership— to believe the dissension and lack of discipline within the Bureau was far from their own building, hours away in an outpost of disgruntled federal agents whose hatred of Hillary Clinton had swayed the big ship of the FBI. It helped that Attorney General Loretta Lynch, hardly a fan of Comey's, firmly believed New York agents were behind the leaks.

Giuliani's sound bite claim on Fox News fed that perception, as had the appearances of James Kallstrom, the former head of the New York field office. And yet try as they might, McCabe, Comey, and others at the FBI found precious little evidence it was New York agents who had tipped off reporters to behind-the-scenes developments in the Clinton cases. As the reporter whose stories got the most scrutiny in that regard, I was more than happy to let people assume the culprits were burrowed somewhere inside the New York FBI office. It reminded me of a line from the first *Indiana Jones* movie: "They're digging in the wrong place."

In December, Carter Page returned to the United States tired but euphoric from another trip to Russia. The FBI was still keenly interested in his activities, so once again Stefan Halper was tasked to connect with him and find out what he could about the former campaign adviser's interactions with influential Russians. Page had gone back to Moscow to give another speech at the New Economic School. His first trip and the reports about his connections to Russia had driven Page out of the campaign, but he was still, at heart, an enthusiastic supporter of improved relations with Russia, and a critic of US policy in that regard.

Talking to Halper again, Page described his latest trip as a week of "18-hour days," and said he planned to return the following month. He added that he'd been invited to Christmas parties at Gazprom and Rosneft, but declined because of all the press attention suggesting he might be under investigation by the FBI. During the conversation, Page told Halper the Russians were "excited but cautious" about the incoming Trump administration. It was a chance for a fresh start and an end to the antagonism that had marked the Obama-Putin years, but Page said the Russians felt they had been "burned a lot in the past" by expecting better relations with the United States, so they were not completely confident Trump would mean a major change between the two countries.

One clear bright spot for the Russians, according to Page, was the reported selection of ExxonMobil CEO Rex Tillerson to be the next secretary of state. The Russians are "almost in awe" of Tillerson, and viewed him as someone "who has real knowledge as opposed to just standard rhetoric that's been in place for 70-some years."

Trying to steer the conversation to the topics of most interest to the FBI, Halper asked Page about the congressional investigations heating up into whether Russians had leaked Clinton emails to try to help Trump win. Carter Page answered in the hypothetical, saying that even if such accusations were true, the emails gave "transparency to the actual corruption" of Clinton and her aides. "Democracy is based on information," Page continued. The difference between Clinton's public and private positions never would have come to light without the email releases, leaving voters with "lies and false information." Page's argument was fairly standard rhetoric among conservatives, and reflected an article of faith among Republicans that stretched back decades: Clinton was corrupt. The emails showed it.

Those two statements require extremely elastic definitions. If anything, most of the emails tended to show how mundane life was behind the Clinton curtain. But there were some, such as the analysis of Clinton's big-money speeches, that stung because they shone a light on just how long Clinton had lived among and taken money from millionaires. But if Republicans hated the kind of deep-pocket politics practiced by Clinton, they hardly objected when their own candidates and former officials moved in the same circles, and took money from Wall Street.

In the time since Halper last met with Page, the notion of creating a Russia-funded think tank seemed to have faltered. Page thought it was possible the New Economic School might support some kind of venture. "This trip proved it," Page said. The New Economic School had significant support from the Russian government at a "high level," and school officials had told him to "come back to us with a proposal."

As in October, Page noted that the public perception of any such effort posed hurdles. "Some people have warned me to be careful with having too much Russia connection for obvious reasons," he said. Page pulled out his personal laptop to show Halper the PowerPoint presentation he'd used in his Moscow lecture. Part of it included Page's riff on Trump's campaign theme of "drain the swamp."

One of Page's slides said it was time to "drain the septic tank" of US-Russia relations. Another was a score card he'd made of previous US administration's positions toward Russia. One purported to show that when she was secretary of state, Clinton had interfered with other governments the same way people had accused Russia of doing to the United States in 2016. Like Putin and an increasing number of Republicans in the Trump era, Carter Page was eager and willing to equate US pro-democracy efforts around the world with the hacking and social media sock puppet campaigns of Russian intelligence.

Page went further, arguing the Russian media arms RT and Sputnik, long viewed by the US intelligence and diplomatic communities as shameless propaganda arms of the Putin regime, may "warrant a Nobel Peace Prize" for bringing transparency that helped "facilitate a pure democracy."

▄▄▄▄▄▄▄▄▄▄▄

After the election, there were few people more upset about the result than Christopher Steele, who blamed the FBI for siding against Clinton. His reports began circulating among a larger group of reporters, lawmakers, and Washington insiders, and as they fell into more hands, they acquired a nickname: the dossier. The latest iteration of the dossier finally became public in early January, shortly after James Comey traveled to New York to warn president-elect Trump that the salacious allegations of Moscow prostitutes could be reported in the press soon.

A staffer for the McCain Institute got a copy of Steele's reports, and shared them with a BuzzFeed reporter. Days after the Comey-Trump discussion in New York, BuzzFeed published its full copy, saying it could not verify the allegations and the document contained some errors, but nevertheless thought the public should see them. Steele, who had previously provided information to reporters and blamed others for leaks, would later say he was flabbergasted by this development, and people he'd trusted had betrayed him by making the reports public. Included in the now public set of accusations was a new one—that Trump's attorney,

Michael Cohen, traveled to Prague in the summer of 2016 to meet with representatives of the Kremlin and associated hackers, all with the goal of helping Trump win the election.

In less than a month, the FBI would be fairly certain this allegation was not true. But in the frenzy of covering the Russia investigation, the Cohen in Prague allegation became a kind of zombie story—it just wouldn't die. Years later, even as Cohen headed to federal prison for a raft of unrelated financial crimes, some reporters and Trump critics would still be trying to find some mix of data points and sourcing to show he had gone to Prague after all.

Days after the dossier's public airing, the FISA court approved another ninety days of electronic surveillance on Carter Page. Unlike the first Page FISA, the renewal did not involve a great deal of internal back-and-forth at Justice and the Bureau. The majority of FISA warrants on individuals get renewed at least once, largely because the bureaucratic process for renewal begins forty-five days before the current order expires, and agents often feel they don't have enough "on the wire" to know one way or another if the target is engaged in the suspected behavior. So in practice, the first renewal of most FISAs usually comes without a ton of new information.

Days after the renewal, Justice Department official David Laufman sat down with a group of FBI investigators and the person who was indirectly responsible for so much of the Crossfire Hurricane case—the person Steele and the FBI referred to as his "primary sub-source." Steele had always made it clear he had a network of sources still plugged into the Kremlin and other circles of power in Russia. When it came to Carter Page, however, it was clear the majority of Steele's information came from one primary sub-source. It was this man who Steele was most worried about exposing, for fear his life could be in danger.

When the FBI finally sat down to speak with the primary sub-source, the most immediate jeopardy was to Steele's reputation. The source told the agents he'd not seen any of Steele's reports until they became public days earlier, and what the dossier said significantly overstated what he had told Steele.

The dossier said the reports of Trump's cavorting with hookers in Moscow had been confirmed by a senior staffer at the hotel, but the primary sub-source said what he'd relayed to Steele was "rumor and speculation" and they had been unable to confirm the story. Not surprisingly, the source also discounted the dossier's claim that Carter Page had been offered a brokerage commission of a 19 percent stake in Rosneft. Ten percent of Rosneft amounted to more than $10 billion. Steele's source said he'd gotten information about a deal like that via text, but when agents examined the texts there was no such mention. Overall, Steele's source's answers indicated the dossier made what was "just talk" sound like concrete facts. Some of it was just the result of "conversations over beers"; the talk of Trump with prostitutes may have been a joke.

Most disappointing for the FBI: Steele's source said that since the election, he'd tried to find corroboration for the claims in the dossier and could not. "Zero," said one agent. The FBI wasn't quite sure what to make of the situation. Had Steele turned boozy gossip and jokes into "the sky is falling" intelligence reports? Had his source, seeing the firestorm unleashed by those reports, simply turtled on the whole thing out of fear of the consequences?

But to the intelligence agents, at a minimum there now seemed something fundamentally sloppy about Steele's reports. For one thing, some of the things stated as fact were, according to Steele's source, just an analytical supposition, or reasonable guesses. Where the dossier claimed the Russians had embarrassing material about Trump with which to blackmail him, Steele's source said that was a "logical conclusion," rather than anything the source had been told.

Blurring source reporting and analytical judgments is a risky proposition in intelligence, as Steele would agree when he was questioned about it later. But the former spy's position was that his source was now retreating from what he'd said before, not that Steele had hyped a bunch of squishy speculation and tried to forge it into something stronger.

Peter Strzok concluded they could no longer assume Steele's source had said all of the things attributed to him in the dossier. Yet three months later, when the FBI again asked to renew the FISA surveillance of Page, the application noted the FBI had interviewed Steele's primary source and "found the Russian-based sub-source to be truthful and co-operative." That was true, but only in the sense that he was truthful about his doubts about the allegations, and cooperative in punching holes in some of the stories Steele had attributed to him.

If Steele's main source was denying or taking back much of what he'd told Steele, which in turn constituted an essential part of the FISA application, why did the agents plow ahead? The agents would later tell investigators they felt the conversation did not nullify all of Steele's work, just gave them pause and concern about the likelihood that any of those allegations would lead anywhere important.

But another explanation lies in the FBI's history of using informants, and the way agent suspicions, once put to paper, can harden into something far weightier than they deserve. One of the best examples dates back to the Cold War, and one of the biggest celebrities of the twentieth century: Frank Sinatra.

In post–World War II America, Sinatra was a rising star, and already on the FBI's radar. After reading an article in 1946 about teenage girls swooning over the young singer with electric blue eyes, Director J. Edgar Hoover scrawled "Sinatra is as much to blame as are the moronic bobby-soxers." At the time, the Bureau was gathering tips from informants that Sinatra was a communist. Red-hunting was gaining steam in the United States, and anxieties over the A-bomb, Russian espionage, and subversives would consume the FBI and the country for years.

The FBI wasn't just suspicious of Sinatra; agents even worried about his dentist. Dr. Abraham Weinstein, whose office was on East Fifty-third Street in midtown Manhattan, had two dental patients who were suspects in a possible Russian espionage ring. Agents conceded it might be a coincidence that Sinatra was also a patient, but they were on top of it nevertheless, marking down in the file when an FBI informant reached out to alert them that Sinatra had made a dentist appointment for the afternoon of April 11, 1946.

As the 1950s began, Sinatra's FBI file was growing with alleged ties to subversives and alleged appearances at events linked to communist sympathizers. The FBI wasn't pursuing him; they were just keeping tabs on him, and silently disapproving. "An unusually reliable source"—often Bureau-speak in the old days for a wiretap—"informed that a yearbook to be published by the American Youth Division of the Communist Party will reportedly contain contributions by Frank Sinatra," read one internal FBI file from the period. The yearbook came and went without any contribution from Sinatra, but the allegation stayed in his secret FBI file for years.

At one point, Sinatra offered his services to the Bureau, saying he was willing to gather information about subversives in Hollywood to become one of their informants. "Sinatra was sensitive about the allegations which had been made concerning his subversive activities," the FBI file said. "Sinatra denies any subversive affiliations or interests on the part of himself, but feels that in view of the publicity which he has received, these subversive elements are not sure of his position, and accordingly, Sinatra feels that he could be of assistance to the Bureau." "We want nothing to do with him," wrote a senior FBI official. Director Hoover agreed.

The FBI's suspicions didn't seem to affect Sinatra's career until 1954, when the army refused his offer to go on a USO tour to entertain the troops posted overseas, saying he was a security risk. Sinatra protested, but to no avail. The following year, he applied for a passport, and as part of the paperwork submitted a sworn statement that he had never been a communist.

Suddenly, the FBI saw an opening. If that sworn statement was a lie, the entertainer could be charged with a crime. So the FBI set out to re-question a number of informants who had, over the years, claimed Sinatra was a member or supporter of the Communist Party. Most of them, when pressed in 1955 about statements they'd made years earlier, denied any actual knowledge of Sinatra's involvement with communists. "He has no facts on Sinatra at all," one agent wrote about an informant who had previously provided derogatory information against him. In an aside that probably said more about the source than the singer, the informant added Sinatra probably should have figured out that some of the people he knew were communists.

Around the country, the FBI questioned more than a dozen informants inside Communist Party circles, including those who had pointed the finger at Sinatra in years past. None had any knowledge of him beyond what they heard and saw on the radio and in the movies. "On reinterview by the Miami office [an informant] reported that the information which he had previously reported was of hearsay nature," a senior FBI official wrote.

The FBI's Sinatra files point to an enduring peril for agents, one that would manifest itself again and again over the years, including in 2016 and 2017. Intelligence gathering is often not that far removed from mere gossip, and gossip, when formalized into secret reports and memos, can take on a sheen of credibility it does not deserve.

But the FBI would not be deterred. In late January, Stefan Halper and Carter Page met once more, and once again the FBI recorded the conversation hoping for an admission of some kind. In their previous conversations, Page had denied any interest in joining the administration, but now he speculated about the possibility he might use any confirmation hearing to attack the allegations against him head-on. The accusations "are not going away," Page said. He planned to meet later that day with White House chief strategist Steve Bannon, and wanted to pitch the idea of an aggressive "forward leaning" offensive against the Russian collusion charges.

Halper tried to let Page down gently, pointing out that the new administration was unlikely to put him through any Senate confirmation, because everyone who disliked his views on Russia "will be rounded up and trotted through in front of the cameras" to defeat him. Their last talk also contained Page's most strident denials of the allegations in the Steele dossier, now that it was public knowledge. The reports were so false, Page said, he wished they'd come out publicly months earlier, because, he believed, all the public allegations against him were based on that. The lurid story about the "pee tape" of Russian hookers urinating for Trump's sexual entertainment "discredits itself so much," Page said.

That morning, the newly minted president had tweeted that he would seek a "major investigation into VOTER FRAUD." Page mentioned the president's tweets, but said the greater fraud was the Steele dossier. "One of the key elements of obstruction of justice is false evidence," Page complained, and the dossier traces back to Clinton, who sent it to "the J. Edgar Hoover building." He compared his situation to that of the civil rights hero Dr. Martin Luther King Jr. "Hoover was all over this guy," and the FBI was now all over him, for nothing more than exercising his free speech, Page told Halper. As Carter Page's strange saga with the FBI ground on for months, he would repeatedly and improbably compare himself to Dr. King.

24

The Storm

THE FBI HAD a cleanup job on its hands on the morning of May 9, 2017. A week earlier, Comey had testified to Congress, and offered seemingly new and damning details about the connections between Clinton's email server, her aide Huma Abedin, and Abedin's husband, Anthony Weiner.

Prior to the hearing, officials had said the emails on Weiner's laptop seemed to have ended up there because Abedin had accessed that email account. What Comey described to Congress, however, was far more nefarious: "Somehow, her emails were being forwarded to Anthony Weiner . . . hundreds and thousands of emails, some of which contained classified information." Comey said at times it appeared the emails were forwarded in order to be printed out so Abedin could then deliver hard copies to Clinton.

But ProPublica had just reported that Comey was wrong—Abedin hadn't forwarded anything like hundreds or thousands of emails. Instead, simply because she had accessed her email account on Weiner's computer, the computer automatically ended up storing vast quantities of her old emails. Comey's remarks suggested Abedin's behavior was much more intentional, and therefore ominous, and her lawyers were furious.

That morning, the FBI was preparing to send a letter to Congress alerting them to Comey's error and setting the record straight. As it happened, I was sitting in a bakery across the street from FBI headquarters—a good place to get breakfast, make calls, and occasionally run into an FBI official without leaving any digital traces. A couple of months earlier, I had left the *Journal* for a job at the *Washington Post*. As I was speaking to a source about Comey's misstatements, I noticed Andy McCabe walking past me on the sidewalk. I decided to follow him at a safe distance, in the hopes my phone call would end in time for me to at least ask him about the issue.

McCabe walked around the corner and went into a coffee shop. For better or worse, my source on the phone was still providing useful information about the Weiner laptop issue, so we kept talking. When McCabe emerged from the coffee shop five minutes later, the source still had plenty to say. I had to make a choice; keep talking on the phone, or drop it to chase McCabe. I chose the person on the phone, thinking they were friendly and cooperative, and the odds were that McCabe, probably still smarting over the Clinton Foundation stories, might not speak to me. So as McCabe sipped his coffee and walked in the shade of E Street, I squinted from across the street but stayed on the phone.

As events unfolded that day, this turned out to be a big mistake. In a few hours, FBI internal investigators, including Inspection Division section chief Voviette Morgan, would question McCabe about a *Journal* story I'd written back in October, specifically the one recounting McCabe's angry August 12 phone call with Matt Axelrod.

The Inspection Division is, in some ways, a bureaucratic backwater of the organization, but it performs essential behind-the-scenes work, trying to ensure the FBI upholds standards throughout its far-flung field offices, foreign postings, and the quieter corners of the J. Edgar Hoover Building. Plenty of FBI agents are not fans of Inspection work, but many managers have to spend some time in Inspection to advance in the organization. Inspection is also the part of the Bureau that handles internal investigations, including leak investigations. At any given time when she was section chief, Morgan was overseeing hundreds of open cases, trying to determine if FBI agents were responsible for leaked information.

This one was an oddity, though, in Morgan's workload. She and another agent had come to McCabe's office on the seventh floor to ask him about a leak investigation he had requested over an inquiry from a short-lived news start-up called Circa. In early 2017, a reporter from Circa had asked the FBI to confirm that at a staff meeting, McCabe had made an angry reference to Trump's national security adviser Michael Flynn, saying something to the effect of "First we fuck Flynn, then we fuck Trump." I had been told the same story, but when I asked people I trusted about it, they told me it was categorically false, so I dropped it.

Behind the scenes, however, McCabe had asked for a leak investigation to see who was making the claim. McCabe told others his rationale was that there were mundane parts of the story that were accurate, even though he had not uttered anything like the wildly inappropriate statement attributed to him.

Around two in the afternoon, Section Chief Voviette Morgan was preparing for the uncomfortable task of interviewing the deputy director of the FBI about leaks. The focus of the questioning was to be the Circa email, but Voviette told one of the agents on the case that she would also ask him about the *Wall Street Journal* story.

The Inspection agents headed up to the seventh floor, passing through the glass doors that guarded the FBI's most senior officials, including Comey and McCabe. Seated around a conference table in McCabe's office, Morgan wrapped up the interview by asking the deputy director about my October 30 story describing tensions between the FBI and Justice Department over the Clinton Foundation. In particular, she steered him to the paragraphs about his phone call with Axelrod, and asked if he had any idea who might have been behind it. At the time, the investigators viewed McCabe as more or less a victim of that particular leak, suspecting someone in the FBI had overheard the call, or found out about it later and gossiped.

McCabe wasn't much help. He told the agents he had "no idea" where the description of the phone call came from, and added that he had told a number of people about the conversation with Axelrod, because he found it so alarming and unusual. The entire exchange about the *Journal* story, one of the agents would later recall, only lasted about five minutes, in part because McCabe's answers seemed so clear cut. Yes, the conversation with Axelrod happened as it was described in the story, and no, he didn't have any idea how a reporter found out about it.

McCabe would later describe the questioning about the *Journal* article as almost a "drive-by" mention as the agents were leaving his office. The interviewers denied that, saying they only discussed the issue at McCabe's conference table, but they acknowledged the topic came up almost in passing at the end of the meeting, and was not the principal focus of it.

At 5:00 P.M., at the end of the same afternoon, President Trump's assistant Rob Porter sent an email to James Comey.

"Dear Director Comey," the message began. "Please find attached a letter from the President." The attached letter notified Comey he had been fired "effective immediately."

> While I greatly appreciate you informing me, on three separate occasions, that I am not under investigation, I nevertheless concur with the judgment of the Department of Justice that you are not able to effectively lead the Bureau.
>
> It is essential that we find new leadership for the FBI that restores public trust and confidence in its vital law enforcement mission.

"I wish you the best of luck in your future endeavors," the president ended the letter. Separately, Trump had also dispatched his longtime bodyguard, Keith Schiller, to the FBI to hand deliver a copy of the letter.

When Porter pressed Send on the email, Comey was at the FBI office in Los Angeles, about to begin a speech to staff assembled around a large command center. But even if he'd been staring at his phone, Comey would not have received the president's letter announcing his dismissal: the White House email to the director had been intercepted by the FBI's spam filter.

Minutes after the email was sent, Andrew McCabe was summoned out of an end-of-day wrap meeting to go talk to Attorney General Jeff Sessions. It was an unusual request, and McCabe assumed he was walking across the street to get yelled at, given the tense state of relations between the White House, Justice Department, and FBI.

"I don't know if you've heard," Sessions began, "but we've had to fire the director of the FBI." No, McCabe hadn't heard, and his mind raced as he was told he was now the acting director of the FBI. When McCabe asked if he should notify the FBI workforce, Deputy Attorney General Rod Rosenstein told McCabe to keep the news to himself until the White House said something. Don't tell anyone, Rosenstein said, "not even your wife."

While McCabe was sitting in the attorney general's office and Comey was speaking to the assembled staffers in Los Angeles, television screens switched to breaking news. "COMEY RESIGNS," declared one. At first, the director thought it was a prank. Then the graphic on the screens changed, to "COMEY FIRED."

As the audience and Comey tried to understand what was happening, the director decided he needed to call his office. So he cut short his remarks and went to a private room to make some calls. Like many of his staff and friends in government, Comey was shocked when he learned the truth. A great deal of that shock was not just the firing, but the brusque manner of it—no phone call, no conversation, just the cheap shot of a public shaming.

On the seventh floor of FBI headquarters, some employees were in tears at the news. Others were furious. Among agents who had spent years, and in some cases their entire careers, chasing Russian intelligence agents, there was a sudden fear that perhaps they would find themselves reassigned to street crime or otherwise punished.

The firing of Comey highlighted a fundamental disconnect between the new administration and the agencies it oversaw. Many people in the Trump White House simply didn't have a good sense of how the departments and agencies worked. Some White House officials were surprised and disappointed to learn that, by firing Comey, they had actually elevated McCabe to the position of director. If there was anyone Trump disliked, it was McCabe. But they were stuck with him, at least for a while. That was far from the only part of the firing process White House officials failed to grasp. Between firing someone by email only to have it caught in a spam filter, and sending a messenger to hand deliver a letter only to find out the intended recipient was three thousand miles away, nothing had gone right for a White House trying to execute a delicate high-visibility maneuver.

When Comey discovered the message in his junk folder the following day, he forwarded it to his now former chief of staff, James Rybicki, with a short note, saying, "History has a sense of humor."

The official rationale for Comey's firing was spelled out in a memo written by Deputy Attorney General Rod Rosenstein, who called the FBI actions in July and October of 2016 a departure from important, long-standing Justice Department practices of fairness.

"Although the President has the power to remove an FBI director," Rosenstein wrote, "the decision should not be taken lightly . . . The way the Director handled the conclusion of the email investigation was wrong. As a result, the FBI is unlikely to regain public and congressional trust until it has a Director who understands the gravity of the mistakes and pledges never to repeat them. Having refused to admit his errors, the Director cannot be expected to implement the necessary corrective actions."

The great irony of the Rosenstein memo is that a great number of officials within both the Justice Department and FBI agreed with that criticism of Comey. He had gone far beyond any Justice Department practice. He was wrong, many current and former law enforcement officials thought. But those same officials also had no faith Comey's firing, coming amid the ongoing investigation into possible Russian contacts with Trump campaign officials, was on the up-and-up. The last thing Trump cared about, those officials reasoned, was unfairness to Clinton.

Later that evening, McCabe was summoned to the White House, where he was ushered into the Oval Office for the first time in his life. Trump sat behind the desk; McCabe took a seat in front of him. Trump told him he had fired Comey, and suggested there were a number of reasons for it. "Are you part of the resistance?" Trump asked. When McCabe said he wasn't sure what the president meant, Trump asked if McCabe had disagreed with Comey's decisions on the Clinton email investigation, though it wasn't clear which decisions he was referring to. McCabe said he'd worked with Comey and was involved in the decisions. Trump asked McCabe if he knew Comey had told him three times the president was not under investigation. Yes, McCabe replied. Trump raised the issue of McCabe's wife running for state senate in Virginia, and seemed to be giving McCabe the option of saying it had been a mistake. McCabe instead defended his wife's decision. Less than twenty-four hours later, Trump would raise the issue again, taunting McCabe by asking how he felt about his wife losing. The whole episode, McCabe thought, was bizarre.

The next day, FBI agents, analysts, and other employees began putting up photos of Comey at their desks, both in headquarters and at various field offices around the country. Long before Comey became director in 2013, it was a tradition among FBI employees to get pictures taken with the director, and to display those pictures in their office or home. Such framed photos weren't necessarily a token of fierce loyalty to a particular director, although they could be. Sometimes, a photo taken with a director many years ago was mostly a way of showing how many years the agent had been at the Bureau. After Comey's firing, the pictures popped up at many more desks and cubicles inside the FBI, and they took on a different meaning: they indicated a quiet protest over his ouster.

McCabe, Baker, and others at the FBI were focused on keeping the four-pronged Russian investigation intact. To McCabe, opening a formal investigation into the president for possible obstruction of justice seemed like an increasingly necessary step to ensure that, even if he was fired the next day, the investigation would continue.

In the wake of Comey's firing, every conversation McCabe had with higher government officials seemed crazier than the last. He was summoned again to the White House, where Trump and senior aides kicked around the idea of the president going to visit FBI headquarters later that week. The acting FBI director would later say he felt he was trapped in a "goofy organized crime movie." The president and his aides were politely pushing McCabe to agree to a presidential visit. McCabe thought it was a horrible idea, but didn't want to say so to the president's face. One of the aides in the room, White House counsel Don McGahn, said the president should only go if McCabe thought it was a good idea. McCabe said yes through gritted teeth, all the while believing such a visit would be a disaster. He was relieved when the planned visit was scrapped.

The following day, the president said in an interview with Lester Holt that he'd been thinking of the Russia investigation when he'd fired Comey, and he felt that even if the firing prolonged the investigation, it was still worth doing. To McCabe and others at the FBI, that seemed evidence the president's true intent in firing Comey was to short-circuit the Russia investigation. They had never believed Comey was fired over his handling of the Clinton investigation, and in the interview the president seemed to be publicly admitting it was connected to the Russia case. The FBI, McCabe decided, would begin a criminal and counterintelligence investigation of the president of the United States.

It was an incredibly tense and emotional time for the FBI, as anger and fear coursed through the conversations among Comey's team. The president, a person close to McCabe told me at the time, "is a madman and has to be stopped." Senior FBI officials viewed the Comey firing as a Rubicon-crossing moment, and feared Trump was hell-bent on bending the Bureau to his will.

Rosenstein was also under enormous pressure, reeling from the public criticism of his own role in writing a memo critical of Comey's handling of the Clinton investigation that was used by Trump as the stated reason for the ouster of the FBI director. Even though he played a critical role in Comey's firing, Rosenstein felt bad about the way it had been done. He also felt he didn't deserve to be blamed for Trump's decision, and was worried McCabe had opened an investigation of the president of the United States without telling him first.

As the Justice Department seemed to be careening off the road, Rosenstein reached for a solution that might placate his critics in Congress and the FBI: he hired Robert S. Mueller III, the former FBI director, to become a special counsel investigating possible conspiracy between Russia and the Trump campaign. Though officials did not say so at the time, Mueller would also be tasked with investigating whether Trump had obstructed justice in that investigation.

The pick helped, but it did not solve the deeper distrust between the Justice Department and the FBI. Rosenstein mused out loud at a meeting if he should secretly record the president, and if members of the cabinet might consider invoking the Twenty-fifth Amendment to replace Trump with the vice president. The dysfunctional relationship between Justice and the Bureau that had greatly exacerbated the election mess of 2016 was, just a year later, in the wake of Comey's firing, far worse. At a tense private meeting between Rosenstein, McCabe, and Mueller, the deputy attorney general suggested the acting head of the FBI recuse himself from the Russia investigation. McCabe, in turn, said it was Rosenstein who should recuse. The two most senior law enforcement officials were starting the biggest case of their careers at each other's throats. Years earlier, Mueller had been talked into extending his time as FBI director for the good of the country. Now, he was being asked to take on a case that seemed to be tearing the Justice Department apart.

Mueller assembled a team of federal law enforcement all-stars. In the beginning, that team included Peter Strzok and Lisa Page. Though they both had qualms about stepping into a pressure-cooker work setting without the familiar structure of FBI headquarters, they both felt the mission was important for their country and for their careers. Yet within about a month they would each leave the special counsel's office. Strzok's departure seemed oddest to his colleagues at the Bureau. The golden boy of counterintelligence had been transferred unceremoniously to Human Resources—a clear demotion. The reason for it would remain a mystery to most of his coworkers.

———

Not long after Comey's firing, I met up with a law enforcement official to commiserate over how crazy life at the FBI had become. Eventually, we began discussing the leak-hunting obsession gripping the FBI, and I wondered out loud how much longer it would affect my work.

"Oh, you—you're going to be under investigation for the rest of your life," the official said, before adding, "Well, not the rest of your life. Just as long as you cover us." It wasn't said with any heat or malice, but a general resignation at the state of things. That year, Attorney General Jeff Sessions would announce the FBI had created a permanent unit of intelligence agents to hunt for leakers in the government. Andrew McCabe, the acting director of the FBI, was about to learn the hard way that once launched, leak probes have a nasty habit of turning in unexpected directions.

Late on a Friday afternoon in the summer of 2017, McCabe sat down for an interview with investigators from the Justice Department's Office of the Inspector General. McCabe's inquisitors had no idea McCabe had already been questioned by FBI agents in May about the *Wall Street Journal* story. The agents showed him texts between Lisa Page and Peter Strzok from late October, when Page wrote that she felt "WAY less bad about throwing him under the bus in the forthcoming CF article." But the IG was unclear what "CF" was a reference to, and asked McCabe.

"I don't know what she's referring to," said McCabe.

"Perhaps a code name?" he was asked.

"Not one that I recall, but this thing is like right in the middle of the allegations about me, and so I don't really want to get into discussing this article with you," McCabe said. He had a point. The stated purpose of the interview was to talk about what Page and Strzok had been texting each other, not what McCabe did. But in this instance, those two topics ran straight into each other. "It seems like we're kind of crossing the strings a little bit," McCabe pointed out.

Was Lisa Page ever authorized to speak to reporters in this time period, the investigators asked McCabe. "Not that I'm aware of," McCabe replied.

When his questioners pointed out that on October 28, Page texted that she was "still on with Devlin," McCabe said, "I was not even in town during those days. So I can't tell you where she was or what she was doing."

A few days later, McCabe called the inspector general's office wanting to clear something up. He wanted them to know, he "may" have authorized Page to talk to me. Shortly after that phone call, Lisa Page sat for an interview with the inspector general's office and freely admitted to being a source for the story. That solved a riddle but also created a bigger problem—if Page had been instructed to talk to me, why had McCabe claimed ignorance, and why had Mike Kortan, the FBI's top spokesman, called the story an unauthorized leak, plain and simple?

Seeking to break the apparent contradiction between Kortan's account and Page's, one of the agents asked Kortan to go back through his emails to see if anything there would explain it. As the interview progressed in Kortan's office, packed with the memorabilia of decades in law enforcement, he began printing out emails from his computer and handing them to the agents. They showed that he and Page had been speaking to me for the story. When the agents came back to question Kortan again the next day, at times Morgan thought he seemed like "a nervous wreck."

The agents were still friendly, and there was no confrontation. Kortan tried to make light of his shoddy memory, saying he was getting old and had forgotten all about it. He should start taking better notes, he said. Kortan gave them more emails, and it was very clear he and Lisa Page had talked to me on background for the Clinton Foundation story.

As the agents left Kortan's office that day, they were struggling to absorb the sudden change. At the start of the investigation everyone had agreed my *Journal* story was an unauthorized leak, and a damaging one. Now, they were being told it was authorized by the top of the organization. One of the agents turned to the other as they walked out of Kortan's office and asked, "What just happened?"

The following day was a Friday, and Morgan's agents decided to have another conversation with Kortan in his office. It was his third interview in as many days, and he tried to explain why his written statement had undergone so many revisions. The two agents, a man and a woman, sat on a small couch, listening to him go through each change, but they were getting impatient. Kortan's explanations, though long-winded, were essentially simple: he had forgotten.

Then the woman agent's phone began to ring insistently. At first she ignored it, but the persistent calls made them think something important was going on. She stepped outside to take the call, and was told McCabe, whom they'd scheduled for an interview at 4:30, wanted to speak to them immediately.

Left alone with Kortan in his office, the other agent decided to take a gamble. "Look, I've known you a long time," he told Kortan. "I've known of you. We haven't worked together. I haven't had the necessity to talk to you in these circumstances, but you're very well respected, and that's how we still feel."

The agent continued in the same vein, telling Kortan it was obvious FBI leadership also admired him because he had held the top press job at the Bureau through two different directors. Then he got to the point: "Is it possible that something got out of control, or something happened, somebody unilaterally made a decision to, to give something they shouldn't have, and once the horse was out of the stall that you found yourself in this position that, that you're actually in a position that you were aware of this and that you're protecting someone?"

Kortan looked at the agent and was about to answer, but at that very moment the woman agent came back in the room and said they had to suspend the interview to go and see McCabe. They left Kortan's office and the unanswered question hung in the air.

The agents walked through the glass doors that marked the FBI's inner sanctum—the offices of the FBI director and his most senior deputies. McCabe greeted them and they sat down at his conference table, where he told them he figured if they spoke now, they might get out of work a little early on a Friday. At the outset, McCabe apologized for how long it had taken to get the agents a revised and signed copy of his statement. Throughout their interactions, McCabe was always unfailingly polite and courteous.

"Here's your statement again," one of the agents said, handing it to him. The agent flagged to him a particular section of the statement, written as a summary of what McCabe told them in their prior May 9 interview about the *Journal* story regarding his phone argument with Matt Axelrod at Justice.

The section read: "Since this event, I have shared the circumstances of this interaction with numerous FBI senior executives and other FBI personnel. I do not know the identity of the source of the information contained in the article. I gave no one authority to share any information relative to my interaction with the DoJ executive with any member of the media."

The agent looked at McCabe. "I want to ask you about this article because we're having conflicting information. And so I need to know from you, did you authorize this article?"

"Yep, I did," McCabe replied. For a moment there was silence as the admission sunk in.

The agents were shocked. Their case had now turned 180 degrees. After initially denying having anything to do with the October 30 story, McCabe was confirming Lisa Page's version—that he had authorized her to talk about his conversation with Axelrod. Silently, the investigators began calculating at what point they would need to stop talking to McCabe, because as a possible suspect, he was entitled to due process. They thought he might need a lawyer.

"Sir, you understand we put a lot of work into this based on what you've told us," one of the agents said. "Long nights and weekends working on this, trying to find out who amongst your ranks of trusted people would do something like this."

McCabe looked down and gently nodded. "Yeah, I'm sorry," he said.

McCabe's apology would later be taken as an admission of guilt by both the inspector general and some of the FBI's critics, but his lawyers would insist the only thing he was apologizing for was the amount of time the agents had spent on the case.

McCabe tried to explain the sudden change in his story as a case of overwork and faulty memory, saying, "There was a lot going on." That would be his central position going forward—that the accusations he misled or lied to the agents was unfounded, because what had really happened was a combination of forgetfulness and misunderstanding in their conversations.

It was an epiphany for the leak hunters. What had started as a search for some mid-level office gossip had led them to the top of the organization. They hadn't gone into the case planning to play gotcha with the acting director of the FBI, but that's where they had ended up. They called their supervisor, Voviette Morgan, and filled her in.

Pretty quickly, the agents' bosses decided they couldn't pursue McCabe any further. There could be a false statement charge involved. It was time to turn the whole thing over to the inspector general. From that moment on, the inspector general pursued the question of whether McCabe had repeatedly lacked candor, a fireable offense, or even lied to federal agents, which was a crime. McCabe insisted he had never knowingly lied to or misled investigators—that a combination of his faulty memory and confused conversations had led investigators to the wrong conclusion.

In early 2018, on the eve of his government pension fully vesting, Andrew McCabe was fired by Attorney General Jeff Sessions. McCabe sued the government for his firing, but civil litigation was only one of his ongoing battles. A grand jury was convened to determine whether to indict him. Almost two years after he was fired, a federal grand jury balked at indicting McCabe right as its term was expiring, to the consternation of a number of senior Justice Department officials.

After years of trying to bring a case against Andrew McCabe, the squeeze was finally over. He would not be charged, prosecutors said in a formal legal notice. On CNN, where McCabe now worked, he said he could not express his relief that a "horrific black cloud that's been hanging over me and my family for almost the last two years" was finally, formally over. The McCabe case had grown out of his own search for who was bad-mouthing him inside the Bureau and ended up boomeranging against him. As the reporter whose conversations were the grounds for the case, it always struck me as an absurd overreach.

In Washington, obsessing about leaks has become an easy means of avoiding discussing the substance of almost any issue. The FBI and Justice Department spent years building up the machinery for perpetual leak-hunting, and McCabe became tangled up in that very machinery, with no apparent sense of irony. In 2019, as a paid CNN contributor, he was asked about Trump's purported lack of memory when it came to WikiLeaks. McCabe said, "It's almost impossible to prove that somebody lied when they are simply saying I don't remember."

McCabe was living proof.

Text Machine

MICHAEL FLYNN, WHO'D LASTED less than a month as President
Trump's national security adviser, strode into the E. Barrett Pretty-
man federal courthouse in Washington on December 1, 2017, wearing a
gray suit and holding hands with his wife. The retired general walked past
a loud phalanx of news cameras and protesters into a packed, hushed
courtroom where he pled guilty to lying to the FBI when agents had interviewed him at the White House nearly a year earlier.

As moving crews were still unloading boxes for the new administration on January 24, Flynn talked to agents Peter Strzok and Joe Pientka
about his conversations a month earlier with the Russian ambassador,
Sergey Kislyak. In his plea, Flynn admitted he'd lied to the agents about
the substance of his discussions with Kislyak on two topics—a UN resolution condemning Israeli settlements as illegal, and his request in late
December 2016 that Russia not retaliate over sanctions the outgoing
Obama administration had slapped on that country for interfering in the
2016 election.

Flynn's guilty plea was a major victory for the Mueller investigation,
because agents and prosecutors now had the cooperation of someone
in Trump's inner circle during the campaign and in the early days of the
administration. For Clinton supporters, the plea delivered a tremendous

sense of schadenfreude. As a Trump surrogate, Flynn had been one of the most enthusiastic cheerleaders for chants of "Lock her up" directed at Clinton over her emails. Now, Flynn was guilty and facing at least the possibility of a prison sentence. Outside the courthouse, a small group of anti-Trump protesters taunted Flynn with cries of "Lock him up!"

"It has been extraordinarily painful to endure these many months of false accusations of 'treason' and other outrageous acts. Such false accusations are contrary to everything I have ever done and stood for. But I recognize that the actions I acknowledged in court today were wrong, and, through my faith in God, I am working to set things right," Flynn said in a statement issued by his lawyers. "My guilty plea and agreement to cooperate with the Special Counsel's Office reflect a decision I made in the best interests of my family and of our country. I accept full responsibility for my actions."

The faith Flynn expressed in his decision that day would curdle in the coming months and years, as he changed lawyers and embarked on a campaign to paint the agents who investigated him as corrupt. A day after his plea, he would start gathering ammunition for those efforts.

The very next day, news would break putting the Mueller team on the defensive. The secret reason for Peter Strzok's demotion had finally been revealed to the outside world, in dueling stories in the *Washington Post* and *New York Times*. Inspector General Michael Horowitz had found the tens of thousands of texts between him and Lisa Page, Andrew McCabe's in-house lawyer. The *Washington Post* reported that they'd used their work phones for these discussions in part to hide from their spouses that they were having an affair.

The political sentiments expressed in the texts appeared to confirm the darkest accusations leveled by Trump and his supporters—that the FBI had been out to get him. Trump had been on the warpath against the FBI since the campaign, but without much to go on. All he could do was toss verbal hand grenades at McCabe and others for suspected political bias. Text conversations like the one in which Page called Trump "a loathsome human" and Strzok replied, "Hillary should win 100,000,000-0" seemed to confirm the spirit of every unfounded accusation the president had made toward the FBI.

Inside the Bureau, the revelations about the texting baffled and angered agents. Strzok was a widely liked and respected agent with an impressive list of successful cases. "How stupid do you have to be?" marveled one of his supervisors. Lisa Page was not an agent, and had ruffled plenty of feathers, but no one thought she was stupid, either. She knew national security law backwards and forwards, and it was incomprehensible to some of her colleagues that she did not see the danger inherent in what she'd done.

Their backgrounds made it even more inexplicable. Page had worked in the FBI's Office of General Counsel, the lawyers' shop whose duties included reminding agents not to put anything in texts that could be discoverable by defense lawyers. Strzok had spent his career in counterintelligence, well aware of the possibility that personally embarrassing information could be exploited by foreign adversaries. If any two types of FBI employees should have known better, their colleagues felt, it was Page and Strzok. Page and Strzok have long maintained that the release of their texts was an unfair attack on them by political leaders at the Justice Department. They insist government employees still have free-speech rights to political opinions, and that their opinions never affected their work on the cases.

The text messages were "a punch in the gut to those of us at the Justice Department and FBI who never thought that two otherwise intelligent and competent people could be so careless and unprofessional," said Gregory A. Brower, a senior FBI lawyer at the time who would go on to spend months dealing with the fallout from the messages.

Across the street at the Justice Department, the texts further exacerbated the distrust and frustration with the Bureau. Prosecutors on the Clinton email team had reminded themselves constantly to be highly circumspect in their comments in any setting, whether it was their own kitchen, a restaurant, or a conference room. When the Clinton case was over, senior Justice Department officials liked to remind the team that Congress and who knows who else would eventually want to go over everything they had done with a fine-tooth comb, so they had better watch their p's and q's at all times. They thought everyone had.

The texts would have an even bigger impact outside the FBI and Justice Department. In the coming days, the back-and-forths between the agent and the senior FBI lawyer would become public, and few would get as much attention as their August 2016 discussion of an "insurance policy." Strzok would spend hours trying to explain to Congress what he meant, and that it was not a reference to some dark cabal or coup by the FBI to keep Trump out of power. But Republicans were incensed, and the text scandal marked a breaking point in the FBI's already strained relationship with Congress.

"The revelation of the texts may have had the most significant and lasting impact on the FBI's standing and credibility in the eyes of the public and in the eyes of Congressional Republicans," said Brower, who in March of 2017 had taken up the unenviable job of leading the FBI's Office of Congressional Affairs. A former Republican state lawmaker in Nevada, Brower had served as a US attorney during the Bush administration, and Comey thought his mix of legal and political skills would help the FBI navigate a difficult time.

To Republicans, the texts were smoking-gun evidence of the FBI's bias against Trump and for Clinton. Inspector General Michael Horowitz would later conclude that, while the texts showed clear political bias, there was no evidence the bias had affected decisions in the Clinton or Trump investigations. That analysis is still scoffed at by many Republicans, who contend it is common sense that the texts show the FBI and the "deep state" government bureaucracy were out to get Trump.

"This belief, now buttressed with actual 'proof,' came to dominate the way the FBI was viewed by supporters of the president on Capitol Hill and around the country," said Brower. The text messages, Brower said, "have done more harm to the Bureau than anything that happened in 2016."

The political problems the texts created for the FBI weren't limited to the facts. By their nature, text messages can be cryptic and open to interpretation by anyone not involved in the conversation. Conservatives read the darkest possible meanings into some of the texts, and a host of conspiracy theories sprouted out of the messages. One of the dumber variants involved my work. Because Page had texted Strzok in October 2016 about being on the phone with me, a meme sprouted up accusing me of taking bribes from the two of them to help Clinton—a comically false premise on multiple levels.

The text controversy would linger for years, as Strzok, Page, and Mc-Cabe each sued the Justice Department over their treatment. Lisa Page resigned from the FBI; Peter Strzok was fired.

Investigating the
Investigators

COMEY HAD BEEN out of the FBI for more than a year when Justice Department inspector general Michael Horowitz released a five-hundred-page report in mid-2018 sharply critical of his handling of the Clinton email case.

"A Review of Various Actions by the Federal Bureau of Investigation and Department of Justice in Advance of the 2016 Election" faulted Comey for "a serious error of judgment" in sending his October 28 letter to Congress announcing the reopening of the email investigation less than two weeks before the presidential election. The decision to give a press conference in July 2016 without telling the attorney general what he planned to say was "extraordinary and insubordinate," Horowitz concluded. But after years of President Trump accusing the FBI, and Comey in particular, of being on a partisan witch hunt against him, Horowitz also found there was "no evidence that Comey's statement was the result of bias or an effort to influence the election."

The report also criticized Loretta Lynch for not being more assertive and reining in Comey. Her explanation that he would have flouted a direct order not to give the press conference, or not to send the October 28 letter, did not pass muster with Horowitz, who was particularly critical of Lynch's public statements after her meeting with former president Bill Clinton at the Phoenix airport.

Comey called the findings "reasonable, even though I disagree with some. People of good faith can see an unprecedented situation differently."

Senior Democrats on the Hill said the findings confirmed what they had long suspected—the FBI had, in the heat of a presidential campaign, put its thumb on the scale. "The stark conclusion we draw after reviewing this report is that the FBI's actions helped Donald Trump become President," Reps. Jerrold Nadler (D-NY) and Elijah E. Cummings (D-MD) said in a joint statement. "As we warned before the election, Director Comey had a double-standard: he spoke publicly about the Clinton investigation while keeping secret from the American people the investigation of Donald Trump and Russia."

At the time Horowitz issued his lengthy report, the Justice Department and FBI were still in the throes of the Russia investigation; that summer, Mueller pressed President Trump's lawyers for a sit-down interview with the president, which would never come, in large part because the Justice Department was unwilling to gamble on subpoenaing Trump, which would likely be challenged in the courts.

The report—and the public reaction to it—was a glaring reminder that the political currents that had swamped the FBI and the country in 2016 were, if anything, even stronger in 2018. Democrats focused on the findings that showed the FBI had hurt, not helped, Clinton. Republicans talked up the parts of the report dealing with anti-Trump comments made by Strzok, Page, and others. At the White House, press secretary Sarah Huckabee Sanders said the report proved the president had been right to be suspicious of Comey and others at the FBI.

With more than five hundred pages to work with, each party found plenty of material to support its own prebaked views of the case. The FBI was biased against Trump. The FBI was unfair to Clinton. There was plenty of evidence for both of those arguments, and no person or party could craft a consensus on any of it.

In April of 2019, the Justice Department released Special Counsel Robert S. Mueller III's report on his findings, which clocked in at a dense 448 pages. The report was divided into two parts, the first dealing with allegations of a possible conspiracy between Russia and the Trump campaign to interfere in the 2016 election, the second dealing with allegations the president may have obstructed justice in the course of that investigation.

On the first count, Mueller concluded that while the Russians wanted to help Trump, and the Trump campaign was happy to get such help, there was not a case for conspiracy between the two sides. "Although the investigation established that the Russian government perceived it would benefit from a Trump presidency and worked to secure that outcome, and that the Campaign expected it would benefit electorally from information stolen and released through Russian efforts, the investigation did not establish that members of the Trump campaign conspired or coordinated with the Russian government in its election interference activities," the report concluded.

After a long, difficult investigation, leading to charges against thirty-four people, six of them former Trump associates or advisers, Mueller had not found collusion. When all was said and done, the single most damning piece of evidence against the Trump campaign was probably his "Russia, if you're listening" declaration on live television at a July 2016 press conference, an announcement that showed what he wanted, and seemed to have spurred a fresh round of hacking efforts by Russian intelligence operatives.

Mueller's findings on the question of obstruction were far more critical of Trump, but also cloaked in dense, hard-to-follow writing that was the Mueller team's solution to a thorny legal problem they never really solved. For years, the Justice Department's Office of Legal Counsel had held that a sitting president could not be indicted, and it was the position of the department where Mueller worked. Following that rule, Mueller's team also concluded that if a president could not be indicted, he could also not be accused of a crime by the department, since such an accusation would be tantamount to a criminal charge. Left unspoken in the report was the obvious inference that it was up to Congress, with the power of impeachment, to decide whether to accuse President Trump of a crime.

"If we had confidence after a thorough investigation of the facts that the President clearly did not commit obstruction of justice, we would so state," Mueller's team wrote. "Based on the facts and the applicable legal standards, however, we are unable to reach that judgment. The evidence we obtained about the President's actions and intent presents difficult issues that prevent us from conclusively determining that no criminal conduct occurred. Accordingly, while this report does not conclude that the President committed a crime, it also does not exonerate him."

It was the most scrutinized and debated paragraph in the report. Was Mueller saying Trump had broken the law, but Justice Department policy barred him from saying so? Was he saying Congress needed to take up the issue with an eye toward impeachment? Or was he saying there was bad conduct, but it ultimately did not rise to the level of a crime? His begrudging, sometimes halting answers at a subsequent congressional hearing did little to clear up those questions. The report would not bridge the gap between conservatives and liberals, between Trump haters and Trump lovers. The president called the findings "total exoneration." One of his main Democratic critics, House Intelligence Committee chairman Adam Schiff, said the report catalogued Trump's "damning conduct."

Later that year, Michael Horowitz, the inspector general, would issue another inch-thick report, this one about the FBI's pursuit of Carter Page. "Review of Four FISA Applications and Other Aspects of the FBI's Crossfire Hurricane Investigation" had been touted by Comey in the days before its release as a kind of vindication against President Trump's feverish accusations against him and his team. "There was no spying on the Trump campaign," Comey declared in a *Washington Post* op-ed.

It was true that Trump's conspiracy theories about the FBI, the Justice Department, and Obama were not borne out by Horowitz's findings, but it was also true that the 343-page document was a very bad day for the Bureau's reputation. "We identified at least 17 significant errors or omissions in the Carter Page FISA applications," and many other errors in the supporting paperwork, the report concluded. "That so many basic and fundamental errors were made," the report said, "raised significant questions regarding the FBI chain of command's management and supervision of the FISA process." It was a failure of FBI agents and their bosses up the chain of command, Horowitz concluded, telling Congress his report "doesn't vindicate anyone at the FBI who touched this, including the leadership."

The former FBI lawyer Kevin Clinesmith, who had been jettisoned from the Russia probe when his politically charged messages were discovered, came in for a particularly harsh assessment. Without naming him, the report made clear the lawyer may have broken the law by altering an internal email to make it appear as if Carter Page had not been a past source of information for the CIA when, in fact, he had. That issue was referred to an outside prosecutor, Connecticut US attorney John Durham, to decide whether to seek criminal charges against Clinesmith.

Horowitz also struck an exceedingly skeptical posture toward Christopher Steele. The FBI should have reassessed Steele's reliability, given all the information it obtained suggesting the allegations in the dossier could not be substantiated. Instead, the FBI told the FISA court that one of Steele's key sources seemed honest and trustworthy.

Another repeated failing by the FBI, the report found, was that when agents used Stefan Halper to feel Carter Page and George Papadopoulos out about a possible conspiracy with Russian hackers, their denials of knowledge about such things were not shared with the FISA court. Whatever might seem incriminating was shared; any statements suggesting their innocence stayed inside the FBI. Those problems only got worse as the investigation continued into 2017, Horowitz found. It was one thing to blow past exculpatory information in the early days; by the time Trump was president, the FBI had amassed a significant amount of information suggesting Steele's assertions and other assertions in the case were just wrong. Yet, rather than tell the court, the FBI plowed ahead.

A subsequent report by the inspector general suggested Trump's claims the FBI was out to get him for political reasons was likely off base, because other, nonpolitical FISA work by the Bureau also did not stand up to scrutiny. After finding so many problems with the high-profile Carter Page case, Horowitz had decided to look at other FISA cases to see if the problem was more widespread.

It was. Of the first twenty-nine FISA applications Horowitz reviewed, problems were found in all twenty-nine. In four of the cases, Horowitz's investigators couldn't even find the required file of supporting documentation meant to ensure the agents' claims to judges were scrupulously accurate.

By 2019, any discussions of how the FBI worked were often drowned out by the political debate about its motives. The conversation had shrunk to such narrowly partisan finger-pointing that no report, analysis, or fact seemed capable of breaking out of binary politics. Even basic words became battlegrounds.

When Attorney General William P. Barr told Congress he thought "spying" had been conducted against the Trump campaign, Comey bristled and said the attorney general was being unfair, telling CBS that Republicans should "breathe into a paper bag." Comey said he had "no idea" what the attorney general was talking about. "The FBI doesn't spy, the FBI investigates. We investigated a very serious allegation that Americans might be hooked up with the Russian effort to attack our democracy."

Yet in 2014, when Comey was asked if the FBI spied on Americans, he was far more comfortable with the word. "Well, not the average person," Comey told a reporter in Alabama. "Now if you're involved in one of the things I'm worried about, if you're trafficking drugs, if you're involved in violent crime, if you're a terrorist or a spy, I would like to be spying on you because I need to know what you're doing. That's our business."

As America edged closer to 2020, a year in which Trump would seek reelection, there were plenty of signs that some in the FBI still struggled with the world of internet-driven media.

Shortly before Christmas 2019, former FBI analyst Mark Tolson stood up in federal court in Alexandria, Virginia, to receive his sentence. "I did what I did to try to protect Director Mueller, who can protect himself," Tolson told Judge Leonie Brinkema. The Tolson case was perhaps the strangest unintended consequence of the Mueller investigation that had consumed Washington for the better part of two years. Tolson's guilty plea to misdemeanor computer fraud and abuse stemmed from his anger that in 2018 two conspiracy theorists had tried to spread the idea that Mueller had sexually assaulted someone.

Conspiracy theorists pose tricky new challenges to news organizations in the age of social media. It can be tempting for reporters or editors to say that if an accusation is circulating on Twitter or elsewhere, then the press should cover it to knock it down. I will confess to being old-fashioned on this issue: if we think we are being used to spread something we know is a lie, I tend to feel that in most cases we should not give the lie a louder megaphone, even if we are using that megaphone to call it a lie. There are a lot of people in my profession whom I respect that see it differently. To me, the farcical Mueller accusation was a classic example.

According to court records, Mark Tolson knew someone who, from a prior work relationship, had access to the email and password of one of the conspiracy theorists. Tolson was so upset about the accusation leveled at Mueller that he offered the email password to a reporter, who declined to take it. Then Tolson went to speak to an FBI manager about his concerns, and offered to share the password information with investigators. This led to the FBI investigating not the conspiracy theorist, but Tolson.

Later that year, Tolson went back to court to be sentenced by Judge Brinkema, who told him sternly: "You can't just rummage through people's accounts." Admitting his wrongdoing, Tolson said he felt that because of the press coverage the rape accusation was getting at the time, "I felt I had to go to the media."

"But as you said," Judge Brinkema reminded him, "Mr. Mueller was perfectly capable of protecting himself . . . And given the overheated environment that we live in these days, you know, that kind of information isn't going to have made a big difference," the judge said, before moving on to her next point. "Whoever the media people were you contacted who turned it down should get a lot of credit because, you know, potentially it was a juicy story, and they certainly conducted themselves ethically. You're actually probably lucky you didn't hit an unethical media person because then the ramifications of this conduct could have been very, very serious."

In another courtroom in late 2019, Donald Trump's longtime friend Roger Stone was found guilty in federal court of witness tampering and lying to Congress—the capstone on a crazy journey that began in August 2016 when he had spoken to a roomful of Florida Republicans, rattling off a series of conspiracy theories before landing on one that resonated—that he had been in touch with WikiLeaks' Julian Assange, and therefore had a notion of what documents would be released next. After publicly declaring his access to Assange, he then spent months scrambling to obscure whether he had been bragging, lying, or some blend of the two. Mueller's team investigated Stone's claim for two years without reaching a conclusion on that point.

In 2016 and the years that followed, conspiracy theories spread like wildfire on social media. The press faces many serious challenges, not least of which is how to deal responsibly with a daily flood of malicious garbage. My own view, which admittedly stems from dealing with such things in the pre-internet era, is that mainstream coverage of such nonsense needs to be much more careful and thoughtful. But readers, viewers, and citizens also play a role in that. If we all just share allegations because "people are saying" something, our actual understanding of the world will be measurably worse. Healthy reading seems to be more important than ever.

The Comey Effect

THREE YEARS AFTER his dramatic firing, which led to the appointment of Robert S. Mueller III as special counsel, James B. Comey was still a subject of public debate, not least because President Trump regularly denounced him as a "crooked cop."

Under Comey's direction, the FBI had investigated one presidential candidate and her opponent's campaign, and in the course of trying to determine if the Trump campaign was planning an "October surprise" ended up tossing perhaps the biggest last-minute curve ball in US election history.

"Wittingly or unwittingly, James Comey's re-opening of the Hillary email investigation was a shocking example of an October surprise," said Sandy Johnson, the former Washington bureau chief of the Associated Press. "The candidate had literally no coherent recourse against the director of the FBI." To Johnson, Comey's decisions smacked of the kind of FBI underhandedness of another era. "It was Hooverian," she said.

When questioned by the investigators within the Justice Department inspector general's office, Comey's defense was that the situation he found himself in was so unique, so unprecedented, that his best option was to toss out the rule book and do what he thought was right. He compared the circumstances of the Clinton probe to "a five-hundred-year flood."

"This is a circumstance that has never happened before," Comey said. "We're criminally investigating one of the candidates for president of the United States . . . You've got the president who has already said there's no there there . . . And so all of that creates a situation where how do we get out of this without grievous damage to the institution?"

From the time he met with a courtroom full of angry defense lawyers in the wake of the 9/11 attacks, Comey has frequently used the argument "What would you have done if you were in my shoes?" to quiet his critics. He did so again in 2016 and 2017, and it is worth considering.

━━━━━━

In August and September of 2016, FBI leadership sent a longtime confidential informant, Stefan Halper, to gather information about any Trump campaign aides conspiring with Russia to interfere in the election. In secretly recorded conversations, both Papadopoulos and Page denied such a conspiracy existed. The FBI decided those denials were not truthful, and kept pursuing the case, applying for and receiving a secret FISA surveillance order against Page in late October.

First, Comey's rationale was based largely on the idea that he faced such an unprecedented situation, an investigation into a presidential candidate in difficult circumstances, that it was the equivalent of a five-century flood. But in Comey's FBI, the flood came not once every five hundred years, but twice in the same month.

His decisions are also in stark contrast to a past FBI case that had similar factors, but ended very differently. In 1992, Bill Clinton was running for president against incumbent George H. W. Bush. H. Ross Perot, a quirky Texas billionaire who hated free trade deals and the Washington establishment, launched what at first seemed like a longshot bid. In the first half of the year, Perot's chances looked surprisingly good, as he garnered support from roughly 33 percent of voters in some polls, a critical threshold in what had become an unusual three-man race. It was the kind of presidential contest television pundits declared unprecedented.

Then in mid-July, as Perot's poll numbers faltered and internal strife seemed to consume his campaign, he abruptly dropped out of the race.

The next month, the head of the FBI office in Dallas, Oliver "Buck" Revell, got a tip. A man named Scott Barnes had approached Perot, saying Bush campaign officials wanted him to bug Perot's phones. Barnes had been joined in his outreach to the Perot camp by David Taylor, a BBC reporter, and they convinced Perot the plot to bug his phones was real. To Revell, the whole thing seemed implausible and downright suspicious. But the allegations, if true, were a serious form of election-year crimes, and he felt the FBI had to investigate quietly, quickly, and carefully.

After sorting out who the various characters were in the strange drama, Revell decided to insert an undercover FBI agent into the conversations to see if the claims were true. After a failed introduction, the undercover agent approached the Bush campaign official who was allegedly eager for illegal recordings of Perot, but the official flatly rejected the overture, and denied he or anyone else in the campaign had asked for such a thing. In fact, the official said, Barnes had offered him tapes already and he'd refused. "There's mischief afoot, and I intend to get to the bottom of it," the Bush campaign official declared, ending the conversation. When Revell listened to the undercover agent's secretly recorded conversation, he felt like a great weight had been lifted from his shoulders, because it meant there was no conspiracy to dig into further.

The next day, when the FBI told the Bush campaign official about the investigation, he was furious, and felt they'd tried to set him up. Agents also interviewed Barnes, who asked for immunity and when it wasn't granted, refused to talk any further. Taylor, the BBC reporter, insisted to agents that he'd only been a reporter chasing a story. And with that, the investigation into the Bush campaign ended, and a new one opened— into whether Barnes and Taylor had committed crimes in trying to set up the Bush campaign.

In the meantime, Perot hadn't given up. He took his suspicions to the 60 Minutes program, which did a piece on the controversy, questioning whether the FBI had acted appropriately. With the blessing of his boss,

Revell spoke on the program, but then faced a leak investigation for doing so. Revell was furious, but much of his anger was still directed at Barnes and the reporter. He wanted them charged with crimes. In the meantime, however, Bush had lost the election, and there was no appetite for such a case among senior Justice Department leaders, including then attorney general William P. Barr.

"President Bush was defeated, and he wanted nothing further to entangle him in the election, and the DoJ and the U.S. Attorney accepted that," said Revell. "I feel that everyone just didn't want to touch it because it was still too fraught with politics, and if we don't take a stand on this, it's going to happen over and over again. Unfortunately, to some extent that is what happened."

In 1997, nearly five years after the case, Barnes gave an interview to the *Dallas Morning News*, admitting to the hoax. "We orchestrated the whole thing," he said. "At the time, I thought it was in the best interests of the country for Bush to be replaced. I thought we needed a new administration."

The parallels to the Crossfire Hurricane case are startling, even down to the involvement of Mueller and Barr. More importantly, 1992 shows the path not taken by Comey. In August and September of 2016, FBI leadership sent an informant to secretly gather information about any Trump campaign aides conspiring with Russia to interfere in the election. In secretly recorded conversations, campaign aides denied any such conspiracy. Yet the FBI decided those denials were not truthful, and kept pursuing the case, applying for and receiving a secret FISA surveillance order against Carter Page in late October that would run on for nearly a year.

Revell's FBI, faced with similar circumstances of a secretly recorded meeting in which the target of the probe denied any interest in the proposed conspiracy, shut down the investigation. In the Crossfire Hurricane case, Comey's FBI recorded not one but multiple denials by different people, in different times and settings. And they still didn't let it go.

Revell said that if he had behaved similarly in 1992 and, after confronting the Bush campaign official in 1992 and recording his denial, asked for court approval to conduct wiretaps on the official or the campaign, "that would have been totally irresponsible, and in my view illegal." The FBI, Revell said, badly misused the FISA process in 2016 and 2017.

There was one key difference since 1992, though. In 2016, the FBI was faced with a very real problem of Russian hacking and election interference. That was not some fever dream or conspiracy theory. The difficulty arose, however, when agents set out to determine if any Americans were working with the Russians, and in doing so, were unwilling to take no for an answer. One of Comey's core arguments in defending his handling of the Clinton and Trump cases is that no one at the FBI had ever seen anything like what he faced. They had. What had never been seen before were the kind of decisions Comey made.

John Pistole, the longest-serving deputy director in the FBI's history, said Comey is a friend, but one who, facing bad options, made serious mistakes with long-term consequences for the Bureau.

"One of the clear lessons is for the FBI not to hold press conferences in the time leading up to the presidential election, or talk about opening a case on one of the candidates," said Pistole. In July 2016, Comey "substituted his judgement for the prosecutor's," and then in October, "he felt like he needed to defend the Bureau from allegations of covering up." Both of those decisions were mistakes, in Pistole's judgment. "I give him credit for being decisive, but it had a high price for himself, and for the Bureau's reputation."

One of Comey's former deputies, Greg Brower, said Comey's decisions were influenced by his work history. Having previously served as the deputy attorney general, Brower said, is key to understanding how Comey behaved as FBI director.

"Previous experience as the DAG is arguably the best and the worst thing an FBI Director can have on his resume," said Brower, because in his old job Comey oversaw the FBI director. While, on the one hand, a former DAG has a tremendous amount of experience with Congress and the White House to draw on, "on the other hand, no one who has ever been the DAG, having had all the power over every aspect of the department, including supervising the FBI, could possibly take on the role of

FBI Director without still thinking of himself as the DAG," said Brower. "I think inevitably this makes any former DAG FBI Director, at least subconsciously, reluctant to fully accept being subordinate to the political appointees across the street." In Comey's own interviews with the inspector general, he made a similar point—when he was considering the announcement of no charges against Clinton, he thought as a DAG.

Cascading misjudgments and missed opportunities led to the ill-fated role of the FBI and the Justice Department in the 2016 election. To this day, many of those intimately involved in the events of 2016 differ as to what the biggest mistakes were, and who is most to blame. They also disagree in their assessments of the damage done to the institutions they care about most. To some, it is unconscionable that the FBI's actions likely tipped the scales to electing Trump the president—partly because they loathe Trump, and partly because they love Comey. For some former senior FBI officials, the worst thing that happened to the Bureau was the ouster of Comey, someone they believe would have made substantial improvements to the Bureau if he had gotten a chance to finish the six years left on his term when Trump fired him. "Things are worse because Comey is no longer the director," said one.

Other law enforcement officials, particularly those with Justice Department pedigrees, believe Comey did lasting, possibly permanent harm to both the FBI and the Justice Department, and the silver lining of the Trump years is that Comey did not stay longer. "In hindsight, it's hard to imagine someone worse suited to be FBI director," said one former official ruefully.

To blame all of the FBI's 2016 failures on Comey is akin to saying Trump has taken the Republican Party hostage. Many of the forces leading to the events of 2016 had been building for years, and boiled over in the added heat of an election campaign. Inside the FBI, long-simmering tensions between criminal investigators and a generation of national security–focused senior executives found an outlet in disagreements over the Clinton cases, fueling distrust and suspicion among small but critically important parts of the organization.

A growing sense of paranoia—about leaks, about their colleagues, and about the Justice Department—gripped many of the FBI agents involved with politically explosive cases. Comey and McCabe were not immune to that paranoia. As Election Day neared, it began to consume them as well.

Throughout the summer and fall of 2016, the leadership of the FBI was badly out of sync with their bosses at the Justice Department. Until Comey's July 5 announcement, Lynch and other senior Justice Department officials were somewhat clueless about how bad the relationship really was. After July, there could be little doubt that Comey did not trust his supervisors, and yet very little was done to address the problem. Like Democrats in Congress, Justice Department leadership wrongly assumed that once the Clinton case was closed, the worst was behind them.

And without realizing it, Congress, too, played a significant role in the meltdown between the Justice Department and the FBI. Years of the GOP hyping cases of political wrongdoing with little evidence of crimes, like the Lois Lerner case, instilled a fear of Capitol Hill even among low-level FBI employees like the Weiner case agent, John Robertson. He was far from alone in that regard. People in different parts of the FBI who didn't know each other at all shared a reflexive worry of being publicly targeted by lawmakers, and it affected how they thought about their own bosses and coworkers. "Earlier in my career, I wouldn't hesitate to tell lawmakers privately what I thought and why," said one retired official. "I cannot say that now. I think it would be foolish to speak that way with some of them."

All of those pressures came to bear on James Comey, Andy McCabe, Loretta Lynch, and Sally Yates in 2016. Even if they had been more adept at handling those problems, the FBI and Justice Department leadership can hardly be blamed for a former congressman with a history of sex addiction unwittingly keeping a digital library of his wife's employer's old emails.

But among current and former law enforcement officials, Comey can and does get blamed for his aggression and self-aggrandizement—for deciding he alone was ethically fit to determine what happened in the Clinton email case on the eve of the election, and for a shocking degree of confidence that he had the reputation, gravitas, and charisma to overcome the political headwinds whipping FBI headquarters.

Faced with the unexpected plot twist of the Weiner laptop, the FBI at first sat on that development, and then rushed to reveal it when it seemed it might leak out. In doing so, Comey made a series of decisions that flew in the face not just of Justice Department practice, but of his own previously stated desire to avoid any October surprise. The same FBI director who refused to add his name to a statement about Russian election interference in early October because he thought it would look political, raced in late October to make it publicly known that he had reopened an investigation of Hillary Clinton. The same FBI that trumpeted one Clinton investigation in late October 2016 launched a leak investigation to try to punish whoever had talked about another one that very same week. And when that leak investigation led back to the person who had launched it, Andy McCabe, he claimed not to remember what he'd done.

For years following the election, pundits and politicians have argued over what role politics played in Comey's decisions. That very question tends to obscure what motivated him most in the period between July and October of 2016. Comey's top priority was not the politics of voter turnout or pollsters, but the politics of the "Bu," and the bureaucracy—keeping the confidence of his own workforce, and avoiding a confrontation with Congress that could lead to his ouster.

The FBI launched its Clinton email investigation thinking it was a straightforward task with a defined target, only to watch it fly off in another direction like an errant missile. Brimming with a sense of their own moral and ethical vigor, FBI officials did not question the ethics of a drone program that led to the alleged killing of a fourteen-year-old boy and other civilians on the borderlands of Afghanistan, but heaped opprobrium on how US officials talked and emailed among themselves about the event. The more challenges FBI officials faced, the more they focused on gossip and intrigue, indulging their own sense of paranoia. To this day, the US government's use of lethal drones is a far more closely guarded secret from Americans than it is to the countries where such drones operate.

When it came to investigating the Trump campaign, FBI bosses were well aware of the high stakes and still proceeded to make a series of errors in judgment so egregious that internal investigators doubted the agents' claims they were honest mistakes.

We live in an age of distrust and suspicion, when conspiracy theories worm their way into news stories on a daily basis. Throughout American society, institutions long held in high or even medium esteem by the public have become regular targets of criticism and doubt, including the FBI and the press. At the FBI, the daily work of chasing hackers, killers, thieves, and kidnappers can feed a general sense of suspicion about the world. But being suspicious of everyone and everything—believing the rest of the world is morally and ethically deficient—brings with it an inherent gullibility. If everything is suspect, it becomes easier to view all sorts of allegations as plausible, from Manchurian candidates to criminal plots to use a private email account.

Comey, McCabe, Lynch, and Yates are all long gone from their jobs at the FBI and Justice Department, but the problems they encountered in 2016 are if anything worse. Trump's attorney general in 2020, William P. Barr, has picked US attorneys from far-flung jurisdictions to second-guess and in some cases override decisions made by career prosecutors, such as in the prosecutions of Roger Stone and Michael Flynn. The distrust and paranoia among law enforcement officials in 2016 pales when compared to that of 2020. After one of Barr's deputies asked a federal judge to toss out Flynn's guilty plea, Trump publicly suggested Comey's successor as FBI director, Christopher A. Wray, was on thin ice. Whoever wins the 2020 election, the once sacrosanct ten-year term of FBI directors may be cut short again.

Some of Comey's biggest critics in law enforcement circles argue that it is a mistake to view him as a rogue moralist or outsize cartoon villain. "He's not some Master of the Universe," one former official said. "He's just a guy who spent too much time in his own head and wouldn't listen to people."

But surveying the institutional wreckage that was wrought, another former law enforcement official felt the consequences of Comey's decisions were severe. "He opened Pandora's box," she said, "and I don't think we'll ever get it closed again."

Acknowledgments

In writing this book, I always kept in mind the two people I most wanted to read it: my father, who as a young man was investigated by the FBI for his opposition to the Vietnam War, and my father-in-law, who was an FBI special agent in the 1970s. I couldn't shake the feeling it was important to recount the hugely consequential events inside the FBI in 2016 in a way that explained what really happened, without any bureaucratic tunnel vision or partisan cherry-picking. If I fell short of that goal in any way, it is not for lack of exemplary role models or colleagues.

As a youngster, I got my first chances in this business from some of the kindest and crassest teachers possible: Stuart Marques, John Mancini, Lisa Baird, Deborah Orin, and Michael Hechtman at the *New York Post*, where friends Dareh Gregorian, Tracy Connor, and Maggie Haberman always had my back. When I thought I was done in this business, Jocelyn Noveck, Tom Hays, Larry Neumeister, and Sonya Ross at the Associated Press convinced me that taking work more seriously could be great fun, too. At the *Wall Street Journal*, Evan Perez, Deborah Solomon, Naftali Bendavid, and others showed me what it means to have sky-high standards and hold fast to them every day.

At the *Washington Post*, I have been incredibly fortunate to work for tremendous editors like Marty Baron, Cameron Barr, Steven Ginsberg, Lori Montgomery, Peter Finn, and Andrew deGrandpre, as well as a small army of the sharpest reporters I've ever seen, including Ellen Nakashima, Shane Harris, Josh Dawsey, Philip Rucker, Ashley Parker, Carol Leonnig, Greg Miller, Tom Hamburger, Sari Horwitz, Julie Tate, Spencer Hsu, Rachel Weiner, and Mark Berman.

There are four people whose help was absolutely essential to this book: Matt Zapotosky is the best partner in crime reporting I could ever want;

Karoun Demirjian was at all times a stellar and resourceful colleague; Rosalind Helderman, in our very first conversation about this book idea, immediately blurted out, "You should call it October Surprise!" and as soon as she said it I knew she was right and I would never forgive her; Adam Entous has been the kind of inspirational colleague and friend who dragged me into some of the best work of my life. I am immensely grateful to them all.

Clive Priddle and Larry Weissman have patiently and brilliantly guided me in making this idea of mine real, and I owe them a tremendous debt that I will try somehow, someway to repay.

Finally, there are two groups of people who have helped me tremendously for twenty-four years and counting. First, the people in the government who take risks to speak to me in a time when obsessive leak-hunting is an easy distraction from the tough questions about how our government works, and how it comes up short. Not all sources are saints, and people make a lot of wildly off-base assumptions about them. But the world is a better place because a great number of people are willing to tell the truth, often at significant personal or professional risk to themselves. I will never forget it. Second, the beat reporters who have shared press rooms with me in courthouses and the Justice Department are the best, weirdest extended family one could ever want. There's no one I would rather compete and commiserate with than folks like Laura Jarrett, Carrie Johnson, Jake Gibson, Mike Levine, Aruna Viswanatha, Sadie Gurman, Eric Tucker, Mike Balsamo, Josh Gerstein, Katie Benner, Adam Goldman, Del Quentin Wilbur, Clare Hymes, Pete Williams, Pierre Thomas, and Paula Reid. Beat reporting is not glamorous, but it is vital, and it is glorious.

Notes

The reporting in every chapter is based on my conversations with people with direct knowledge of the events described, as well as internal FBI emails, 302s, other documents, and two lengthy Justice Department Inspector General reports about the events of 2016. The overwhelming majority of the people who spoke to me were unwilling to do so on the record, given the nature of their jobs, the topics discussed, and the ongoing leak investigations surrounding FBI interactions with the press generally, or me in particular. Not everyone's memory of every interaction is the same. Where there is a disagreement, the account reflects the disagreement. In some instances where individuals were unwilling to speak with me or discuss certain subjects, I have noted in the text where those descriptions are based principally on an Inspector General interview.

CHAPTER 1. MISSILE FIRE

As the sun began to set: Amnesty International, "Will I Be Next? US Drone Strikes in Pakistan," October 2013, https://www.amnesty.org/download /Documents/12000/asa330132013en.pdf.

Counterterrorism officials were confident: Associated Press, "US Drone Strike Kills 12 in Pakistan," July 6, 2012, https://www.cbsnews.com/news/us-drone -strike-kills-12-in-pakistan/.

The US government kept the drone strike program: Adam Entous, "Obama Kept Looser Rules for Drones in Pakistan," *Wall Street Journal*, April 26, 2015, https://www.wsj.com/articles/obama-kept-looser-rules-for-drones-in -pakistan-1430092626.

Hillary Clinton had issued an apology: Eric Schmitt, "Clinton's 'Sorry' to Pakistan Ends Barrier to NATO," *New York Times*, July 3, 2012.

At the time of that particular strike: Adam Entous and Devlin Barrett, "Emails in Clinton Probe Dealt with Planned Drone Strikes," *Wall Street Journal*, June 9, 2016, https://www.wsj.com/articles/clinton-emails-in-probe-dealt -with-planned-drone-strikes-1465509863.

"put the recent difficulties . . .": "Ties Still Raise Tough Questions: Clinton," Reuters, July 8, 2012, https://www.reuters.com/article/us-pakistan-usa/u-s -pakistan-ties-still-raise-tough-questions-clinton-idUSBRE86702H2012 0708.

The three-year anniversary: Justice Department Office of the Inspector General, "A Review of Various Actions by the Federal Bureau of Investigation and Department of Justice in Advance of the 2016 Election," June 2018, https://www.justice.gov/file/1071991/download.

The implications of Steinbach's move: Email from Michael Steinbach to John Giacalone, "State email FOIA—UNCLASSIFIED," May 21, 2015.

But the Clinton investigation: Federal Bureau of Electronic Communication, "Opening of Full Investigation on Sensitive Investigative Matter (SIM)," July 10, 2015.

CHAPTER 2. THE COMEY EFFECT

Comey decided that one way: Justice Department Office of the Inspector General, "The September 11 Detainees: A Review of the Treatment of Aliens Held on Immigration Charges in Connection with the Investigation of the September 11 Attacks," June 2003, https://oig.justice.gov/special/0306/.

"We also have to work . . .": Transcript of NBC's *Meet the Press*, September 16, 2001, https://www.washingtonpost.com/wp-srv/nation/specials/attacked/transcripts/cheney091601.html.

As the DAG, Comey worked well: Transcript of James Comey testimony before the Senate Judiciary Committee, May 15, 2007, https://gulcfac.typepad.com/georgetown_university_law/files/comey.transcript.pdf.

Comey took another important step: Ray Dalio, *Principles: Life and Work*, 2017, Simon & Schuster.

"Most of my friends . . .": John Cassidy, "Mastering the Machine," *New Yorker*, July 18, 2011.

"I went to Bridgewater in part . . .": "Confirmation Hearing on the Nomination of James B. Comey, Jr. to Be Director of the Federal Bureau of Investigation," July 9, 2013, https://www.govinfo.gov/content/pkg/CHRG-113shrg23750/pdf/CHRG-113shrg23750.pdf.

CHAPTER 3. THE RISE OF ANDY MCCABE

"I did not have an answer . . .": Remarks from Robert S. Mueller III at Georgetown University, June 20, 2014.

In 2009, Mueller showed: Evan Perez and Siobhan Gorman, "Interrogation Team Is Still Months Away," *Wall Street Journal*, January 22, 2010, https://www.wsj.com/articles/SB10001424052748704423204575017760430119880.

In her role as a hospital doctor: Michael Laris and Laura Vozzella, "In Va., Fight over Medicaid Expansion Continues," *Washington Post,* February 24,

2014, https://www.washingtonpost.com/local/virginia-politics/2014/02/24/988697ea-9d59-11e3-b8d8-94577ff66b28_story.html.

The meeting took place less than one week: Michael S. Schmidt, "Hillary Clinton Used Personal Email Account at State Dept., Possibly Breaking Rules," *New York Times*, March 2, 2015, https://www.nytimes.com/2015/03/03/us/politics/hillary-clintons-use-of-private-email-at-state-department-raises-flags.html.

In October 2015: Virginia Department of Elections campaign finance reports for McCabe for Senate, https://cfreports.elections.virginia.gov/Committee/Index/287f263b-8ae3-e411-a05b-984be103f032.

CHAPTER 4. BUT THEIR EMAILS

The FBI agents wanted to talk to Munter: FBI 302 of Interview of Cameron Munter, March 10, 2016. https://vault.fbi.gov/hillary-r.-clinton.

the FBI scheduled an interview with Hoagland: FBI 302 of Interview of Richard Hoagland, March 15, 2016, https://vault.fbi.gov/hillary-r.-clinton.

In that session, Munter explained: FBI 302 of Interview of Cameron Munter, April 25, 2016, https://vault.fbi.gov/hillary-r.-clinton.

Not everyone was content: "Hillary Clinton Email Archive," WikiLeaks, March 16, 2016.

CHAPTER 5. LORETTA AND JIM

a sit-down interview with Bret Baier: Bret Baier, "Lynch. No 'Artificial Deadline' on DOJ's Clinton Email Probe," Fox News, February 29, 2016, https://www.foxnews.com/politics/lynch-no-artificial-deadline-on-dojs-clinton-email-probe.

Peter Strzok, the case agent: Matt Zapotosky and Devlin Barrett, "'You Stepped in It Here': How Anti-Trump Texts Ruined the Career of the FBI's Go-to Agent," *Washington Post*, August 14, 2018, https://www.washingtonpost.com/world/national-security/you-stepped-in-it-here-how-anti-trump-texts-ruined-the-career-of-the-fbis-go-to-agent/2018/08/13/eb1868be-9401-11e8-a679-b09212fb69c2_story.html.

Lisa Page had come to the FBI: Majority Staff of the Senate Committee on Homeland Security and Governmental Affairs, "The Clinton Email Scandal and the FBI's Investigation of It," Appendix C, February 7, 2018, https://www.hsgac.senate.gov/imo/media/doc/Appendix%20C%20-%20Documents.pdf.

During this same time period: Krishnadev Calamur, "Justice Department Won't Charge IRS' Lois Lerner with Criminal Contempt," NPR, April 1, 2015,

https://www.npr.org/sections/thetwo-way/2015/04/01/396872364/justice
-department-wont-charge-irs-lois-lerner-with-criminal-contempt.

CHAPTER 6. AN ALREADY BIG FIRE

a *Washington Post* headline: Ellen Nakashima, "Russian Government Hackers Penetrated DNC, Stole Opposition Research on Trump," *Washington Post*, June 14, 2016.

The day after the *Post* story: US Department of Justice, "Report on the Investigation into Russian Interference in the 2016 Presidential Election, Volume I of II," 107, March 2019, https://www.justice.gov/storage/report.pdf.

That afternoon, Loretta Lynch boarded: KNXV, "Quite the Meeting on the Tarmac," June 29, 2016, https://www.youtube.com/watch?v=sRWDP-PWunE.

"What on earth . . .": Aspen Ideas Festival, "Loretta Lynch: A Conversation on 21st Century Policing, Civil Rights, and Criminal Justice Reform," July 1, 2016, https://www.youtube.com/watch?v=xGY5x9w-aLM.

In general, Clinton insisted: FBI 302 of Interview of Hillary Clinton, July 2, 2016. https://vault.fbi.gov/hillary-r.-clinton.

CHAPTER 7. RADICAL TRANSPARENCY

"Good morning . . .": My transcription of Comey's statement as seen on C-Span, https://www.youtube.com/watch?v=ghph_361wao. For the government's prepared text version, see "Statement by FBI Director James B. Comey on the Investigation of Secretary Hillary Clinton's Use of a Personal E-Mail System," July 5, 2016, https://www.fbi.gov/news/pressrel/press-releases/statement-by -fbi-director-james-b-comey-on-the-investigation-of-secretary-hillary -clinton2019s-use-of-a-personal-e-mail-system [fbi.gov].

As he delivered that line: Adam Entous and Devlin Barrett, "The Last Diplomat," *Wall Street Journal*, December 2, 2016, https://www.wsj.com/articles /the-last-diplomat-1480695454.

Another, previously undisclosed case: Krishnadev Calamur, "India-U.S. Row over Diplomat's Arrest in New York Escalates," NPR, December 17, 2013, https://www.npr.org/sections/thetwo-way/2013/12/17/251944983/india-u-s -row-over-diplomats-arrest-in-new-york-escalates.

In fact, that very day: Justice Department Office of the Inspector General, "Review of Four FISA Applications and Other Aspects of the FBI's Crossfire Hurricane Investigation," December 2019, https://www.justice.gov/storage /120919-examination.pdf.

In June 2016, one of Steele's clients: Adam Entous and Devlin Barrett, "Clinton Campaign, DNC Paid for Research That Led to Russia Dossier," *Washington*

Post, October 24, 2017, https://www.washingtonpost.com/world/national
-security/clinton-campaign-dnc-paid-for-research-that-led-to-russia
-dossier/2017/10/24/226fabf0-b8e4-11e7-a908-a3470754bbb9_story.html.

CHAPTER 8. ASYMMETRICAL POLITICS

Moyer would come to regret: Transcript of Interview of Sally Moyer, Joint
Session of the House Judiciary Committee and House Committee on Government Reform and Oversight, October 23, 2018, https://dougcollins.house
.gov/sites/dougcollins.house.gov/files/10.23.18%20Moyer%20Interview_
Redacted%20DJ.pdf.

"Hillary Clinton created this mess": House Committee on Government Reform and Oversight hearing, "Hillary Clinton Email Investigation, Part 1,"
C-Span, July 7, 2016, https://www.c-span.org/video/?412315-1/fbi-director
-james-comey-testifies-hillary-clinton-email-probe.

CHAPTER 9. RUSSIA WAS LISTENING

In London, Australian diplomat: Interview of Alexander Downer, Sky News,
May 9, 2019, https://www.youtube.com/watch?v=ygckFL8m2Ws.

"What I don't have patience for . . .": Mike Levine, "FBI Director Says Decision
to Forgo Charges against Hillary Clinton 'Wasn't That Hard' to Make," ABC
News, July 26, 2016, https://abcnews.go.com/US/fbi-director-decision-fo
rgo-charges-hillary-clinton-wasnt/story?id=40895203.

The "if you're listening" line: Jason Leopold, et al., "The Mueller Report's Secret Memos," BuzzFeed News, November 2, 2019, https://www.buzzfeednews
.com/article/jasonleopold/mueller-report-secret-memos-1.

As the FBI prepared: FBI Electronic Communication, "Crossfire Hurricane,"
July 31, 2016, https://www.judicialwatch.org/documents/jw-v-doj-reply
-02743/.

"I can't wait to hear . . .": Remarks of Roger Stone to the Southwest Broward
Republican Organization, August 8, 2016, https://www.youtube.com/watch
?v=6gM_cyROnto.

CHAPTER 10. PREDICATE

Peter Strzok was back: Evan Perez, "Feds Investigate Manafort Firm as Part of
Ukraine Probe," CNN, August 19, 2016.

As the Crossfire cases: Karoun Demirjian and Devlin Barrett, "How a Dubi-
ous Russian Document Influenced the FBI's Handling of the Clinton Probe,"

Washington Post, May 24, 2017, https://www.washingtonpost.com/world
/national-security/how-a-dubious-russian-document-influenced-the-fbis
-handling-of-the-clinton-probe/2017/05/24/f375c07c-3a95-11e7-9e48-c4f
199710b69_story.html.

"First on CNN . . .": Drew Griffin, Pamela Brown, and Shimon Prokupecz, "First
on CNN: Inside the Debate over Probing the Clinton Foundation," CNN,
August 11, 2016, https://www.cnn.com/2016/08/11/politics/hillary-clinton
-state-department-clinton-foundation/index.html.

"EXCLUSIVE: Joint FBI-US Attorney Probe . . .": Richard Pollock, "Exclusive:
Joint FBI-US Attorney Probe of Clinton Foundation Is Underway," Daily
Caller, August 11, 2016, https://dailycaller.com/2016/08/11/exclusive-joint
-fbi-us-attorney-probe-of-clinton-foundation-is-underway/.

a *New York Times* story: Jo Becker and Mike McIntire, "Cash Flowed to Clinton
Foundation amid Russian Uranium Deal," *New York Times*, April 23, 2015,
https://www.nytimes.com/2015/04/24/us/cash-flowed-to-clinton-founda
tion-as-russians-pressed-for-control-of-uranium-company.html.

The eleventh of August: Tom Hamburger, Robert Costa, and Ellen Nakashima, "Cambridge Perch Gave FBI Source Access to Top Intelligence Figures—and a Cover as He Reached Out to Trump Associates," *Washington
Post*, June 5, 2018, https://www.washingtonpost.com/politics/cambridge
-university-perch-gave-fbi-source-access-to-top-intelligence-figures--and
-a-cover-as-he-reached-out-to-trump-associates/2018/06/05/c6764dc2
-641e-11e8-99d2-0d678eco8c2f_story.html.

While the FBI was pursuing: US Department of Justice indictment, *U.S. v. Internet Research Agency* et al., February 2, 2018, https://www.justice.gov/file
/1035477/download.

While the pieces seemed: Devlin Barrett, "FBI in Internal Feud over Hillary
Clinton Probe," *Wall Street Journal*, October 30, 2016, https://www.wsj.com
/articles/laptop-may-include-thousands-of-emails-linked-to-hillary
-clintons-private-server-1477854957.

CHAPTER 11. DANGLE

Supervisory Special Agent Joe Pientka: Mike Levine and John Santucci,
"Trump to Receive First Classified Briefing," ABC News, August 16, 2016,
https://abcnews.go.com/Politics/trump-receive-classified-briefing-tomor
row/story?id=41419607&cid=clicksource_4380645_1_hero_headlines_bsq
_image.

Eight days after Stefan Halper: Steven Mufson and Tom Hamburger, "Trump
Adviser's Public Comments, Ties to Moscow Stir Unease in Both Parties,"
Washington Post, August 5, 2016, https://www.washingtonpost.com/business
/economy/trump-advisers-public-comments-ties-to-moscow-stir-unease

-in-both-parties/2016/08/05/2e8722fa-5815-11e6-9aee-8075993d73a2_story
.html.

"Are we going to see it . . .": Fox News interview with Julian Assange, "Assange Talks 'Revealing the Truth' through WikiLeaks," Fox News, August 25, 2016, https://www.foxnews.com/transcript/assange-talks-revealing-the-truth-through-wikileaks-ramos-neutrality-not-always-an-option-for-journalists.

Four Democratic lawmakers: Tyler Pager, "House Democrats Ask FBI to Investigate Any Trump Connection to Cyberattacks," Politico, August 30, 2016, https://www.politico.com/story/2016/08/democrats-fbi-connection-trump-cyberattacks-227555.

The microphone was working: Robert Costa et al., "Secret FBI Source for Russia Investigation Met with Three Trump Advisers during Campaign," *Washington Post*, May 18, 2018, https://www.washingtonpost.com/politics/secret-fbi-source-for-russia-investigation-met-with-three-trump-advisers-during-campaign/2018/05/18/9778d9f0-5aea-11e8-b656-a5f8c2a9295d_story.html.

CHAPTER 12. TRAVELLERS CLUB

George Papadopoulos met Stefan Halper: George Papadopoulos, *Deep State Target: How I Got Caught in the Crosshairs of the Plot to Bring Down President Trump*, Diversion Books, 2019.

CHAPTER 13. FISA

"U.S. Intel Officials . . .": Michael Isikoff, "U.S. Intel Officials Probe Ties between Trump Adviser and Kremlin," Yahoo! News, September 23, 2016, https://www.yahoo.com/news/u-s-intel-officials-probe-ties-between-trump-adviser-and-kremlin-175046002.html.

Prior to the Yahoo! story: Glenn Simpson and Peter Fritsch, *Crime in Progress: Inside the Steele Dossier and the Fusion GPS Investigation of Donald Trump*, Random House, 2019.

"The FBI does not believe . . .": FBI Records, "In Re: Carter W. Page, a U.S. Person," 2016, https://vault.fbi.gov/d1-release/d1-release/view.

CHAPTER 14. LAPTOP

"They do say, before you come on this squad . . .": *Inside the FBI*, Episode 2: Deviant Crimes, NBC, 2017, https://www.nbc.com/inside-the-fbi-new-york/video/deviant-crimes/3510338.

Working out of his cubicle: Alana Goodman, "EXCLUSIVE: Anthony Weiner Carried on a Months-Long Online Sexual Relationship with a Troubled 15-Year-old Girl," *Daily Mail*, September 21, 2016, https://www.dailymail .co.uk/news/article-3790824/Anthony-Weiner-carried-months-long-online -sexual-relationship-troubled-15-year-old-girl-telling-hard-asking-dress -school-girl-outfits-pressing-engage-rape-fantasies.html.

"In recent weeks, this line of attack . . .": House Judiciary Committee Hearing, "FBI Oversight," C-Span, September 28, 2016, https://www.c-span.org /video/?415887-1/fbi-director-james-comey-testifies-oversight-hearing.

CHAPTER 15. ARE YOU KIDDING ME?

"The U.S. Intelligence Community is confident . . .": Department of Homeland Security, "Joint Statement from the Department of Homeland Security and Office of the Director of National Intelligence on Election Security," October 7, 2016, https://www.dhs.gov/news/2016/10/07/joint-statement-depart ment-homeland-security-and-office-director-national.

the *Washington Post* reported, with accompanying audio: David Fahrenthold, "Trump Recorded Having Extremely Lewd Conversation about Women in 2005," *Washington Post*, October 7, 2016, https://www.washingtonpost.com /politics/trump-recorded-having-extremely-lewd-conversation-about-women -in-2005/2016/10/07/3b9ce776-8cb4-11e6-bf8a-3d26847eeed4_story.html.

WikiLeaks released emails from Hillary Clinton's: Laura Koran, Dan Merica, and Tom LoBianco, "WikiLeaks Posts Apparent Excerpts of Clinton Wall Street Speeches," CNN, October 8, 2016, https://www.cnn.com/2016/10/07 /politics/john-podesta-emails-hacked/index.html.

"Stone pointed his finger at me . . .": William Cummings, "Podesta Suggests Trump Campaign in Cahoots with the Russians," *USA Today*, October 12, 2016, https://www.usatoday.com/story/news/politics/onpolitics/2016/10/12 /trump-campaign-had-advance-warning-russian-backed-wikileaks -dump/91931602/.

when he sat for a television interview: Jim DeFede, "Trump Ally Roger Stone Admits 'Back-Channel' Tie to WikiLeaks," CBS, October 12, 2016, https:// miami.cbslocal.com/2016/10/12/trump-ally-roger-stone-admits-back -channel-tie-to-wikileaks/.

CHAPTER 16. A LETTER TO HIMSELF

That lunch hour, he sat down at a computer: Email from SA John Robertson to himself, October 20, 2016, confidential source.

CHAPTER 17. ROLLER COASTER

The pushback from McCabe: Devlin Barrett, "Clinton Ally Aided Campaign of FBI Official's Wife," *Wall Street Journal*, October 24, 2016, https://www.wsj.com/articles/clinton-ally-aids-campaign-of-fbi-officials-wife-1477266114.

That morning, McCabe attended: Devlin Barrett, "Internal Justice Department Probe Eyes McCabe's Role in Final Weeks of 2016 Election," *Washington Post*, January 30, 2018, https://www.washingtonpost.com/world/national-security/internal-justice-department-probe-eyes-mccabes-role-in-final-weeks-of-2016-election/2018/01/30/db2ea8f0-05c7-11e8-8777-2a059f168dd2_story.html.

That afternoon, Jill McCabe: Transcript of Interview of John Giacalone, Joint Session of the House Judiciary Committee and House Committee on Government Reform and Oversight, June 21, 2018, https://dougcollins.house.gov/sites/dougcollins.house.gov/files/6.21.18%20Giacalone%20Interview_Redacted.pdf.

"This still reads to me like someone . . .": Email from James Comey to Andrew McCabe, October 24, 2016, https://vault.fbi.gov/deputy-director-mccabe-office-of-professional-responsibility-investigation/deputy-director-mccabe-office-of-professional-responsibility-investigation-part-08-of-09.

"Overview of Deputy Director McCabe's . . .": FBI Memo, "Overview of Deputy Director McCabe's Recusal Related to Dr. McCabe's Campaign for Political Office," October 24, 2016, https://www.judicialwatch.org/wp-content/uploads/2017/10/JW-v-DOJ-McCabe-ethics-01494-pg-10-11-2.pdf.

CHAPTER 18. LEAK HUNTING

"We have just learned," Trump declared: "Presidential Candidate Donald Trump Rally in Sanford Florida," C-Span, October 25, 2016, https://www.c-span.org/video/?417444-1/donald-trump-campaigns-sanford-florida.

A day earlier, the front page: Matt Apuzzo, Adam Goldman, and William Rashbaum, "Justice Dept. Shakes Up Inquiry into Eric Garner Chokehold Case," October 24, 2016, https://www.nytimes.com/2016/10/25/nyregion/justice-dept-replaces-investigators-on-eric-garner-case.html.

That night, as he often did in 2016: Fox News interview with Rudy Giuliani, "Trump Surrogate on 'America's Newsroom': 'We've Got a Couple of Things Up Our Sleeve,'" Fox News, October 27, 2016, https://www.youtube.com/watch?v=L-4mDUS1a9w.

CHAPTER 19. THE WORLD OF REALLY BAD

McCabe later told investigators: US Department of Justice Office of Inspector General, "A Report of Investigation of Certain Allegations Relating to Former FBI Deputy Director Andrew McCabe," February 2018, https://oig .justice.gov/reports/2018/020180413.pdf.

Page in particular: Transcript of Interview of Lisa Page, Joint Session of the House Judiciary Committee and House Committee on Government Reform and Oversight, July 13, 2018, https://dougcollins.house.gov/sites/doug collins.house.gov/files/Lisa%20Page%20interview%20Day%201.pdf.

CHAPTER 20. "THE DEATH OF ME"

"Dear Messrs Chairmen . . .": FBI letter to congressional leaders, October 28, 2016, https://www.washingtonpost.com/apps/g/page/politics/oct-28-fbi -letter-to-congressional-leaders-on-clinton-email-investigation/2113/.

Later that afternoon: Cameron Joseph, "FBI Reopens Clinton Email Investigation after It Discovers New Info on Aide Huma Abedin's Device in Her Husband Anthony Weiner's Sexting Probe," *New York Daily News*, October 28, 2016, https://www.nydailynews.com/news/politics/anthony-weiner-sexts -lead-fbi-reopened-clinton-email-probe-article-1.2849177.

"Someone in the chain of command . . .": Email from SA John Robertson to himself, October 28, 2016, confidential source.

"Your actions in recent months . . .": Mike DeBonis, "Harry Reid Says Comey 'May Have Broken the Law' by Disclosing New Clinton-related Emails," *Washington Post*, October 30, 2016, https://www.washingtonpost.com/news /powerpost/wp/2016/10/30/harry-reid-says-comey-may-have-broken-the -law-by-disclosing-new-clinton-emails/.

"Justice Officials Warned . . .": Sari Horwitz, Tom Hamburger, and Ellen Nakashima, "Justice Officials Warned FBI That Comey's Decision to Update Congress Was Not Consistent with Department Policy," *Washington Post*, October 29, 2016, https://www.washingtonpost.com/world/national-security /justice-officials-warned-fbi-that-comeys-decision-to-update-congress-was -not-consistent-with-department-policy/2016/10/29/cb179254-9de7-11e6 -b3c9-f662adaa0048_story.html.

CHAPTER 21. HALLOWEEN

"A Veteran Spy Has Given . . .": David Corn, "A Veteran Spy Has Given the FBI Information Alleging a Russian Operation to Cultivate Donald Trump,"

Mother Jones, October 31, 2016, https://www.motherjones.com/politics/2016/10/veteran-spy-gave-fbi-info-alleging-russian-operation-cultivate-donald-trump/.

"Investigating Donald Trump . . .": Eric Lichtblau and Steven Lee Myers, "Investigating Donald Trump, FBI Sees No Clear Link to Russia," *New York Times*, October 31, 2016, https://www.nytimes.com/2016/11/01/us/politics/fbi-russia-election-donald-trump.html.

On Monday, Baker went to see McCabe: Transcript of Interview of James Baker by US Department of Justice Office of the Inspector General, December 18, 2017, https://s3.amazonaws.com/storage.citizensforethics.org/wp-content/uploads/2020/02/02160255/CREW-March-2020-Production Part1.pdf.

"William J. Clinton Foundation . . .": FBI FOIA records, November 1, 2016, https://vault.fbi.gov/william-j.-clinton-foundation.

"to mitigate the appearance . . .": Letter from Senator Charles Grassley to FBI director James Comey, October 28, 2016, https://www.judiciary.senate.gov/imo/media/doc/2016-11-02%20CEG%20to%20DOJ%20IG%20(Conflicts%20Review).pdf.

CHAPTER 22. MARGIN OF ERROR

"So while one can debate the magnitude . . .": Nate Silver, "The Comey Letter Probably Cost Clinton the Election," FiveThirtyEight, May 3, 2017, https://fivethirtyeight.com/features/the-comey-letter-probably-cost-clinton-the-election/.

That morning, the *Wall Street Journal*: Devlin Barrett and Christopher Matthews, "Secret Recordings Fueled FBI Feud in Clinton Probe," *Wall Street Journal*, November 2, 2016, https://www.wsj.com/articles/secret-recordings-fueled-fbi-feud-in-clinton-probe-1478135518.

reporters had zeroed in: Matt Zapotosky, "Rudy Giuliani Is Claiming to Have Insider FBI Knowledge. Does He Really?," *Washington Post*, November 4, 2016, https://www.washingtonpost.com/news/post-nation/wp/2016/11/04/rudy-giuliani-is-claiming-to-have-insider-fbi-knowledge-does-he-really/.

"Based on our review . . .": Letter from FBI director James Comey to congressional leaders, November 6, 2016, https://vault.fbi.gov/director-comey-letter-to-congress-dated-november-6th-2016/director-comey-letter-to-congress-dated-november-6-2016/view.

In Michigan, Donald Trump edged out: Federal Elections Commission, "Official 2016 Presidential Election Results," January 30, 2017, https://transition.fec.gov/pubrec/fe2016/2016presgeresults.pdf.

CHAPTER 23. HANGOVER

The examination of FBI employees' phone records: Email from Pete Strzok to Andy McCabe, December 22, 2016, https://s3.amazonaws.com/storage .citizensforethics.org/wp-content/uploads/2020/02/28220125/McCabe -Release-2-28-20-Part-3.pdf.

As the pressure on Comey and McCabe: Wayne Barrett, "Meet Donald Trump's Top FBI Fanboy," Daily Beast, November. 3, 2016, https://www.thedailybeast .com/meet-donald-trumps-top-fbi-fanboy.

The latest iteration of the dossier: Evan Perez et al., "Intel Chiefs Presented Trump with Claims of Russian Efforts to Compromise Him," January 11, 2017, https://www.cnn.com/2017/01/10/politics/donald-trump-intelligence -report-russia/index.html.

A staffer for the McCain Institute: Ken Bensinger, "These Reports Allege Trump Has Deep Ties to Russia," BuzzFeed News, January 10, 2017, https:// www.buzzfeednews.com/article/kenbensinger/these-reports-allege-trump -has-deep-ties-to-russia.

Most disappointing for the FBI: Tom Hamburger and Rosalind Helderman, "Hero or Hired Gun? How a British Former Spy Became a Flash Point in the Russia Investigation," *Washington Post*, February 6, 2018, https://www .washingtonpost.com/politics/hero-or-hired-gun-how-a-british-former -spy-became-a-flash-point-in-the-russia-investigation/2018/02/06/94ea 5158-0795-11e8-8777-2a059f168dd2_story.html.

"Sinatra is as much to blame . . .": FBI FOIA release of files regarding Frank Sinatra, 1998, https://vault.fbi.gov/Frank%20Sinatra.

CHAPTER 24. THE STORM

But ProPublica had just reported: Peter Elkind, "James Comey's Testimony on Huma Abedin Forwarding Emails Was Inaccurate," ProPublica, May 8, 2017, https://www.propublica.org/article/comeys-testimony-on-huma-abedin -forwarding-emails-was-inaccurate.

This one was an oddity: US Department of Justice Office of the Inspector General Interview of Voviette Morgan, December 20, 2017, https://s3.amazonaws .com/storage.citizensforethics.org/wp-content/uploads/2020/02/28215630 /McCabe-Release-2-28-20-Part-1.pdf.

"Dear Director Comey": Email from Rob Porter to James Comey, May 9, 2017, confidential source.

While McCabe was sitting: Andrew McCabe, *The Threat: How the FBI Protects America in the Age of Terror and Trump*, Macmillan, 2019.

As the audience and Comey: James Comey, *A Higher Loyalty: Truth, Lies, and Leadership*, Flatiron Books, 2018.

When Comey discovered the message: Email from James Comey to James Rybicki, May 10, 2017, confidential source.

"Although the President . . .": Memorandum from Deputy Attorney General Rod Rosenstein, "Restoring Public Confidence in the FBI," May 9, 2017, https://www.bbc.com/news/world-us-canada-39866767.

The pick helped, but: Adam Goldman, and Michael Schmidt, "Rod Rosenstein Suggested Secretly Recording Trump and Discussed 25th Amendment," *New York Times*, September 21, 2018, https://www.nytimes.com/2018/09/21/us/politics/rod-rosenstein-wear-wire-25th-amendment.html.

At a tense private meeting: Matt Zapotosky and Devlin Barrett, "Rosenstein-McCabe Feud Dates Back to Angry Standoff in Front of Mueller," *Washington Post*, October 10, 2018, https://www.washingtonpost.com/world/national-security/rosenstein-mccabe-feud-dates-back-to-angry-standoff-in-front-of-mueller/2018/10/10/8a7e99fe-ccac-11e8-a3e6-44daa3d35ede_story.html.

Seeking to break: US Department of Justice Office of the Inspector General Interview with Mike Kortan, December 22, 2017, https://s3.amazonaws.com/storage.citizensforethics.org/wp-content/uploads/2020/02/28220125/McCabe-Release-2-28-20-Part-3.pdf.

After years of trying: Matt Zapotosky et al., "Justice Dept. Won't Charge Andrew McCabe, the Former FBI Official Who Authorized the Investigation of President Trump," *Washington Post*, February 14, 2020, https://www.washingtonpost.com/national-security/justice-dept-wont-charge-andrew-mccabe-the-former-fbi-official-who-authorized-the-investigation-of-president-trump/2020/02/14/8ab3aac0-4f48-11ea-bf44-f5043eb3918a_story.html.

CHAPTER 25. TEXT MACHINE

Michael Flynn, who'd lasted: Carol Leonnig et al., "Michael Flynn Pleads Guilty to Lying to FBI on Contacts with Russian Ambassador," *Washington Post*, December 1, 2017, https://www.washingtonpost.com/politics/michael-flynn-charged-with-making-false-statement-to-the-fbi/2017/12/01/e03a6c48-d6a2-11e7-9461-ba77d604373d_story.html.

The very next day: Karoun Demirjian and Devlin Barrett, "Top FBI Official Assigned to Mueller's Russia Probe Said to Have Been Removed after Sending Anti-Trump Texts," *Washington Post*, December 2, 2017, https://www.washingtonpost.com/world/national-security/two-senior-fbi-officials-on-clinton-trump-probes-exchanged-politically-charged-texts-disparaging-trump/2017/12/02/9846421c-d707-11e7-a986-d0a9770d9a3c_story.html.

Inspector General Michael Horowitz had found: US Department of Justice Office of Inspector General, "Report of Investigation: Recovery of Text Messages from Certain FBI Mobile Devices," December 2018, https://oig.justice.gov/reports/2018/i-2018-003523.pdf.

CHAPTER 26. INVESTIGATING THE INVESTIGATORS

"There was no spying . . .": James Comey, "The Truth Is Finally Out. The FBI Fulfilled Its Mission," *Washington Post*, December 9, 2019, https://www .washingtonpost.com/opinions/james-comey-the-truth-is-finally-out-the -fbi-fulfilled-its-mission/2019/12/09/614df00c-1aad-11ea-8d58-5ac3600 967a1_story.html.

The former FBI lawyer: Ellen Nakashima, Matt Zapotosky, and Devlin Barrett, "Justice Dept. Watchdog Finds Political Bias Did Not Taint Top Officials Running the FBI's Russia Probe but Documents Errors," *Washington Post*, November 22, 2019, https://www.washingtonpost.com/national-security /justice-dept-watchdog-finds-political-bias-did-not-taint-top-officials-run ning-the-fbis-russia-probe-but-documents-other-errors/2019/11/22/4b2f 51de-0d48-11ea-97ac-a7ccc8dd1ebc_story.html.

A subsequent report: US Department of Justice Office of the Inspector General, "Management Advisory Memorandum for the Director of the Federal Bureau of Investigation Regarding the Execution of Woods Procedures for Applications Filed with the Foreign Intelligence Surveillance Court Relating to U.S. Persons," March 2020, https://oig.justice.gov/reports/2020/a20047.pdf.

Yet in 2014: Carol Robinson, "FBI Director Talks Football Analogies, Homegrown Terrorism, Spy Stuff in Birmingham," AL.com, January 14, 2014, https://www.al.com/spotnews/2014/01/fbi_director_talks_football_an.html.

Shortly before Christmas: Rachel Weiner, "Former FBI Analyst Tells Court He Was Trying 'to Protect Mueller' by Snooping on Conservative Activist's Email," *Washington Post*, December 20, 2019, https://www.washington post.com/local/public-safety/former-fbi-analyst-tells-court-he-was-trying -to-protect-mueller-by-snooping-on-conservative-activists-email/2019/12 /20/5d5f143e-234b-11ea-86f3-3b5019d451db_story.html.

CHAPTER 27. THE COMEY EFFECT

In 1992, Bill Clinton: Oliver "Buck" Revell, *A G-Man's Journal*, Atria, 1998.

Index

DEVLIN BARRETT is a reporter with the *Washington Post*, where he writes about the FBI and the Justice Department. He was part of a team that won a Pulitzer Prize in 2018 for National Reporting, for coverage of Russian interference in the US election. In 2017 he was a co-finalist for both the Pulitzer for Feature Writing and the Pulitzer for International Reporting. He has covered federal law enforcement for more than twenty years, and has worked at the *Wall Street Journal*, the *Associated Press*, and the *New York Post*. He lives in Virginia.

PublicAffairs is a publishing house founded in 1997. It is a tribute to the standards, values, and flair of three persons who have served as mentors to countless reporters, writers, editors, and book people of all kinds, including me.

I. F. STONE, proprietor of *I. F. Stone's Weekly*, combined a commitment to the First Amendment with entrepreneurial zeal and reporting skill and became one of the great independent journalists in American history. At the age of eighty, Izzy published *The Trial of Socrates*, which was a national bestseller. He wrote the book after he taught himself ancient Greek.

BENJAMIN C. BRADLEE was for nearly thirty years the charismatic editorial leader of *The Washington Post*. It was Ben who gave the *Post* the range and courage to pursue such historic issues as Watergate. He supported his reporters with a tenacity that made them fearless and it is no accident that so many became authors of influential, best-selling books.

ROBERT L. BERNSTEIN, the chief executive of Random House for more than a quarter century, guided one of the nation's premier publishing houses. Bob was personally responsible for many books of political dissent and argument that challenged tyranny around the globe. He is also the founder and longtime chair of Human Rights Watch, one of the most respected human rights organizations in the world.

·   ·   ·

For fifty years, the banner of Public Affairs Press was carried by its owner Morris B. Schnapper, who published Gandhi, Nasser, Toynbee, Truman, and about 1,500 other authors. In 1983, Schnapper was described by *The Washington Post* as "a redoubtable gadfly." His legacy will endure in the books to come.

Peter Osnos, *Founder*